Jean-Pierre Prévost

# How to Read the P

SCM PRESS LTD

Translated by John Bowden from the French
*Pour Lire Les Prophètes*, published 1995 by Novalis
and Les Editions du Cerf

The illustrations on pages 17, 35, 39, 53, 83, and 125
are by Guylaine Malo. The illustrations on pages 7, 11,
19, 27, 72, 77, 79, 87, 97, 115, 117, 121, and 129 are by
Gustave Doré.

*Nihil obstat:* Anton Cowan
            Censor
*Imprimatur:* David Norris
            Vicar General
            10 April 1996

The *Nihil obstat* and *Imprimatur* are a declaration that a
book or pamphlet is considered to be free from doctrinal
or moral error. It is not implied that those who have
granted the *Nihil obstat* and *Imprimatur* agree with the
contents, opinions or statements expressed.

0 334 02592 3

First published in English 1996
by SCM Press Ltd,
9–17 St Albans Place, London N1 0NX

Typeset at The Spartan Press Ltd,
Lymington, Hants
and printed in Great Britain by
Redwood Books, Trowbridge, Wiltshire

# Contents

# Introduction

'A virgin most pure, as the prophets do tell, hath brought forth a baby, as it hath befel . . .' These words from a traditional Christmas carol largely represent the view that has long prevailed among Christians about the biblical prophets. They are credited above all, if not exclusively, with having announced the one who is at the heart of our faith, Jesus the Christ. At the same time, the prophets become the heralds of the Messiah, and there is interest in them to the degree that they predicted and prepared for his coming.

This view of the prophets is confirmed and to some degree perpetuated by the lectionary of the Roman liturgy, in which the texts of the prophets, and principally that of Isaiah, have a privileged place in the season of Advent and Christmas: the biblical prophets become the bards par excellence of the Christian hope.

However, little is known about the prophets themselves and their specific message. To all intents and purposes, all that is remembered of Hosea, Micah, Isaiah, Jeremiah and the rest is that they spoke of the Messiah, and there is no thought of the specific historical context of each prophet and the particular colouring which he gave to his message. When announcements are made in church like 'A reading from the Book of Amos' or 'A reading from the Book of Habakkuk', or 'A reading from the Book of Zephaniah', I get the impression that many people switch off. Very often they do not

have the least idea of the time and place in which these prophets lived. Did they live in the eighth century before Jesus Christ or in the sixth? In a period of peace or prosperity? In Judah or Israel? In the reign of a just king or that of an oppressor? Were they countrymen or townsfolk? Were they courtiers or commoners? Were they regional heroes or major figures on the national and international scene?

Even more serious is the fact that liturgical custom necessitates a selection of quite brief passages which do not in themselves make it possible to grasp the complexity and totality of the message of a prophet.

Basically, as far as the prophets are concerned, even now we are still in the position of the Ethiopian eunuch who, as the Acts of the Apostles tells us, was reading the scroll of Isaiah, more specifically one of the Servant Songs. 'And the eunuch said to Philip, "About whom, pray, does the prophet say this, about himself or about someone else?" Then Philip opened his mouth, and beginning with this scripture he told him the good news of Jesus' (8.34–35).

This is the question that we will be asking throughout this book: 'Of whom is the prophet speaking like this? Of himself or of someone else?' Is he speaking of his time and only for his time? Is he speaking of himself, purely and simply in the first person? Or is he speaking of a community and in its name?

# Prophets in Freedom

The question has often been asked in our day: 'What does one have to do to be a prophet?' In other words, is there a foreseeable way by which one comes to adopt the role of a prophet? Are there techniques that can be learned? Or even a profile and an itinerary to follow?

If we look at the profile and the itinerary of the biblical prophets, we soon see that there is no laid down model, stereotype or fixed itinerary leading infallibly to prophecy. The biblical prophets had very different religious careers. Not only did they come from all kinds of backgrounds, but their spheres of life and their training, their religious experiences, their manner of communication and their style of speaking varied greatly. Reading their writings and those of their disciples, one could say that 'all roads lead to prophecy', since the prophets show so much originality and freedom.

Let's look at the profiles of some of them in order to get a better idea of this amazing diversity in the ways that lead to prophecy.

## Isaiah

is a married man, a court diplomat. He is in the thick of the action where decisions are taken. At the time when his vocation as a prophet emerges, he seems to be in full possession of himself, sure of himself: 'Send me, Lord!' (Isa.6.8). He is a man of great decisions and great political and religious debates. He is also one of the greatest poets of the Bible.

## Jeremiah

is young. He has all the enthusiasm and the verve of youth. He will soon become fascinated by the promises of Josiah's religious reform. But he remains fearful and vulnerable. In a way he is very 'human'. He will come to experience the disappointments of an abortive religious reform, the disquiet of times of war and exile, the weight of a solitary life – he receives the order to remain celibate (Jer.16.1) – and he will know persecution by his compatriots, in particular by the religious authorities of Jerusalem. He, too, is a poet of towering genius, but he does not

have Isaiah's assurance, and no prophet has 'confessed' better than he the way in which the mission with which he has been entrusted tears him apart: 'Why is my pain unceasing, my wound incurable, refusing to be healed? Truly you have become to me like a deceitful brook, like waters that fail' (Jer.15.18).

## Ezekiel

is a member of the priestly class which was so severely affected by the capture and destruction of the temple. But this priest is not purely a cultic official. He can identify at great depth the sense of trial inflicted on his people and communicate it with powerful imagery and unusual symbols. Though his work sometimes seems to us confused and takes on the aspect of a fantastic epic which is difficult to decipher, he has the merit of leaving the well-trodden ways and addressing his contemporaries vividly. A contemporary of Jeremiah, he differs from him particularly by his marital status, since he was a happily married man before he had the tragic experience of mourning a wife whom he cherished as 'the joy of (his) eyes' (Ezek.24.16). He also differs from Jeremiah by virtue of the mission conferred on him to proclaim the word of God in the land of exile, as one of those deported to Babylon.

## Hosea

has experienced a difficult and tormented marriage. God himself invited him to take in marriage 'a woman who is a prostitute' (Hos.1.2). That is not what one would normally expect of a prophet of God! But it is precisely through the difficulties, the misfortunes and the 'impossibilities' of his experience as a husband and father that the prophet is to discover the tenderness and faithfulness of God.

## Amos

a countryman with intense and colourful language, had nothing about him which indicated the prophet. Furthermore, he claims that he did not seek this role:

↓

↓
'I am no prophet nor a prophet's son; but I am a herdsman and dresser of sycamore trees' (Amos 7.14). In a sense, nothing prepared him for his mission. However, this man, who came late to prophecy, was able to find a clear and firm language in which to denounce the nonsense of triumphalist liturgies which easily adjusted to the unjust and oppressive treatment reserved for the very poorest (5.21–24).

*Jonah*

And what are we to say of the recalcitrant Jonah, a prophet 'despite himself'? He did not carry much conviction, poor thing! At least he had his little ideas on salvation, and he kept to them. He did all he could to escape his mission. But even against his will, prophecy asserted itself, and the people of Nineveh understood and accepted his message. However, despite the resounding success of his brief intervention in the streets of Nineveh and the sudden conversion of the whole city, Jonah was still not content and prayed to die. Hardly edifying for a man of God who should rather have been rejoicing at witnessing such prodigal demonstrations of mercy!

So there is no predetermined course to follow, nor are there barriers which could get in the way of being a prophet. Among the prophets of the Bible we find both men and women (see the box 'Prophecy in the Feminine'); young men (Samuel and Jeremiah) and old men (Samuel, in his old age and the aged Simeon), or people of a mature age; fully active men (Amos, Hosea, Isaiah, Ezekiel), 'career' prophets living among other prophets, like Elisha; and 'surprise prophets' like Eldad and Medad (Num.11.26–27) or Amos; people deeply rooted in their milieu (Hosea, Isaiah, Ezekiel) and 'uprooted' people, working outside their original sphere (Balaam, Amos, Jonah). The prophets came from different social classes: Amos is a countryman and a cultivator; Isaiah is a diplomat who has access to the royal court and from whom the city of Jerusalem has no secrets; Ezekiel is a priest, as is Jeremiah, at least by descent; and Deborah is a judge, fighting and involved in the resistance.

Thus the Bible presents us with a rich mosaic of prophecy, and no one can *a priori* be excluded from this vocation which is so important for the life of believing communities.

Like Philip, we too shall maintain the Christian perspective and see in what way the prophets also form part of the 'good news of Jesus the Christ'.

To present 'the prophets' in a single volume is an enormous challenge, and first of all I ask these giants of biblical literature to excuse me for the necessarily summary treatment I shall give them. Such a venture would seem excessive did I not have the consolation of at least being able to achieve the major objective of the series of which this volume is a part: 'How to Read'. For this is an invitation to read. Nothing can replace reading the actual text of the prophets. This volume simply aims to make people want to read the prophets, to read them one by one in their entirety. At the same time it suggests tools which can be used to enter into a fruitful reading of their texts.

So the book will be in two parts, of unequal

length, in order to give due priority to the actual texts of the prophets. Introductory questions have been reduced to a minimum: only two chapters. The first, which presupposes a continuous reading of the prophetic texts, seeks to bring out the main characteristics of the biblical prophets. The second takes into account the deep affinities between the message of the prophets and that of Jesus: they refer to each other, and each sheds light on the other.

The second part will allow some of the greatest figures of biblical prophecy to have their say: Amos, Hosea, Isaiah, Jeremiah, Ezekiel. At the end of this account comes a chapter which reflects on the prophets of the return, i.e. those who contributed to the rebuilding of Jerusalem – both the city and the community! – after 538. Jonah, who does not claim to be a great prophet, has been included for his originality and for the very profound theological lesson which he teaches us, in a way which is both critical and playful.

In each case, with the exception of Jonah and the prophets of the return, the study will be made in three stages. The first stage will be essentially about the prophet in his time and, I would say, in his book. Then, three key texts will be presented to help us to start on and, I hope, follow up, the study of each of these prophets. Finally, special attention will be paid to the way each of the prophets talks about God. Just as in the Gospels it is interesting to discover the Jesus of Mark, Matthew, Luke and John, so it is clear that one of the most fruitful approaches to the study of the prophets could be one which allows us to grasp the image of God which motivates and controls all that they do and say. I hope that this book will make it possible to discover some of these fascinating and diverse features of the God of the prophets, without which we could not understand the God of Jesus.

| The prophets in history | |
|---|---|
| Prophet | Ministry (BCE) |
| 1. Amos | 750 |
| 2. Hosea | 750 |
| 3. Isaiah | 740–700 |
| 4. Micah | 740 |
| 5. Nahum | 660 |
| 6. Zephaniah | 630 |
| 7. Jeremiah | 626–587 |
| 8. Habakkuk | 600 |
| 9. Ezekiel | 593–570 |
| 10. Obadiah | 580 |
| 11. Haggai | 520 |
| 12. Zechariah | 520 |
| 13. Joel | ??? (between 600 and 200!) |
| 14. [Jonah] | a fictitious story presenting an eighth-century prophet |
| 15. Malachi | 400 |

| Some important dates for placing the prophets | |
|---|---|
| Chronology (BCE) | Events |
| 1200–1000 | Period of the Judges and Samuel |
| 1000 | David, king of Judah and Israel |
| 970 | Solomon, king of Judah and Israel |
| 933 | Division into two kingdoms Israel = northern kingdom Judah = southern kingdom |
| 722–721 | Capture of Samaria and end of the northern kingdom |
| 597 | Capture of Jerusalem by Nebuchadnezzar and first deportation to Babylon |
| 587 | Destruction of the temple by Nebuchadnezzar and second deportation to Babylon |
| 538 | Edict of Cyprus, end of exile and return to Jerusalem |

# 1

# What is a Prophet?

That is the question which interests us, though we shall not be in a position to give a full answer to it until the end of this study. It is a question which does not interest us in a purely biographical or psychological sense, but in a literary and theological sense. We want to get to know the texts and what they set out to say from the perspective of faith.

## The prophets in the Bible

In this chapter, the first question to arise is this. What do we mean by 'the prophets' in an expression like 'How to Read the Prophets'? What will be the object of our study?

Here the Bible has surprises in store for us. The biblical definition of prophets, and more specifically of prophetic books, does not necessarily coincide with ours. The Hebrew Bible, which contains thirty-nine books, adopted a tripartite division which is different from the arrangement in the 'Old Testament' with which Christians are familiar: the Law (the Pentateuch = the first five books), the Prophets and the Writings. So there are an impressive number of books (thirty-four of them) which the Jewish tradition put either with the Prophets or with the Writings. Of this number the Jewish tradition kept twenty-one to form this second part of the Bible, which it denotes by the general title 'the Prophets'. In speaking here of 'prophets' or 'the prophetic literature' we shall be referring to all these twenty-one books of the Hebrew Bible.

The most amazing thing about this classification, as far as we are concerned, comes right at the beginning of the collection. There we find six books which beyond question we would not tend to define as prophetic: the books of Joshua, Judges, Samuel (I and II) and Kings (I and II). A first reading might incline us to put them in the third section with, for example, the books of Chronicles or those of Ezra and Nehemiah. How could they stand comparison with the majestic poetry and incisive oracles of prophets like Amos, Isaiah or Jeremiah?

However, we can understand how these books came to be associated with the prophetic tradition. On the one hand, despite its title, I and II Kings, which comprises forty-seven chapters in all, is just as much the history of the prophets as it is of the kings, with the famous interventions of Elijah, Elisha, Isaiah and Nathan, to mention only the leading figures. In fact, at least half of these forty-seven chapters introduce one or more prophets. Similarly, the two books of Samuel give a prime place to two great figures of early prophecy, Samuel and Nathan. On the other hand, on a deeper level, we discover that in these six books history is constantly read and reread in a prophetic manner. Here the prophets intervene precisely in order to invite another reading, a theological reading, of the history lived out by the kings and the people of Israel and Judah.

There remain the other fifteen books. Isaiah, Jeremiah and Ezekiel are no surprises; they have

## The Books of the Hebrew Bible

*The Law*

Genesis
Exodus
Leviticus
Numbers
Deuteronomy

*The Prophets*

*The former prophets*
Joshua
Judges
I and II Samuel
I and II Kings

*The latter prophets*
Isaiah
Jeremiah
Ezekiel
Hosea
Joel
Amos
Obadiah
Jonah
Micah
Nahum
Habakkuk
Zephaniah
Haggai
Zechariah
Malachi

*The Writings*

Psalms
Proverbs
Job
Song of Songs
Ruth
Lamentations
Koheleth (Ecclesiastes)
Esther
Daniel
Ezra
Nehemiah
I and II Chronicles

always been recognized as the great classics of biblical prophecy. On the other hand, from a Catholic perspective it is surprising not to find the name of Daniel on an equal level as a fourth prophet. However, his book is later than those of the other prophets and belongs more with wisdom and apocalyptic writings.

Then come the Twelve, often referred to as minor prophets, not because their message is less important but more prosaically because of the brevity of their individual writings.

We are going to draw on these twenty-one books in speaking of prophecy. But when the time comes to introduce each of the books, for evident reasons of space we shall be concentrating on the fifteen books attributed to individual prophets, i.e. to those who are usually called the writing prophets.

More fundamentally, we shall seek to discover who the prophets are, in the sense of 'What makes the prophets prophets?' Can we draw up an 'identity card' for them which allows us to distinguish true prophecy from false, and give a better definition of what should be understood today by prophet or prophecy?

### The meaning of terms

The etymology of the English word 'prophet' is very instructive. It is a composite word derived from the Greek, formed from a preposition (*pro*) and the name of an agent (*phetes*), the latter derived from a root which means 'say'. So prophesying has something to do with 'saying'. It is essentially a verbal activity.

But how are we to interpret the preposition *pro*? In Greek, it has three main meanings: 1. temporal, 'before'; 2. spatial, 'in front of'; 3. vicarious or representative, 'in place of' (as, for example in 'pro-cathedral', 'pro-proctor'). In the case of the word prophet and its derivatives in English, Christian tradition has clearly favoured the first sense, the temporal sense, thus giving it the meaning of 'predict' and 'prediction'. The prophets thus become those who spoke in advance, who predicted events to come, and, in a quite particular

Elisha sees Elijah taken up into heaven (II Kings 2.11f.)

way, the coming of the Messiah and the different aspects of his mission.

However, present-day biblical research – and the study which we shall be undertaking here will take the same direction – links biblical prophecy more with the two other senses of the preposition *pro*. On the one hand, the spatial sense would denote the vital link between the prophet and the community, the prophet and the people. The prophet is the one who speaks *before* the community, who addresses a community. He is the one who adopts a position in relation to the people, who puts himself in front of them in order to confront them with the demands of the covenant.

On the other hand, the 'representative' sense indicates that the prophet is not acting on his own initiative or on his own authority. He has been sent by God and must speak in God's name. The prophet speaks in the name of another, as a spokesman (or spokeswoman).

But there is more than vocabulary. A wider study of the whole of the writing prophets and other prophetic figures that we find in the prophetic literature leads us to perceive a certain number of constants or characteristics which define prophecy. So now let's try to trace the profile of the biblical prophets.

## Men of the Word

This first characteristic is the one that best defines the mission of the prophets. They are not scribes, but men of the word. They are people who have spoken, who have come forward, and whose ministry has been devoted to the service of the word. Nowadays we would say that they were 'professionals of the word'.

'Of the word', written with a lower case w. Amos, Hosea, Micah, Jeremiah and Ezekiel take up the word in turn and express it each according his style and his convictions, and with his own distinctive genius.

But their words seek to be first and foremost an echo of the Word (with a capital W). For the prophets claim to speak in the name of an Other.

Ten of the fifteen books of the writing prophets have the expression 'Words of X' or 'Word of the Lord to X for Y' in their titles. Furthermore, this general title is confirmed in the majority of the individual sayings of the prophets, which are usually introduced or concluded with one of the three following formulae:

- The word of the Lord came to X . . . (around 110 times)

- Thus says the Lord (436 times)

- Oracle of the Lord (more than 200 times; usually translated in English versions as 'says the Lord')

The prophets bring the Word of another. They are messengers, spokesmen. So their hearers are invited to receive their words as an expression of the Word of God: 'Hear the word of the Lord' (Jer.2.4).

Furthermore, it could be said that the Word is their sole passion, in both senses of the word. That is, the Word is what brings them alive, animates them and leads them to commit themselves to transforming the world and changing the future of their people. But it is also their passion in the sense that it is the Word that makes them suffer. It is because of the Word that they are persecuted and rejected.

No one has expressed better than Jeremiah this paradox of the Word which brings both happiness and suffering to the prophets:

When I found your words,
I devoured them.
Your words became a joy to me,
and made me deeply happy.
Your name has been proclaimed over me,
Lord, God of hosts.

I did not sit in the company of merry-makers,
nor did I rejoice.
I sat alone, constrained by your hand,
for you filled me with indignation.

Why is my pain unceasing,
my wound incurable,
refusing to be healed?
Truly you have become for me like a deceitful brook,
like waters that fail (Jer.15.16–18).

His contemporary Ezekiel expresses the same conviction in the form of an image. The Word is a book on which the prophet has to feed (Ezek.3.1–3) and which tastes sweet (the sweetness of honey) and bitter in turn. That is how the word of all the biblical prophets is presented: essentially good news of God proclaimed to the poor, it nevertheless remains terribly demanding for all.

## Men of the present

Men of the Word, the prophets are also men of the present. People have tried to make them diviners, proclaiming the 'great adventure', those who knew the course of events in advance and predicted it. But that is not the case.

The prophetic books do not devote themselves to an interpretation of the map of heaven or to wise calculations which would make it possible to read the future. On the contrary, they apply themselves to deciphering the present. In this connection it is instructive to re-read the headings of the books of the writing prophets. The editors have taken trouble to put in these the chronological frameworks in which the prophets worked.

Thus, for example, for Hosea, 'The word of the Lord was addressed to Hosea the son of Beeri, in the days of Uzziah, Jotham, Ahaz, and Hezekiah, kings of Judah, and in the days of Jeroboam the son of Joash, king of Israel' (1.1); or for Isaiah, 'The vision of Isaiah the son of Amoz, which he saw concerning Judah and Jerusalem, in the days of Uzziah, Jotham, Ahaz, and Hezekiah, kings of Judah' (1.1); or, much later, for Ezekiel, 'In the thirtieth year, in the fourth month, on the fifth day of the month, as I was among the exiles by the river Chebar, the heavens were opened, and I saw visions of God. On the fifth day of the month (it was

the fifth year of the exile of King Jehoiachin), the word of the Lord came to Ezekiel the priest, the son of Buzi, in the land of the Chaldaeans by the river Chebar' (1.1–3).

These chronological references are absolutely indispensable for understanding what follows. The Word of God is not timeless and should not be detached from the history which gave it birth. So it is important to read prophecy in the present; before even wanting to apply it to our times, or to Christianize it, we must first listen to it in its original context.

The prophets are not diviners. The Septuagint, the Greek translation of the Hebrew Bible, understood this when it preferred the term *prophetes* to *mantis* (as in cheiromancy) to translate the Hebrew *nabi*. The Greek *mantis* has the connotation of 'diviner'. On the other hand, if we read all the prophetic oracles we see that in fact not much space is given over to prediction; so little, indeed, that one could well not notice it. It is very rare that we hear a prophet venturing to date the fulfilment of his oracles. On the contrary, these oracles are usually introduced with a very flexible formula which in no way presumes a real calendar of events: 'In those days', or 'In that day', or 'Days will come . . .'

The prophets are not futurologists. They are interested first and foremost in the present, their own present and that of their audience. What interests them is not divining the future but changing the present. The prime concern of their oracles is the present history of their people.

That does not mean that the prophets are confined to the horizon of their own history. They are equally passionate about the future, but this is a future with which they have contact. They reject a determinist reading of history, and they believe that the future is connected with the initiative of God and the response of human freedom.

If the word of the prophets had eternal value, one prophet would have been enough: as an extreme, one could have been content with the words of Moses, of Elijah or Isaiah. But precisely because the prophetic word arises for a given era and in response to precise needs, there have been a great variety of spokesmen: Amos, Hosea, Micah, Isaiah, Joel, Jeremiah, Ezekiel, Jonah, Malachi, and so on: 'In many and various ways God spoke of old to our fathers by the prophets; but in these last days he has spoken to us by a Son . . .' (Heb. 1.1–2). 'In many and various ways.' Not all spoke at the same time and in the same way. Just as we have the gospel of Jesus Christ in four different versions, so the treasure of biblical prophecy has been handed on to us by a multitude of witnesses and literary forms.

It is also interesting to note how biblical prophecy has come down through time and marked the major stages of the history of salvation. Israel had the good fortune to have prophets for the major transitional periods of its history. First, of course, there was *the* prophet, Moses, and his sister Miriam, a prophetess, at the time of the liberation from Egypt and the journey in the wilderness. There was also Deborah in the time of the Judges, the only judge who is said also to have been a prophetess, who led the history of Israel for forty years. When the time came for Israel to give itself a king, it was the prophet Samuel who guided the destiny of the people. The period of the monarchy, from David to Jehoiachin, i.e. until the exile to Babylon, was the period of prophecy *par excellence*. There were great prophets at the time of the exile and at its heart (Jeremiah, Ezekiel) as there also were for the return (Deutero–Isaiah, Haggai, Malachi, Zechariah). Certainly prophecy died out in the course of the three last centuries before Jesus Christ, but the expectation of a great prophet was no less lively.

So we have to say that the prophetic movement is an extremely lively one. Misunderstood and persecuted, nevertheless the prophets had a following. Circles of disciples received their sayings and re-read them in the light of the new situations which they were called on to live out. Prophecy engenders prophecy. It is not enough to repeat the oracles of the prophets of the past. These oracles require to be meditated on, assimilated and then adapted to meet the needs of the moment.

## Men of vision

If for the prophets the word has priority, we must not neglect another dimension of their experience and their activity. For the prophets are also seers, or better, visionaries. Furthermore it is by this title of seer (Hebrew *ro'eh*) that the prophet was first known in Israel: 'Formerly in Israel, when a man went to inquire of God, he said, "Come, let us go to the seer"; for he who is now called a prophet was formerly called a seer' (I Sam 9.9). We should note in this passage the distance in time between the 'now' of the final redactor of I Samuel and the 'formerly' of the time of Saul. In this passage, prophecy does not seem yet to have been freed from divinatory practices.

But it is not in this sense that the prophets are finally to assert themselves as seers. Their 'visions' are of quite a different order from that of divination.

You may be surprised to learn that the book of the great prophet Isaiah is entitled 'Vision of Isaiah' and not 'Words of Isaiah' or 'Word of the Lord which came to Isaiah'. And in a way which is strangely similar, the heading of the book of Amos has 'Words of Amos . . . words which he saw . . .' In fact chapters 7 to 9 of Amos report to us a series of five visions which support his final plea for the conversion of Israel.

Even the calling of Jeremiah is based on a visionary experience and an interpretation of what the prophet sees:

And the word of the Lord came to me, saying, 'Jeremiah, what do you see?' And I said, 'I see an almond branch.' Then the Lord said to me, 'You have seen well, for I am watching over my word to perform it.'

The word of the Lord came to me a second time, saying, 'What do you see?' And I said, 'I see a boiling pot, facing away from the north' (Jer. 1.11–13).

Deborah (Judg. 4–5)

# Prophecy in the Feminine

The twenty-one books which form the central section of the Hebrew Bible called 'the Prophets' have made us familiar with the great masculine figures of prophecy: Amos, Hosea, Isaiah, Jeremiah, Ezekiel and so on. The headings of individual books, which serve as signatures, in all probability contain no feminine name. This is a fact which can be deeply deplored today, but it is hardly surprising in the religious and institutional context in which the Hebrew Bible was formed.

That having been said, even for the Hebrew Bible prophecy is by no means the exclusive prerogative of men. Women prophesied and were recognized within their communities as prophetesses. What wouldn't we give today to rediscover just one of their writings! In them we would certainly find one more proof of the remarkable freedom of the breath of prophecy.

But who are these prophetesses? In the Old Testament we find a total of five of them: Miriam, Deborah, Isaiah's wife, Huldah and Noadiah.

Let's examine the role of each of these briefly.

**Miriam** is known to us as the sister of Aaron and Moses, and we can understand how the biblical tradition has favoured her two brothers, one of whom was to remain the greatest charismatic figure in the history of Israel and the other of whom is the great ancestor of priestly power. However, given the stature of these two spiritual leaders of the chosen people, the role given by the texts of the book of Exodus to Miriam seems all the more important.

First — and this was not the case with her two famous brothers — Miriam is introduced by a title which indicates her role within the community, 'prophetess'. What we are in fact told in Ex.15.20, the first explicit mention of Miriam, is this: 'Then Miriam, the prophetess, the sister of Aaron, took a timbrel in her hand; and all the women went out after her with timbrels and dancing. And Miriam sang to them: "Sing to the Lord, for he has triumphed gloriously; the horse and his rider he has thrown into the sea."'

Here is a significant and calm recognition of the status of Miriam within the community; it seems to be taken for granted. Note also in the passage the solidarity of Miriam with 'all the women' and the fact that they sing together the first couplet of the famous 'Song of Moses' which he sang 'with the people of Israel' (Ex.15.1).

In another episode during the course of the journey in the desert, Miriam will be involved in a controversy over the privileged authority of her brother Moses (Num.12.1–16). Along with Aaron, she openly criticizes Moses' conduct in his marriage with a Nubian woman and challenges the exclusiveness of his charisma: 'Has the Lord indeed spoken only through Moses? Has he not spoken through us also?' (v.2). This criticism did not succeed in pleasing the Lord, whose 'anger was kindled against them, and he departed; and when the cloud removed from over the tent, behold, Miriam was leprous . . .' (vv.9,10). It is strange that of the two challengers, only Miriam is punished. But at the same time, as the Jewish tradition has stressed, Miriam seems to enjoy a special status. Though she cannot in any way lay claim to the privileged status of Moses, the man in whom the Lord trusts and who 'sees the form of the Lord', while Miriam and the other prophets have access to God only through a 'vision' or a 'dream', i.e. in 'hidden language', the fact remains that the journey of the people in the wilderness could not be continued 'till Miriam was brought in again' (v.16)!

**Deborah** (Judg.4–5) has nothing to fear from the plethora of judges of greater or lesser fame whose memory is celebrated in the book of Judges. First of all as a judge: she can boast of having succeeded in what seems to represent the ideal of success for a judge, namely to have brought peace to the country for a period of forty years (Judg.3.11, 30; 5.31; 8.28). Then, of all the judges who ruled over the country (Judg.1–21), she is the only one to have combined the functions of judge and prophet: 'Now Deborah, a prophetess, the wife of Lappidoth, was judging

↓

Israel at that time. She used to sit under the palm of Deborah between Ramah and Bethel in the hill country of Ephraim; and the people of Israel came up to her for judgment' (Judg.4.5). Finally, of all the judges, she is also the only one to whom a song has been attributed (Judg.5). This is one of the oldest poems in the Bible, which has some similarities with the song of victory sung by Moses (Ex.15). And like Moses before her, she does not sing it alone: 'Then sang Deborah and Barak the son of Abinoam on that day . . .' (Judg.5.1). In Exodus we had Moses and Miriam, and Moses took the initiative. Here the perspective of the masculine and feminine roles is to some degree reversed; we have Deborah and Barak, but it is manifestly Deborah who takes the initiative.

Then comes the **wife of Isaiah**, the only 'prophetess' whose name we do not know. With Noadiah, she is also the one about whose prophetic career we know least. She effaces herself completely behind her husband Isaiah, the giant of prophecy, and only comes out of the shadows when mention is made of another son to be born to the couple: 'And I went to the prophetess, and she conceived and bore a son' (Isa.8.3). From such effacement there are those who conclude that the feminine noun prophetess (Hebrew *nebiah*) has the more restricted sense here of 'wife of the prophet'. This is not completely impossible, but it would be somewhat surprising and would be a unique instance. It is hard to see why here too the noun should not have its functional sense rather than the more restricted relational sense of 'wife of the prophet'.

Then, at the time of King Josiah and what has been called the 'Deuteronomic reform' around 625, we must surely emphasize the exceptional role played by the prophetess **Huldah** in the discovery of the Book of the Law (II Kings 22). When the king could very well have appealed to the prophet Jeremiah, the officers of the temple, whom he had sent to 'consult the Lord', chose rather to resort to the services of 'Huldah the prophetess, the wife of Shallum the son of Tikvah, son of Harhas', who 'dwelt in Jerusalem in the New Quarter' (II Kings 22.14). Her particulars are given in the way customary in the headings of the prophetic books. Further-more she is the only woman in the whole of the Old Testament to whom formal oracles are attributed with the traditional introduction, 'Thus says the Lord, the God of Israel . . .' (II Kings 22.15, 16, 18), and the classical conclusion, 'Says the Lord' (II Kings 22.20). It was from her instructions that the great reform undertaken by Josiah was to stem (II Kings 23). It is also interesting to note that some chapters later the author of II Kings refers again to the prophecies of Huldah with the general formula 'according to the word of the Lord which he spoke by his servants the prophets' (II Kings 24.2).

**Noadiah** is mentioned in the prayer of Nehemiah: 'Remember Tobiah and Sanballat, O my God, according to these things that they did, and also the prophetess Noadiah and the rest of the prophets who wanted to make me afraid' (Neh.6.14). Here 'remember' takes on a double meaning: while in the case of the other prophets it denotes a negative retribution, it keeps its usual sense of benevolent and protective concern in the case of Tobiah, Sanballat and Noadiah.

To these five women we should also add the name of the prophetess Anna who, although she is mentioned in the writings of the New Testament (Luke 2.36–38), by her age ('she had reached the age of eighty-four') and attachment to the temple ('she did not depart from the temple, worshipping with fasting and prayer night and day') belongs to the period that we call the Old Testament. If the evangelist Luke does not record her words, as he does those of Simeon, he nevertheless gives her an important role in the announcement of Jesus 'to all who were looking for the redemption of Jerusalem'.

That is the portrait of prophecy in the feminine which can be derived from the Old Testament. We are still far from a full blossoming and a full participation, but there are happy glimpses of a new time when women and men will be able to prophesy equally: 'And it shall come to pass afterward, that I will pour out my spirit on all flesh; your sons and your daughters shall prophesy, your old men shall dream dreams, and your young men shall see visions. Even upon the menservants and maidservants in those days, I will pour out my spirit' (Joel 3.1–2).

Of all the prophets, Ezekiel is certainly the most powerful visionary. The opening of his book sets the tone: 'The heavens were opened, and I saw visions of God' (Ezek.1.1). If the Lord calls on him to listen, he also calls on him to look and to interpret his vision.

Finally, the little book of Obadiah is also presented to us as a vision.

So the prophet is a visionary. In other words, he learns to read events and see them in God's way. He is, as was once said of Balaam, 'the man with the penetrating gaze'. Where others have a complacent or disillusioned view, the prophet presents a view which is both critical and refreshing. This is the sense in which we must re-read the enigmatic passage in Isaiah in which the prophet is compared to a watchman:

One is calling to me from Seir,
'Watchman, what of the night?
Watchman, what of the night?'
The watchman says,
'Morning comes, and also the night.
If you will inquire, inquire;
come back again' (Isa.21.11–12).

### Men of the spirit?

Perhaps you will be amazed at the question mark here. After all, doesn't the expression 'man of the spirit' occur quite literally in Hosea 9.7, specifically in parallel with the word 'prophet'? Isn't it customary to speak of the prophetic spirit? However, a careful reply must be given to the question raised.

First of all we must note the extreme reserve of the classical prophets (those who have been included in the canon of scripture) in this connection. Of all the writing prophets, only Ezekiel makes explicit reference to the spirit in giving an account of his prophetic mission. There is complete silence in the others, including Isaiah and Jeremiah. Certainly, it will be said that the spirit was at work in them, but they did not describe their own prophetic experience as an experience of the spirit. And on the few occasions when they allude to the

Spirit, it is always in a polemical or ironical context, when they are reacting to the ecstatic or divinatory techniques of those whom they regard as false prophets (Hos.9.7–9; Micah 2.6–11; 3.5–8; Jer.5.10–17).

Does that mean that the spirit is not significant in the experience of the biblical prophets and therefore we must abandon the term 'prophetic spirit'? Certainly not, for there is also a biblical tradition in which the spirit plays a major role in prophecy. One might think above all of the beginnings, with the spirit which is imparted to Moses and then to the elders (Num.11.25), then of the transmission of prophetic authority from Elijah to Elisha (II Kings 2.15) and above all to Ezekiel, who acts directly under the influence of the Spirit: 'a spirit came upon me . . .' (Ezek.2.2; 3.12, 24; 11.5). The link between the spirit and prophecy will be even clearer in the New Testament, with the reading which Peter makes of Joel 3.1–5 on the day of Pentecost: 'And in the last days it shall be, God declares, that I will pour out my spirit upon all flesh, and your sons and your daughters shall prophesy, and your young men shall see visions, and your old men shall dream dreams; yes, and on my menservants and my maidservants in those days I will pour out my spirit; and they shall prophesy' (Acts 2.17–18).

But at any rate let us remember that the spirit who inspired the prophets does not seem to have been offended by the fact that they spoke so little of him in giving an account of their call to the prophetic ministry.

### Witnesses and signs for the people

To make the Word of God understandable to their contemporaries, the prophets did more than speak. They performed actions and translated the word by their lives.

If it was above all their oracles and their oral preaching which were remembered, some of their gestures and symbolic actions struck the popular imagination all the more. The prophets had the gift of performing actions which shook, aroused, intrigued and provoked the people to change.

Isaiah certainly made the population of Judah think when he appeared in public, at the time of the Syro–Ephraimite crisis (around 730), with his son Shear-yashub (Isa.7), whose name means 'A remnant will return'. So for him the situation was not desperate. However, shortly afterwards he was to announce a contrary situation, this time bringing with him his son Maher-shalal-hash-baz, whose name can be translated 'Prompt-prey-near-spoil' (Isa.8); hope now gives place to disquiet. Then, later in his career, we are told that he walked around Jerusalem naked and without shoes for three years (Isa.20).

Jeremiah also performed a certain number of symbolic actions. He hid a waistcloth that was going rotten in the cleft of a rock to symbolize the present corruption and the lamentable state of the people (Jer.13). He watched with the greatest interest the potter at work in his workshop and understood the care which God takes to form the human creature with his own hands. This also led him to become aware of the fragility of the work which emerges from the hands of the potter and of the divine wrath which was on the point of bursting out against Judah. But also, at the height of the exile, Jeremiah acquired a field in Anathoth, his home village, to show that there was no need for despair and that normal life would soon resume its course (Jer.32). However, it was Ezekiel who proved the champion of symbolic actions. He has an undeniable talent for mime in performing a whole series of actions announcing the rigours of the imminent exile: he shuts himself up in his house, depicts a city under siege, lies only on his left side, prepares his bread in wretched conditions and shaves himself with a drawn sword (Ezek.4; 5). He also goes out, in the full sight of all, with the typical bundle of clothes carried by those who are deported (Ezek.12).

But there are not only outward symbolic actions. There are also those which are deeply rooted in life, in the very existence of .the prophet. We might think, for example, of the difficult loves, marriage and remarriage of Hosea (Hos.1–3), or of the weight of loneliness which Jeremiah feels when God calls on him to renounce marriage, at least for a time, because of the misfortune which will soon fall upon the house of Judah (Jer.16). And his contemporary Ezekiel has to mourn his wife with extreme detachment (Ezek.24), again because of the gravity of the tragedy which strikes his people.

So one is not a prophet at the level of lip service, but in one's flesh and one's tears, one's loves and failures, in all that makes up a human life. The biblical prophets are of this race, the race of those who have suffered and struggled in solidarity with a people who are deeply afflicted.

## Disturbing people

As we know, the prophets never had an easy life. That is not surprising, since they had been chosen always to be in the front line. Contestants by nature, they were necessarily engaged in conflict, with their fellow prophets, or with the kings whom they denounced, or the temple authorities, or finally the people themselves. In a way Ahab was right when he accused Elijah of being 'the troublemaker of Israel' (I Kings 18.17).

No sphere of the collective history of Israel escapes the challenge of the prophets.

In foreign policy, the prophets denounce the alliances with the neighbouring powers, like Egypt or Assyria:

'Woe to the rebellious children,' says the Lord,
'who carry out a plan, but not mine;
and who make a league, but not of my spirit,
that they may add sin to sin;
who set out to go down to Egypt,
without asking for my counsel,
to take refuge in the protection of Pharaoh,
and to seek shelter in the shadow of Egypt.
Therefore shall the protection of Pharaoh turn to your shame,
and the shelter in the shadow of Egypt to your humiliation.
Already your leaders are at Tanis,
the envoys have reached Hanes.

They will all be deceived
by a people that cannot profit them,
that brings neither help nor profit,
but shame and disgrace' (Isa.30.1–5).

Called to intervene on the political scene, the prophets were never afraid to point out the falsity of this kind of alliance sought by the kings of Israel and Judah. On the other hand, Jeremiah, alone against the rest, called for submission to the king of Babylon (Jer.27).

Critical of power, the prophets attacked constantly and systematically all that they considered an abuse of power and injustice:

Your princes are rebels
and companions of thieves.
Every one loves a bribe
and runs after gifts.
They do not defend the fatherless,
and the widow's cause does not come to them
(Isa.1.23).

Run to and fro through the streets of Jerusalem,
look and take note!
Search her squares to see
if you can find a man,
one who does justice
and seeks truth (Jer.5.1).

Gilead is a city of evildoers,
tracked with blood (Hos.6.8).

Assemble yourselves upon the mountains of Samaria,
and see the great tumults within her,
and the oppressions in her midst.
'They do not know how to do right,' says the Lord,
those who store up violence and robbery in their strongholds (Amos 3.9–10).

Hear, you heads of Jacob
and rulers of the house of Israel!
Is it not for you to know justice? –
You who hate the good and love the evil,
who tear the skin from off my people,
and the flesh from off their bones (Micah 3.1–2).

Religion, too, attracts extremely severe criticism from the prophets. Not because they are against the religion of their time or right on its periphery, but because they see all its lying aspects. What they denounce is the formalism and triumphalism of a worship which is contradicted by a life of injustice and infidelity:

When you spread forth your hands,
I will hide my eyes from you;
though you make many prayers,
I will not listen;
your hands are full of blood (Isa.1.15).

This people honours me with its lips,
but its heart is far from me (Isa.29.13).

I hate, I despite your feasts,
and I take no delight in your solemn assemblies
(Amos 5.22).

They utter mere words;
with empty oaths they make covenants;
so judgment springs up like poisonous weeds
in the furrows of the field (Hos.10.4).

But it is not only the political and religious leaders who are the cause of this. What the prophets deplore is the faithlessness of a whole people and the widespread failure to know the covenant and its demands. In the face of this situation, the prophets even speak of God putting his people on trial.

Hear the word of the Lord, O people of Israel;
for the Lord has a controversy with the inhabitants of the land.
There is no faithfulness or kindness,
and no knowledge of God in the land (Hos.4.1).

Ah, sinful nation,
a people laden with iniquity,
offspring of evildoers,
sons who deal corruptly.
They have forsaken the Lord,
they have despised the Holy One of Israel,
they are utterly estranged.
Why will you still be smitten,
that you continue to rebel?

The whole head is sick,
and the whole heart faint (Isa.1.4–5).

Around the exile, the portrait will be hardly any better, when Jeremiah gives the surname 'apostasy' to Israel (Jer.3.6), while Ezekiel is warned that he will have to deal with a 'rebellious house'.

## Men of unconditional hope

Serious though the infidelities of the people may be, the prophets are not the kind of people who accept them and believe that all is now lost. The severity of their denunciations and their threats is aimed at rousing the people in order to lead them back to the truth and help them to rediscover happiness. If the prophets have chosen to speak, it is certainly not to 'quench the smoking flax' (Isa.42.3). They have an unconditional hope. This is not a naive and tolerant hope, but a bold and demanding one.

The theme of conversion remains one of the leitmotifs of prophetic preaching: 'Return, apostate Israel, says the Lord, I will not look upon you with anger' (Jer.3.11); 'Return, O Israel, to the Lord your God, because your fault has made you stumble' (Hos.14.2); 'On that day you shall not be put to shame because of the deeds by which you have rebelled against me' (Zeph.3.11). It could be said that even an outspoken prophet like Amos was the 'prophet of the eleventh hour'. For all the prophets, in fact, a conversion of the people is always possible. Otherwise, it stands to reason, why prophesy? A prophet as recalcitrant as Jonah must end up by accepting this; even the wicked Ninevites choose the way of conversion, and Nineveh is not destroyed.

However, this is only one side of the coin, that of the conversion of the people. There is another even more important one, that of the future which God is preparing for his people. The prophets constantly proclaim the restoration of the people and a salvation for all nations. In connection with this we can profitably re-read the conclusions of the books of the writing prophets. Eleven books out of the fifteen end with grandiose perspectives of salvation: the people is gathered together, healed, consolidated and saved, and the nations ascend to Jerusalem to form the vast people of the saved.

Do the prophets have an unconditional hope? This was certainly thought to be the case by Ben Sirach, some two centuries before Jesus Christ:

> May the bones of the twelve prophets
> revive from where they lie,
> for they comforted the people of Jacob,
> and delivered them with confident hope
>
> (Sirach 49.10).

Balaam

# 2

# From the Prophets to Jesus – the Same Gospel?

It might seem premature or somewhat illogical now to look at the relationship between the prophets and the New Testament. We are used to having the prophets presented in chronological order, so that we look first at all the prophetic writings before discussing their impact on those of the New Testament.

However, since the aim of this book is to make you want to read the prophets, it seems to me that there is no better way in to them than this. The best answer to the questions which inevitably arise in a Christian setting in our day, 'Do we have to read the prophets? If for us Jesus is the prophet *par excellence*, do the prophets of the Old Testament still have anything to teach us? And if so, how do we read them?', is beyond doubt that in so doing we will be faithful to the New Testament, to the gospel of Jesus Christ. And this is the most decisive argument. Even a brief reading of the Gospels will soon show that the prophets and their message were a constant point of reference of the utmost importance for Jesus and the New Testament writers.

## The witness of the prophets in the New Testament

In fact, the place occupied by the prophets and their writings in the New Testament is quite remarkable. Purely from a statistical point of view, we can identify some 400 quotations or allusions; this is not only a great many, but makes the prophets by far the best represented group of writings in the New Testament.

But there is more than these statistics, and better. It is clear that for the New Testament authors the books of the prophets are part of an inspired scripture, and that with the Law they contain the essentials of revelation: Matthew, Luke, John and Paul readily use the expression 'the Law and the Prophets' (seventeen times in all) to refer to the overall witness of scripture. Moreover, it is this joint witness of the 'Law and the Prophets' that is signified by the presence of Moses and Elijah at the Transfiguration of Jesus (Mark 9.4 par.). On the other hand, without wanting to minimize the fundamental role of the Law, the New Testament writers quite frequently – forty-five times in all – refer solely to the collective witness of the prophets to justify the conduct or the teaching of Jesus.

The New Testament, and Jesus in particular, is also fond of evoking great popular prophetic figures like Elijah (thirty times) and Elisha (once). Even if these two ancestors of biblical prophecy did not leave any writings, the saga of their prophetic oracles and actions is sufficiently alive in the memory of Jesus' hearers for them to be referred to as a way of making Jesus' actions and gestures more understandable. Luke did not fail to emphasize at the beginning of the ministry of Jesus (ch.4) the parallel between Jesus and the prophets Elijah and Elisha:

The Transfiguration of Jesus (Mark 9.4)

But in truth, I tell you, there were many widows in Israel in the days of Elijah, when the heaven was shut up three years and six months, when there came a great famine over all the land; and Elijah was sent to none of them but only to Zarephath, in the land of Sidon, to a woman who was a widow.

And there were many lepers in Israel at the time of the prophet Elisha; and none of them was cleansed, but only Naaman the Syrian (4.25–27).

So the rejection of Jesus by his people in Nazareth is not a new phenomenon in Israel: Elijah and Elisha suffered an identical fate. But the comparison does not stop there. In citing the example of the two prophets Jesus also means to bring out the 'paradox of salvation'. Misunderstood or rejected in the midst of their people, the authentic prophets receive a favourable welcome in a foreign land and, thanks to them, the nations bordering on Israel have access to salvation.

The phenomenon of the quotations is no less interesting. Certainly the prophet Isaiah is the one who is quoted most often: twenty-two times by name and five other times where the reference, although not explicit, is certain. Second after him is a more unexpected figure – Jonah (ten times)! After that we find, in order, Jeremiah (three times), Hosea (once) and Joel (once). These are the writing prophets who are explicitly mentioned.

That the prophets are quoted, and quoted relatively frequently in the New Testament, is evidence in itself, provided that one reads the New Testament attentively. However, more important than the number of references or illusions, we cannot ignore the positive value that the New Testament attaches to the witness of the prophets. In fact the quotations which the New Testament authors have drawn from their writings are far more than just ornamental and aesthetic. In other words, when the prophets are quoted, it is not simply to enliven the text and make it more atractive to read, but solely to express the good news of Jesus Christ better. Here we should note the so to speak strategic importance of the biblical quotations taken from the prophets. Let's look at several examples.

First of all in Mark. On the lips of Jesus, the parables, which already in his time were a well-attested genre in the Bible and in Jewish literature, take on a quite special colouring. In a sense one can say that Jesus' parables of the kingdom are fully characteristic of his language. However, Jesus' contemporaries did not always succeed in grasping their meaning. Confronted with this paradoxical fact (Jesus excelled in presenting parables, but people did not understand them!), Mark did not hesitate to invoke the witness of Isaiah, whose preaching also had to come to terms with the resistance and incomprehension of its first hearers:

And he said to them, 'To you has been given the secret of the kingdom of God, but for those outside everything is in parables; so that they may indeed see but not perceive, and may indeed hear and not understand; less they should turn again and be forgiven' (Mark 4.11–12; cf. Isa.6.9–10, Aramaic text).

So it is the essentials of Jesus' preaching (here Mark gives us not only Jesus' first parable, but a fuller collection) which are put in the context of the reception of prophetic preaching in the past.

A little later, again in the Gospel of Mark (ch.7), Jesus takes the Pharisees severely to task for all their traditions (ablutions and all kinds of ritual purifications):

And he said to them, 'Well did Isaiah prophesy of you hypocrites, as it is written, "This people honours me with their lips, but their heart is far from me; in vain do they worship me, teaching as doctrines the precepts of men." You leave the commandment of God, and hold fast the tradition of men' (Mark 7.5–8; cf. Isa.29.13, Greek text; the same quotation is used in Matt.15.8–9).

Once again, Jesus uses a saying of the prophet Isaiah to back up his denunciation of the excesses of a ritual which expresses more concern for outward purity than for inward purity, and to present his own vision of a purity which comes 'from within . . . from the human heart' (Mark 7.21). In other words, Jesus bases himself on the witness of the prophets in order to distance himself better from the religion of the Pharisees. In such a context the word of Isaiah takes on a new dimension and in a way serves to define the novelty of the religion put forward by Jesus.

Jesus differed from the Pharisees on another major point: his attitude to sinners. On this point it is again to the witness of a prophet, Hosea, that Matthew appeals to justify Jesus' conduct, which was a source of scandal for the Pharisees:

And when the Pharisees saw this, they said to his disciples, 'Why does your teacher eat with tax collectors and sinners?' But when he heard it, he said, 'Those who are well have no need of a physician, but those who are sick. Go and learn what this means, "I desire mercy, and not sacrifice." For I came not to call the righteous, but sinners' (Matt.9.11–13; cf. Hos.6.6; Matthew takes up the same quotation in 12.7).

In Luke, the whole mission of Jesus is set explicitly in the context of an oracle of the prophet Isaiah:

And he came to Nazareth, where he had been brought up; and he went to the synagogue, as his custom was, on the sabbath day. And he stood up to read; and there was given to him the book of the prophet Isaiah. He opened the book and found the place where it was written:

'The spirit of the Lord is upon me,

because he has anointed me to preach good news to the poor.

He has sent me to proclaim release to the captives

and recovering of sight to the blind,

to set at liberty those who are oppressed,

to proclaim the acceptable year of the Lord.'

And he closed the book, and gave it back to the attendant, and sat down; and the eyes of all in the synagogue were fixed on him. and he began to say to them, 'Today this scripture has been fulfilled in your hearing' (Luke 4.16–21).

This is a programmatic text carefully chosen by Luke: the mission of Jesus is presented as good news to the poor, in line with the gospel message formulated in the third section of the book of Isaiah (61.1). Everything in this text is aimed at emphasizing the solemnity of the moment. Jesus leaves no doubt about the meaning which must henceforward be attached to the passage which he has just read, 'Today this scripture has been fulfilled in your hearing.' It is certainly fulfilled, but not without new features, since Luke attributes to Jesus a slightly abbreviated quotation of the text of Isa 61.1, deliberately omitting the words 'the day of vengeance of our God' after 'the acceptable year of the Lord'. In Luke, the mission of Jesus is primarily and solely a mission of salvation. This dimension of salvation, already very marked in the original oracle of the prophet Isaiah, is here reinforced and taken to its supreme fulfilment.

Put on the lips of Jesus, the quotations from the prophets have a strictly theological function. The number of quotations and the importance attached to them by the evangelists confirms the validity of the prophet's perspective on God and his demands on believers. Jesus agrees with the prophets on essentials: he shows complete solidarity with them, and appeals to the same God. When, for example, we find in Hosea the phrase 'I desire mercy and not sacrifices', we already have a very high idea of God and the primacy of the commandment to love. This is already an anticipation of the New Testament: the prophet anticipates the experience of a God of mercy with whom Jesus will speak in perfect harmony. The prophets of the Old Testament already sensed the mystery of a God who wants 'mercy and not sacrifices', the religion of the heart and not of external practices, just as they already made known, in their day, 'the good news to the poor' and the 'deliverance of the captives'.

## An example of Christian re-reading of the prophets

We saw earlier that the prophets very rarely risked making predictions. But in that case, why have they so often been said to have predicted Christ? And isn't it true that the Gospels themselves do not fail to emphasize that Jesus performed such and such an action precisely 'in order that what the Lord had said by the prophet X or Y should be fulfilled . . .'?

There has in fact been much 'psychologizing' of the texts of the prophets. Because of the way in which people have thought of the inspiration of scripture, they have attempted to rediscover in the prophet's consciousness a clear and definite perception of very distant events. Now nothing is less certain than that the prophets had such a consciousness.

One example – though it contains a number of references – will be enough to illustrate this statement: Matthew 1–2. Contrary to what might be expected, these two chapters about the childhood of Jesus are far from naive; on the contrary, they present themselves as a well-constructed narrative, rich in a very developed theology. Matthew, who, as we know well, had Jewish roots and was concerned to answer questions and objections from Jewish circles, feels the need to show that Jesus fulfils the Jewish scriptures. He does this in a brilliant way by inserting, into each of the five episodes of the childhood of Jesus (the annunciation to Joseph, the visit of the magi, the flight into Egypt, the massacre of the children of Bethlehem and the return from Egypt to Nazareth), a word of scripture which is introduced each time by a solemn and unequivocal formula: 'that what the Lord had spoken by the prophet should be fulfilled . . .' (or an equivalent formula). While he did not hesitate to quote the Law and the Psalms, here he refers only to the prophets. His reading, or better his re-reading, is done in a prophetic key.

Let us look briefly at the texts which Matthew quotes and his interpretation of them:

- In 1.23:

  Behold a virgin shall conceive and bear a son,
  and his name shall be called Immanuel (which means, God with us) (Isa.7.14).

- In 2.6:

  And you, O Bethlehem, in the land of Judah,
  are by no means least among the rulers of Judah;
  for from you shall come a ruler
  who will govern his people Israel (Micah 5.1).

- In 2.15:

  Out of Egypt have I called my son (Hos.11.1).

- In 2.18:

  A voice was heard in Ramah,
  wailing and loud lamentation,
  Rachel weeping for her children;
  she refused to be consoled,
  because they were no more (Jer.31.15).

- In 2.23:

  'He shall be called a Nazarene' (a quotation of unknown origin!)

This small group gives an excellent indication of the work that the evangelists did in quoting the prophets.

First, the very fact of the quotations bears witness to a great respect for scripture. The quotations play a strictly theological role and serve as a framework of interpretation for Matthew.

Secondly, there is no doubt of Matthew's biblical, specifically prophetic, culture. Four different prophets are brought in, and it is certainly necessary to know their books well to identify the specific verses.

Thirdly, along with the evangelist's respect for scripture we must also note his extreme freedom. In the Jewish tradition inherited by Matthew the prophetic word is not fixed. It is in constant evolution, and is constantly subjected to exercises in re-reading and updating. In fact, two of Matthew's five quotations differ quite significantly from the earliest versions of the prophetic text. Thus, for example, in the Immanuel oracle Matthew prefers the Greek version of the Septuagint, which speaks of a 'virgin', where the Hebrew text of Isaiah spoke more generally of a 'young woman'. And as for the status of Bethlehem among the clans of Judah, it is easy to see that Matthew has completely changed the focus of Micah's oracle: where the eighth-century prophet was speaking of an insignificant hamlet, Matthew, beginning from what he knows of Jesus, makes Bethlehem the greatest of the clans of Judah. But where Matthew shows even more signs of freedom, indeed imagination, is in the last quotation, 'He shall be called a Nazarene.' People have searched in vain: no prophet said such a thing, nor any biblical writer. We can understand why Matthew did not mention a particular prophet, but was content with a vague 'which was spoken by the prophets'. He just did not have any biblical quotation, and because he couldn't find one which met his needs, he made it up!

So these few examples take us to a more basic question. What is the meaning of the expression 'that the word of the prophet might be fulfilled'?

## Jesus a prophet?

The New Testament authors resorted to a multitude of titles in speaking of Jesus: Master, Son of Man, Son of the Most High, Son of God, Messiah, to mention only the main ones. Of course the title 'prophet' has also been applied to him (seventeen direct and explicit references). However, the question arises in broader terms.

First of all, it is clear that having long suffered from 'the silence of prophecy', in the time of Jesus people were eagerly awaiting the return not only of a prophet but of the prophet who was to be the successor to Moses. Thus the priests and Levites sent from Jerusalem by the Pharisees take their enquiry to John the Baptist: 'And they asked him, "Who are you? Are you Elijah?" He replied, "I am not." "Are you the prophet?" He answered, "No"' (John 1.21). The question inevitably arose over John the Baptist, in whom some felt that they could already recognize Elijah or one of the prophets.

So it is not surprising to see that the same question was raised about Jesus and that people answered it in different ways. Peter's confession of faith alludes to these different popular responses:

'Now when Jesus came into the district of Caesarea Philippi, he asked his disciples, "Who do people say that the Son of man is?" And they said, "Some say John the Baptist, others say Elijah, and others Jeremiah or one of the prophets"' (Matt.16.13–14). Sometimes the response is more affirmative, as after the feeding of the five thousand, when, according to John's version, the crowds recognized in Jesus the prophet who was to come: 'When the people saw the sign which he had done, they said, "This is indeed the prophet who is to come into the world"' (John 6.14).

So one thing is certain: Jesus was often regarded by the crowds as one of the prophets, doubtless like others before him (such as John the Baptist), and there were those who went so far as to recognize in him the prophet *par excellence*, who had been so ardently awaited after the death of Moses. Through the indirect testimony of the crowds, it is clear that for Christians Jesus is a prophet, indeed the greatest of them. After Easter and Pentecost the testimonies could not be more explicit. For example, one of the disciples on the Emmaus road refers to 'Jesus of Nazareth, who was prophet mighty in deed and word before God and all the people' (Luke 24.19).

## 'Something greater than Jonah is here . . .'

Jesus was undeniably a prophet. However, as with all the traditional titles attributed to him from the Old Testament, the title prophet does not go far enough. Jesus is in effect *the* prophet raised by God to succeed Moses, but he is greater than Moses: 'The Law was given by Moses, grace and truth have come by Jesus Christ' (John 1.17). He is also the long-expected Messiah, but here, too, he is Messiah in an unexpected way. Jesus falls completely in line with the prophets and deserves to be compared with the greatest of them. However, a remarkable new quality shines out in him: 'The men of Nineveh will arise at the judgment with this generation and condemn it; for they repented at the preaching of Jonah, and behold, something greater than Jonah is here' (Matt.12.41).

# 3

# Amos: The 'Roaring' Voice

## I.  A prophet to rediscover

### Amos, the unknown

It can hardly be said that the Christian tradition has been much inspired by the terse statements of the man who is usually recognized as the earliest of the writing prophets. However, he was a genius who has given us a book in which the main characteristics of biblical prophecy are already outlined.

Amos, the unknown . . . If we were to survey people in church on Sunday, for example in the Catholic tradition, and were to ask 'Who is the prophet Amos? What was his message?', I fear that the answers would be embarrassed and somewhat evasive. And indeed the Roman lectionary accords him a very minor place: a total of 13 verses spread over a period of three years. That is a very small proportion of the 146 verses which the book of Amos contains (less than ten per cent!). It is easy to see that the lectionary has been concerned to treat the congregation gently and that the most challenging statements of the prophet – specifically those about worship – have no chance of being heard in our liturgical assemblies.

There is no reason why we should be particularly surprised at this, since from the moment that Amos, this countryman whom nothing seemed to destine for the world of prophecy (7.12–15), spoke out in the kingdom of Israel around 750 BCE, his incendiary statements have not ceased to disturb people. The 'conflict at Bethel', in which the prophet was severely criticized by the priest Amaziah, an official at the royal sanctuary, is a good illustration of the fate that Amos's oracles have tended to meet with in the Christian tradition: 'Go, seer, flee away to the land of Judah, and eat bread there and prophesy there' (7.12). In fact people are ready to give him the title prophet, but not at home: only 'there'! Isn't this what has happened for the most part to the book of the earliest of the prophets? It is part of the canonical Christian scriptures, but has to some degree been neutralized by a highly parsimonious use of it.

It is a fact that the book of Amos has long been ignored or misunderstood by Christians. The Church Fathers, for example, commented little on it and were more than selective in their quotations. It seems that two major reasons worked against the prophet of Tekoa. On the one hand it was thought that his message was too hard to receive, and because of this it faded into the background by comparison with the hope offered by the Gospels and the Christian message. On the other hand – and this has beyond question been a more determinative factor – it is hard to see how a book

24

without any messianic oracle could have been exploited in a Christian setting. As I commented in the introduction to this volume, the Christian tradition first looked in the prophets for what could proclaim Christ. So it became difficult to appeal to the book of Amos, which seems to contain no christological echo.

In the more recent history of interpretation, it could also be said that the book of Amos has been used to support or reject (depending on the case) arguments in the great theological controversies. Thus for example the famous Dominican Savonarola in his conflict with Rome chose to base his preaching in Lent 1496 – two years before his condemnation and execution – on the book of Amos. At the time of the Reformation, Luther and Calvin did not fail to invoke the prophet's oracles in their denunciation of the triumphalism and abuses of Rome, in particular over anything relating to worship. And since the Reformers felt at ease with the prophet's sayings, it is no surprise that the theology which emerged from the Counter–Reformation left in the shadows a book which was deemed too revolutionary.

## The rediscovery of a prophet

Happily, things have changed since the beginning of the century. On the one hand, progress in the sphere of biblical study has made a better appreciation of prophecy possible. And on the other hand, the challenges of the modern world have led to great questioning among Christians and at the same time have restored a dramatic vividness to the message of the prophets, who are so profoundly concerned with questions of human dignity, social justice and freedom, with a preferential option for the poorest. That has helped to bring out of the shadows the uncompromising and unsparing message of Amos.

It was above all on the Protestant side, at the heart of a Germany confronted with the aberrations of Nazism and the Second World War, that the prophet Amos was to regain his status and arouse from torpor a Christian conscience which had fallen

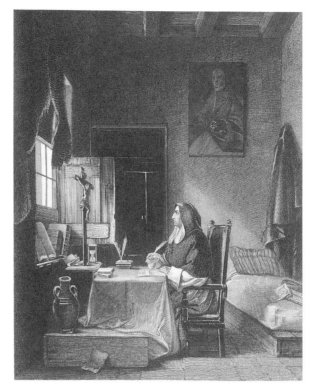

Savonarola, by A. H. Payne
(Mary Evans Picture Library)

asleep or even been complicit in the atrocities committed by Hitler's regime. Famous exegetes and theologians, like Vischer, Lüthi and Barth, then had the courage to make the indignant cry of the prophet of Tekoa and his vibrant protest on behalf of the poor and the oppressed heard once more.

On the Catholic side, the biblical renewal endorsed by Vatican II (1960–1965) at last opened the door to a rediscovery of the treasures of the Bible and marked a new start of interest in the prophets. There was more and more talk of a church which would prophesy and, following the line of the conciliar Constitution on the Church in the Modern World, a new sensitivity to relations between faith and social justice began to make itself felt. Out of a concern to be faithful to the gospel of Jesus Christ, Christians felt the need to involve themselves in the transformation of social structures. This awareness led to base communities, organizations for social justice and development, movements in favour of human rights, and the various theologies of liberation. The time of the prophets had come, and that of Amos in particular.

## The prophet and his setting

The heading of his book already gives us a good picture of the person with whom we shall be concerned: 'The words of Amos, who was among the shepherds of Tekoa, which he saw against Israel in the days of Uzziah king of Judah and in the days of Jeroboam the son of Joash, king of Israel, two years before the earthquake' (1.1). Manifestly written after the body of the book, this summary gives us the main particulars of the prophet, his time and his message.

First of all the prophet's name, Amos. This name is unique in the biblical tradition, and although its etymology takes us back to a root which means 'carry' – also attested in the name Amaziah (II Chron.17.16), i.e. Yahweh carries, Yahweh raises up (his people) – the editors of the book of Amos do not elaborate in any way on its theological significance. On the other hand, they tell us of Amos's work, 'one of the shepherds', and this is confirmed by the prophet's own words (7.14–15). Indeed Amos is even more explicit, since he also says that he was a 'dresser of sycamore trees'. So he was essentially a cultivator, a man of the earth, and in all probability was relatively well off, since he reared both small and large cattle and had another source of income in the sycamores.

Amos is from 'Tekoa', a few miles from Bethlehem, and therefore not very far from Jerusalem. The town was fortified by King Rehoboam (II Chron.11.5–6), and in the time of Jeremiah would still seem to be a stronghold (Jer.6.1). However, it was situated on the edge of a desert – which moreover bore the name of 'the desert of Tekoa' (II Chron.20.20). According to II Sam.14, the town was also renowned for its tradition of wisdom.

So Amos comes from the southern kingdom, the capital of which was Jerusalem. However, he would have nothing to do with that city. His whole ministry was to unfold in the northern kingdom, the capital of which was Samaria. Thus Amos had plenty to disturb him: in addition to the virulent content of his oracles, he had against him the fact that he was no more at home in Bethel than in Gilgal or Samaria. If it is true that 'no one is a prophet in his own country', in the case of Amos it does not seem that coming from elsewhere was a better guarantee of success.

The historical and social setting in which Amos worked can easily be deduced from the heading and then quite certainly from the content of his oracles. The particulars could hardly be more precise: 'in the days of Uzziah king of Judah and in the days of Jeroboam the son of Joash, king of Israel, two years before the earthquake'. This last piece of information is certainly not easy for us to identify, but it must have been a memorable event for those for whom the book was intended. According to the known chronology of the kings in question, Uzziah and Jeroboam, the prophet's ministry would thus have to be put between 787 and 740; the 760s are usually mentioned as the decade in which the prophet of Tekoa must have exercised his ministry.

Now what must we remember of this period, and more particularly of what happened in the northern kingdom, in the reign of Jeroboam II? It was essentially a period of prosperity and ease, not to mention the expansion of frontiers (II Kings 14). There was a uniquely favourable situation unknown since the great days of Solomon, which would not be repeated before the exile.

The book of Amos is full of allusions to this extremely prosperous situation: the fever of commercial activities, the frenzy of banquets and festivities, the unbridled luxury of the houses of the rich, the triumphalism of worship, and so on. This was the sight which presented itself to the prophet as to all comers. But behind this abundance of riches was hidden a quite different reality. It was that of the lack of conscience and the euphoria of the rich, the abuses of power and the exploitation of the poor by the ruling classes; and also the reality of

Amos

# A Prophet among the Wise Men?

As we have already seen, Amos is the earliest writing prophet. In a way he invented the ways of written prophecy. However, that did not prevent him from drawing on other sources of the religious tradition of Israel. Among these sources mention should first be made of the different traditions of wisdom. Such is their influence on Amos that it invites us to reconsider the links between prophets and wise men. Although there has often been a tendency to contrast prophets and wise men, in the Bible they supplement one another, and the book of the prophet Amos attests a remarkable affinity with the themes and techniques of the wise men of Israel.

Thus, for example, he resorts to rhetorical or didactic questions:

Do two walk together,
unless they have made an appointment?
Does a lion roar in the forest,
when he has no prey?
Does a young lion cry out from his den,
if he has taken nothing?
Does a bird fall in a snare on the earth,
when there is no trap for it?
Does a snare spring up from the ground,
when it has taken nothing?
Is a trumpet blown in a city,
and the people are not afraid?
Does evil befall a city,
unless the Lord has done it? (3.3–6)

Do horses run upon rocks?
Does one plough the sea with oxen?
But you have turned justice into poison
and the fruit of righteousness into wormwood
(6.12).

In each case the answer is obvious and easily derived from the reader's experience. Such a procedure is typical of the wise men: we find it often in the books of Job, Proverbs and Koheleth (Ecclesiastes), and it is not surprising to find it again very frequently on the lips of Jesus, the wise man of Nazareth.

A second procedure which Amos seems to have borrowed from the wise men is that of progressive numerical formulas which recur throughout chapters 1 and 2: 'For three transgressions and for four . . .' It is in fact among the wise that this type of numerical sequence, aiming at highlighting its last element, is to be found (see Prov.15–31).

Like the wise men, Amos also excels in pedagogical exhortations. Certainly his denunciations are vigorous, but he can also indicate the right way:

Seek good and not evil,
that you may live;
and so the Lord, the God of hosts, will be with you,
as you have said.
Hate evil, and love good,
and establish justice in the gate . . . (5.14–15).

Here we might be hearing the customary recommendations of Proverbs with the classical contrast between good and evil, the theme of seeking and the emphasis on life, which has a privileged place in the creed of the wise men.

Of course we must avoid exclusiveness here, and it is certain that Amos drew on other traditions than wisdom. However, the important affinities between Amos and biblical wisdom invite us to interpret more flexibly the frontiers which scholars thought that they had discerned between prophets and wise men. Amos is definitely a prophet. Nevertheless, he shows an amazing familiarity with the wise men. Amos, the prophet of the incisive saying, loses none of the wisdom of his land. Given his origins, which would in no way seem to predispose him to prophecy (7.14), shouldn't we say, rather, that in him we see a wise man who has ventured among the prophets?

a cult which was rotten to the core, in which outward actions were contradicted by a life which accepted the worst injustices and most extreme forms of idolatry and immorality.

These are precisely the things that Amos denounced so vividly, to such a degree that the title of his book could recall that this was a collection of 'words . . . *against* Israel . . .' Yes, the 'word of the Lord' can be a 'word against', each time the rights of the poor are flouted and the demands of the God of the covenant are not recognized.

Finally, a last valuable indication in the title: the collection is called both 'words' and 'visions', even by an unexpected formula ('words which he saw . . .'). This also helps us to see the literary genre and structure of the book, since the central part between the prologue (1.1–2) and the epilogue (9.11–15) is rightly divided into two sections, the first being devoted to the 'words' i.e. the prophet's oracles against the nations and against Israel (1.3–6.13), and the second relating five of his visions.

# II. Three texts for understanding Amos

Once we know the main particulars of the prophet Amos, we can go more deeply into the study of his texts and his message. Here are three texts which have been chosen for their singularity or, if you like, their originality in the religious and social context of eighth-century Israel, and their topicality for our age and our own religious developments. As we read them, it will not be difficult to hear the voice, percussive and sometimes disturbing, of the prophet of Tekoa, which itself is no more than the echo of another voice which 'roars' from Zion–Jerusalem . . .

## 1. Israel in the dock
### (Amos 2.6–16)

6 *Thus says the Lord:*
*For three transgressions of Israel, and for four,*
*I will not revoke the punishment;*
*because they sell the righteous for silver,*
*and the poor for a pair of shoes –*
7 *they that trample the head of the needy into the*
*dust of the earth,*
*and turn aside the way of the humiliated;*
*a man and his father go in to the same maiden,*
*so that my holy name is profaned;*
8 *they lay themselves down beside every altar*
*upon garments taken in pledge;*

*and in the house of their God they drink*
*the wine of those who have been fined.*
9 *Yet I destroyed the Amorite before them,*
*whose height was like the height of the cedars,*
*and who was as strong as the oaks;*
*I destroyed his fruit above,*
*and his roots beneath.*
10 *And I brought you up out of the land of Egypt,*
*and led you forty years in the wilderness,*
*to possess the land of the Amorites.*
11 *And I raised up some of your sons for prophets,*
*and some of your young men for Nazirites.*

Is it not indeed so, O people of Israel?
*says the Lord.*

12 *But you made the Nazirites drink wine,*
*and commanded the prophets,*
*saying, 'You shall not prophesy.'*

13 *Behold, I will press you down in your place,*
*as a cart full of sheaves presses down.*

14 *Flight shall perish from the swift, and the strong*
shall not retain his strength,
*nor shall the mighty save his life;*

15 *he who handles the bow shall not stand,*
*and he who is swift of foot shall not save himself,*
*nor shall he who rides the horse save his life;*

16 *and he who is stout of heart among the mighty*
*shall flee away naked in that day, says the Lord.*

---

## Privilege or responsibility?

Amos's Israelite hearers must have applauded his very first oracles (1.3–2.5), since these are directed against their immediate neighbours and long-standing enemies: Damascus, the Philistines, Moab, Judah and the others. The prophet hardly spared them: each is vividly condemned for its war crimes and violations of human rights, and has a most sombre future predicted for it.

Such bad news could not be displeasing to Israel, which wanted nothing better than to see its enemies defeated or reduced to impotence. Better still, Israel believed that it was itself sheltered from such condemnation, sure as it was of being the chosen people and therefore of having God 'on its side'.

It is precisely this conception of the covenant – and not the fact of the covenant itself – that the prophet Amos is now to attack so vigorously. It is no chance that the oracle against Israel has been put here, in eighth place. On the one hand Israel sees itself set on a level with other nations and judged as they are: the fact of being a people chosen by God does not in any way dispense it from the moral and religious criteria by which the other nations are judged. Quite the contrary.

On the other hand, we can feel that there is a deliberate progression in the oracles and that the main target is in fact Israel, whom the prophet is accusing of far too complacent a reading of its 'election' by God. Israel is the main target of Amos's attack: a comparison with the previous oracles leaves no doubt about that.

First of all, we have to see that here, in contrast to the seven previous oracles, the reasons for the accusation are listed. Whereas for the other nations there is only one reason for the accusation, in the case of Israel the prophet gives a list of four 'transgressions'. Here is a fullness which has not been felt in the previous oracles. A second notable difference comes from the nature of the crimes with which Israel is charged. Whereas in the case of the other nations these were always what would now be called 'war crimes', Israel finds itself accused of crimes of another order; this time they are social disorders within the community, committed against brothers, neighbours, friends. Finally, and this adds to the seriousness of these crimes, there is the fact of the covenant in which God has taken the initiative. Indeed, Amos invokes Yahweh's actions for Israel as circumstances which aggravate its crimes. Far from being a privilege, the covenant is first and foremost a demand: 'Be holy, for I the Lord your God am holy' (Lev.19.2). Israel is all the more to be condemned because it has failed to recognize, has even denied, the good things that God has done for it (Amos 2.9–10).

## Flouting the rights of the poor . . .

As I said above, the accusations made against Israel relate to the sphere of social life. They are serious, and the samples given by the prophet are typical. While they are not exhaustive, the accusations are clearly more developed (the original Hebrew uses the causal conjunction 'because' four times): some commentators even see here a series of seven accusations, as if the prophet had wanted to indicate that the evil committed by Israel has reached its peak. But whatever the number of crimes of which Israel is accused, it is easy to see that these are serious injustices and different ways of exploiting the poor.

One of the main keys to reading this passage is the vocabulary used by the prophet to speak of the poor: in turn they are designated as needy, humble (or more literally humiliated), and weak. This language, which will be taken up by the whole of the prophetic tradition and the tradition of the psalms, says a lot about the way in which the Bible speaks of the poor.

Each of these three terms emphasizes a particular dimension of poverty. First of all, the poor are seen as needy, i.e. they are deprived of goods and financial resources. This is a poverty which could be called physical or economic, actual poverty. But in the Bible this actual poverty is often the result of a social context created by abuses of power and injustice. This is the second aspect of poverty, a poverty which could be described as sociological. In this sense the poor of the Bible are the 'humble', that is to say those who have been humiliated, those who have been impoverished. So it would be more correct to speak of the 'impoverished', of those who have had to suffer under a system in which the riches of some are necessarily balanced by the impoverishment of others. And finally, Amos and the biblical tradition also call these same 'impoverished' people 'weak', in the sense that poverty makes them more readily vulnerable and exposed to difficult social conditions, not by reason of their moral deficiencies.

It is true that the terms remain interchangeable and that it is not always easy to see whether one or other of these three nuances underlies a particular Hebrew word. But what matters is to see that a prophet like Amos forces us to abandon any simplistic reading of the phenomenon of poverty. Often used in apposition with one another, these three terms emphasize the complexity of this phenomenon and invite us to seek its deepest roots.

### Israel flouts the 'rights of Yahweh'

In taking up the defence of the poor, Amos finds himself taking up the defence of his God. For these two causes are linked. In other words, the 'theologal', i.e. anything concerned with the relationship with God (faith and religion), depends on the theological, i.e. the perception of the mystery of God. This a scheme which we often find again in the New Testament. For example, the parables of Jesus first put forward an image of God (merciful, patient, generous, etc.) and then derive from that the demands on the life of believers: they have to forgive, show tolerance and patience, give freely and without counting the cost.

That is rather like what happens here. Amos finds the behaviour of Israel all the more serious because it has always benefited from the benevolence of Yahweh, who has successively delivered it from Egypt (v.10), been with it in the wilderness and the conquest of the promised land (v.9), and finally guided it by sending prophets and Nazirites (v.11). So there is nothing arbitrary or capricious about Yahweh's demands. On the contrary, they are based on a concrete commitment on his part which calls for a response. Yahweh is right to expect fruits of justice from his people, because he is the one to whom Israel owes its existence.

---

## 2. 'Prepare to meet your God, O Israel!'
### (Amos 4.1–13)

1 *Hear this word, you cows of Bashan,*
*who are in the mountain of Samaria,*
*who oppress the needy,*
*who crush the poor,*

*who say to their husbands,*
*'Bring, that we may drink!'*
2 *The Lord God has sworn by his holiness*
*that, behold, the days are coming upon you,*

31

when they shall take you away with hooks,
   even the last of you with fishhooks.
3 And you shall go out through the breaches,
   every one straight before her;
   and you shall be cast forth into Harmon,
   says the Lord.
4 Come to Bethel, and transgress;
   to Gilgal, and multiply transgression;
   bring your sacrifices every morning,
   your tithes every three days;
5 offer a sacrifice of thanksgiving of that which is
      leavened,
   and proclaim free will offerings, publish them;
   for so you love to do, O people of Israel!,
   says the Lord God.
6 I gave you cleanness of teeth in all your cities,
   and lack of bread in all your places,
   yet you did not return to me,
   says the Lord.
7 And I also withheld the rain from you
   when there were yet three months to the harvest;
   I would send rain upon one city,
   and send no rain upon another city;
   one field would be rained upon,
   and the field on which it did not rain withered;
8 so two or three cities wandered to one city
   to drink water, and were not satisfied;
   yet you did not return to me,'
   says the Lord.

9 I smote you with blight and mildew;
   I laid waste your gardens and your vineyards;
   your fig trees and your olive trees the locust
      devoured;
   yet you did not return to me,
   says the Lord.
10 I sent among you a pestilence after the manner of
      Egypt;
   I slew your young men with the sword;
   I carried away your horses,
   and I made the stench of your camp go up into your
      nostrils;
   yet you did not return to me,
   says the Lord.
11 I overthrew some of you,
   as when God overthrew Sodom and Gomorrah,
   and you were as a brand plucked out of the
      burning;
   yet you did not return to me,
   says the Lord.
12 Therefore thus I will do to you, O Israel,
   because I will do this to you,
   prepare to meet your God, O Israel!
13 For lo, he who forms the mountains, and creates the
      wind,
   and declares to man what is his thought;
   who makes the morning darkness, and treads on the
      heights of the earth –
   the Lord, the God of hosts, is his name!

---

## Accounts to settle

Taken out of context, the phrase 'Prepare to meet your God, O Israel' could suggest a gratifying experience, like the numerous theophanies which punctuated the history of Israel for its greater happiness (Jacob's dream at Bethel, the burning bush, Sinai, the shining cloud, the consecration of the temple, and so on). But it is nothing of the sort. The preparations to which the prophet alludes here have a military aspect. Here is real mobilization for a fight, or, if you like, a challenge at the beginning of a formidable encounter. The imminent encounter with God will be testing for Israel, which will have to face judgment and recognize its wrongs if it wants to have any chance of survival. The hour has come for Israel to settle its accounts!

## Where is the caricature?

Chapter 4 of Amos, which is a real plea for the renewal of the covenant, begins with extremely harsh words. Has the prophet exaggerated? Is he a past master in the art of caricature, to the point of treating the rulers of the capital (Samaria, capital of the northern kingdom) as 'cows of Bashan'? Or again could he have taken irreverence to the point of making a direct attack on the equally culpable behaviour of their spouses?

But what if the caricature were elsewhere? What if it were in this disturbing reality of a corrupt society which 'oppresses the needy and crushes the poor' (v.1) and is only concerned with its own pleasures? What if the caricature were also in these pseudo-liturgies in which God feels betrayed (vv.4–5)? The prophet does not mince his words, and he has a consummate way of using irony.

He does it first of all by attacking more than venerable sanctuaries, Bethel and Gilgal. The first is connected with the memory of the patriarchs (Abraham, Gen.12.8; Jacob, Gen.35.6,14,15), and in itself represents a privileged place for meeting God. But under Jeroboam II, the sanctuary of Bethel was built as a rival to that of Jerusalem. It became a political symbol where the priests became officials in the service of the king. Amos, who was chased off by one of these priests (7.13), denounces this state of affairs and questions Bethel's status as an authentic cult place. Gilgal, a name which is less familiar to Christian readers, is also a name of happy memory, since it is linked with the crossing of the Jordan (Josh 4.19–24) and the celebration of the first passover in the land of Canaan (5.10–12).

These two sanctuaries thus have a rich religious past. But in the time of Amos they had become the theatre of a cult which was completely devoid of meaning. Not without irony, the prophet in fact describes them as 'transgressions', with the same word that he used in the first two chapters to speak of the 'transgressions' of the nations and of Israel. And as if this judgment were not severe enough, Amos adds to the irony by emphasizing the degree to which God distances himself from these cultic practices: 'your transgressions, your sacrifices, your tithes, . . . for so you love to do . . .' It is clear: there is nothing in the cult which pleases God.

| Amos 4 | Leviticus 26 |
|---|---|
| 1. I *gave* you . . . (6) | 1. I will *give* you rains in their season . . . (4, 6, 17, 19, 26, 29, 30, 31) |
| 2. . . . *lack of bread* in all your places | 2. When I break your *staff of bread* . . . (26) |
| 3. And I also withheld the rain from you . . . (7) | 3. I will give you rains in their season . . . |
| 4. . . . two or three cities wandered to one city to drink water, and were not satisfied (8) | 4. . . . and you shall eat, and not be satisfied (26) |
| 5. I *smote* you . . . | 5. . . . I myself will *smite* you sevenfold for your sins (24) |
| 6. I *sent* among you a *pestilence* after the manner of Egypt . . . (10) | 6. I will *send pestilence* among you . . . (25) |
| 7. I slew your young men with the *sword* . . . (10) | 7. I will bring a *sword* upon you . . . (25; see also 33.36–37) |

## A conversion which is to be expected

Verses 6–11 present a somewhat unusual vision of the history of Israel. In them the prophet gives a long description of the interventions of God, but from the perspective of punishment and testing, in terms which recall the most famous punitive actions (vv.10–11), 'when God overthrew Sodom and Gomorrah' and the plagues of Egypt, as well as the solemn curses which had been attached to the conclusion of the Sinai covenant (Lev.26, see box on previous page). If the history of Israel is a history of salvation, marked by beneficent interventions on the part of God, it is also a history of infidelity and hardening.

As the prophet presents them, each of God's initiatives aimed at bringing Israel back to the right way has been marked by failure: '. . . but you did not return to me' (vv.6, 8, 9, 10, 11). This is a terrible observation, but one which just as much reveals the basically pedagogical purpose of the interventions of a God who expected and desired a conversation that never came about. Never? Perhaps we should say not yet. The encounter with God to which the people are invited (v.12) will be equally decisive and (who knows?) perhaps the people will finally understand and choose to return to God.

When the dramatic tension is at its height – how will the encounter of Israel with its God turn out? For judgment or for salvation? – a flicker of hope finally appears. The last words of the oracle form a vibrant and joyful profession of faith (v.13) in this God who in his sovereignty dominates the created universe (he 'treads on the heights of the earth') and whose freedom is joined with that of human beings in the unfolding of history (he 'declares to man what is his thought'). The prophet could not imagine a better motivation for leading Israel to conversion and to the renewal of the covenant.

---

## 3. 'I hate, I despise your pilgrimages'
### (Amos 5.21–27)

21 *'I hate, I despise your pilgrimages,*
*and I cannot feel your solemn assemblies.*
22 *When you offer me your burnt offerings and cereal offerings,*
*nothing pleases me,*
*from the peace offerings of your fatted beasts*
*I turn away my eyes.*
23 *Take away from me the noise of your songs;*
*to the melody of your harps I cannot listen.*
24 *But let justice roll down like waters,*

*and righteousness like an overflowing stream.*
25 *Did you bring me sacrifices and offerings for forty years in the wilderness,*
*O house of Israel?*
26 *But you have brought Sakkuth your king, and Kaiwan your star-god,*
*your images, which you made for yourselves;*
27 *therefore I will take you into exile beyond Damascus,'*
*says the Lord, whose name is the God of hosts.*

---

## Unprecedented . . .

Rarely in the history of Israel will more radical criticism of everything relating to the cult and the liturgy have been heard. Amos does not attack marginal phenomena or secondary devotions, but what is most sacred: feasts, offerings, prayers. Nothing escapes his criticism. In this brief passage we find an unusual concentration of cultic terms (no less than eight in the first three verses), for the most part taken from Leviticus – the book which was authoritative in Israel when it came to regulating the liturgy: pilgrimages, assemblies, burnt offerings, sacrifices, offerings of fatted beasts, songs, melody, harps. That's a lot. In fact all that is missing is the smell of incense (though that may be implicit in the 'I cannot feel your solemn assemblies') and an explicit mention of the temple as a holy place.

To understand the drift of the prophet's criticism, it is enough here to put it under three headings: feasts, offerings, music and singing.

Amos attacks on a broad front, first of all mentioning pilgrimages and assemblies. The first reference is to no more and no less than the three great annual feasts (Passover, Pentecost, Tabernacles, Ex.23.14–17) which require a pilgrimage to Jerusalem. Now it must be remembered that king Jeroboam, father of Jeroboam II, had decided to organize his own pilgrimages to Bethel as competition for the prescribed pilgrimages to Jerusalem. The second term, assemblies, denotes the same feasts, but here considered from the aspect of one of their most solemn features, the 'closure for the festival', which normally implied the ending of work (Lev.23.36; Isa.1.13) and the calling of the sacred assembly.

The three terms which follow (burnt offerings, sacrifices and offerings of fatted beasts) are typical of the cult connected with the temple. They are more attached to the daily liturgy which took place at the temple, and can very well be understood as communal liturgical services rather than celebrations of a more private kind.

The list ends with another form of cultic expression, music and singing. The vocabulary used by the prophet thus reflects what we find in the unparalleled treasury of biblical prayer formed by the Psalms and the two books of Chronicles, which are particularly full of liturgical reminiscences.

In short, practically no level of liturgical tradition has been spared by Amos's vigorous criticism. Now all these practices – and not the principle of the cult itself – are not only challenged by the God of Amos but rejected outright: 'I hate, I despise'. This is total repudiation, as is also confirmed by the negative connotation of the verbs with which Amos describes the reaction of God to the cult practised by Israel: 'I cannot feel, nothing pleases me, I turn my eyes from, I cannot listen . . .'

## Authentic worship

The prophet's attack seems quite devastating, and once the shock-wave of his oracles has passed, the question remains: if this worship, now practised by Israel, is rejected by God, what must be substituted for it? Amos asked himself the question and gave it a remarkable answer which was to inspire the whole of the prophetic tradition, with his immediate successors like Isaiah and Micah, right down to Jesus: 'But let justice roll down like waters, and righteousness like an overflowing stream!' That is the true worship which pleases God, extended and confirmed by a commitment to right and justice. Isaiah will make very similar proposals (Isa.58), and so too will even Jesus, when he reminds the Pharisees that the commandment to love comes before observance of the rules for ritual purity (Mark 7.1–13). The God of the prophets has nothing to do with a cult which does not change life in any way and which is deaf to the cry of the poor.

Amos

# III. The God of Amos

## A God who 'roars' (1.2)

The expression might seem bold, even offensive, compared with our image of God and his usual way of speaking. There is nothing very elegant about it which might invite us to listen. Who could be interested in listening to a God who 'roars'?

However, it is good that Amos tells us that God 'roars'. He is in fact the first to use this verb of God and to apply to God the image of the 'lion' and its formidable cry, sowing terror and disarray in the towns and deserts of the ancient Near East: 'The Lord roars from Zion, and utters his voice from Jerusalem; the pastures of the shepherds mourn, and the top of Carmel withers' (1.2).

Now this voice which roars is none other than that of the prophetic message, hard, incisive, disturbing, at the opposite extreme from complacency and compromise. The word of God which comes to Amos and through him is a formidable word, a severe warning, in which everything – except for the last five verses – is reproach and threats: 'The lion has roared, who will not fear? The Lord God has spoken, who will not prophesy?' (3.8).

## A God who has his reasons for losing patience

The God of the covenant (Ex.34.6) presented himself as a God who is 'slow to anger and rich in mercy'. Amos is well aware of that, since twice he gives us a long list of the divine benefits for his people (2.6–16; 4.6–11): the exodus from Egypt, protection in the desert and the conquest of Canaan, the sending of prophets and consecrated men. But this is where the drama lies. Despite these numerous benefits, Israel has multiplied transgressions and has remained insensitive to the calls to conversion: '. . . but you did not return to me' (the expression recurs five times in the passage 4.6–11).

Not only has Israel failed to recognize its God; even worse, the sin of the people has come to a climax. This is the meaning of the expression 'for three transgressions and for four'.

So the situation is extremely grave. Mention is made of the end:

> And when a man's kinsman, he who burns him, shall take him up to bring the bones out of the house, and shall say to him who is in the innermost parts of the house, 'Is there still any one with you?' he shall say, 'No'; and he shall say, 'Hush! We must not mention the name of the Lord.' For behold, the Lord commands, and the great house shall be smitten into fragments, and the little house into bits (6.11).

Throughout the book of Amos we feel the tension mount, and it seems that nothing will be able to contain the divine fury: 'I will not revoke the punishment . . .' (a refrain which crowns the eight oracles of the first two chapters). Delay is no longer possible: 'The Lord said to me, "The end has come upon my people Israel; I will never again pass by them"' (8.2).

## A God who suffers over the fate of the poor

Even if he rarely uses the technical vocabulary of the covenant, the prophet is nevertheless a witness to the God of the exodus, aware of the cry of the poor and wounded by any form of oppression. In making himself the defender of the poor, Amos is only showing the demands of the God of the covenant and for the first time displaying what is to become one of the dominant features of the religion of the writing prophets.

Always in the name of the God who took him 'from following the flock' (7.15) and called him to prophesy, Amos vigorously denounces the irresponsible ambition and comfort of the rulers, the quest for profit beyond all justice and the violence done to the poor:

> Proclaim to the strongholds in Ashdod,
> and to the strongholds in the land of Egypt,
> and say, 'Assemble yourselves upon the mountains of Samaria,
> and see the great tumults within her,
> and the oppressions in her midst.
> They do not know how to do right,' says the Lord,
> 'those who store up violence and robbery in their strongholds' (3.9–10).

> Hear this word, you cows of Bashan,
> who are in the mountain of Samaria,
> who oppress the needy, who crush the poor,
> who say to their husbands,
> 'Bring that we may drink' (4.1).

> Hear this, you who trample upon the needy,
> and destroy the humiliated of the land,
> saying, 'When will the new moon be over,
> that we may sell grain?
> And the sabbath,
> that we may offer wheat for sale,
> that we may make the ephah small and the shekel great,
> and deal deceitfully with false balances,
> that we may buy the needy for silver
> and the poor for a pair of sandals,
> and sell the refuse of the wheat?' (8.4–6).

## A God who remains free to forgive

As we have seen, the oracles of Amos are full of reproaches and threats, dominated by the perspective of an inescapable and formidable judgment. Does that mean that the people are delivered over without mercy and without hope of salvation to the wrath of God which makes itself heard through Amos's voice?

The glimmers of hope are sparse, but they are not completely absent from the book. First of all, even if the prophet's statements are extremely severe, they do not end up in condemnation pure and simple. The prophet speaks so loudly and so strongly because he hopes that he can still change the course of history in some way. Far from accommodating to the infidelities and injustices of his people, he seeks to arouse the people. By making them see the nonsense of their behaviour towards the poor, at the same time he makes them see the only way which can lead them to happiness: 'Seek the Lord and you will live' (5.6); 'Seek good, and not evil, that you may live; and so the Lord, the God of hosts, will be with you, as you have said' (5.14). The end envisaged is conversion, which is here translated into terms of the re-establishment of justice: 'Let justice roll down like waters, and righteousness like an everflowing stream!' (5.24).

To this general aim, which is basically positive, must be added the prophet's love for his people and the solidarity which drives him to intercede concretely for them: 'Then I said, "O Lord God, cease, I beseech you! How can Jacob stand? He is so small"' (7.5; see also 7.23). Even at the height of the turmoil, the prophet cannot but love his people and he always returns to interceding on their behalf.

Now if he does intercede, and in terms which are both sober and moving, it is because he knows well the God whom he is addressing. This God is a God who more than any other also loves this people and remains free to forgive it. When the sentence seems irrevocable, the prophet does not lose hope for the people and hangs on with all his might to the sovereign freedom of God, who can change his mind and forgive: 'Hate evil, and love good; and establish justice in the gate; it may be that the Lord, the God of hosts, will be gracious to the remnant of Jacob' (5.15).

The last word of God cannot be one of condemnation and definitive rejection. Twice the prophet intercedes, and twice his prayer is heard: 'The Lord repented concerning this; "It shall not be," said the Lord' (7.3). 'The Lord repented concerning this; "This also shall not be," said the Lord' (7.6). So there is a 'remnant' from which the healing and restoration of the people could take place (9.11–15):

'except that I will not utterly destroy the house of Jacob' (9.8).

## A God of sovereign freedom and power

The fragments of hymns scattered through the book (4.13; 5.8; 9.6) continue to intrigue commentators. But whatever conclusions are drawn about their original form and content, it has to be agreed that they present a powerful and coherent vision of God. First of all, they are true professions of faith in honour of the God of the covenant: 'The Lord, God of hosts is his name.' By immediately adding the title 'God of hosts', Amos indicates that this is also the creator God. The God of the exodus, who is a God of history and a saviour God, must not be opposed to the creator God. For it is the same 'God of hosts' who 'forms the mountains, and creates the wind, who makes the morning darkness' and 'declares to man what is his thought' (4.13).

## A God who shows the way of life

The God of Amos is not content with 'roaring'. If he chastizes his people and addresses them bluntly, he can also be a teacher and show his people the only way which can lead them to salvation: 'Seek the Lord and you will live . . . seek good and not evil . . . hate evil, and love good, and establish justice in the gate . . .' (5.4, 6, 14, 15). And when he predicts that days will come when the people will experience 'a famine and a thirst for hearing the words of the Lord' (8.11–12), he gives a glimpse of what would be the supreme scourge. Expressed here we can recognize the only attitude capable of giving the people supreme happiness, which consists in being grasped by this same word.

## A God who takes in hand the future of his people

The book of Amos, like the books of almost all the prophets which come after him, ends on prospects of restoration which allow the most splendid hopes (9.11–15). In addition to the emphasis on God's initiative ('I will repair, I will raise up, I will rebuild'), note the beauty of the imagery, drawn directly from the world of the prophet of Tekoa and his disciples, a country world in which the work of building and rebuilding is an everyday matter, and a pastoral world in which life beats to the rhythm of the earth and the seasons:

'In that day I will raise up the booth of David that is fallen
and repair its breaches,
and raise up its ruins,
and rebuild it as in the days of old;
that they may possess the remnant of Edom
and all the nations who are called by my name,'
says the Lord who does this.
'Behold the days are coming,' says the Lord,
'when the ploughman shall overtake the reaper
and the treader of grapes him who sows the seed;
the mountains shall drip sweet wine,
and all the hills shall flow with it.
I will restore the fortunes of my people Israel,
and they shall rebuild the ruined cities and inhabit them;
they shall plant vineyards and drink their wine,
and they shall make gardens and eat their fruit.
I will plant them upon their land,
and they shall never again be plucked up
out of the land which I have given them,'
says the Lord your God (Amos 9.11–15).

# 4

# Hosea, Witness to a Crazy Love

## I. A prophet and his loves

### A shocking story!

One cannot open the book of Hosea for the first time without feeling a real shock. First of all there is the shock of the story, dramatic and eventful, of an unconventional couple, Hosea the prophet, and Gomer, described as a 'woman given to prostitution'. There is also the shock of the language and imagery, taken directly from the language of love, which does not fail to astonish in the context of the Bible. But above all there is the shock of seeing this story applied to God and God's relations with his people. Could God love in such a strange way?

The story of Hosea has seemed incredible to more than one Christian, and in the course of Bible studies, though people have claimed to be fascinated by what the prophet says and his vision of a God of tenderness, I have often heard comments like, 'That's a fine story . . . but only a story', on the assumption that no self-respecting prophet would ever have launched out on such an adventure.

The story of Hosea is quite shocking, not to say provocative, as was the story of his people at the moment when the prophet appeared on the scene in Israel. But this is also an overwhelming story of human emotions and revelations about the true face of God. This story may seem incredible, but it is our story and the story of our God. It is a true story. So even before we begin our investigation of this prophet and his story, and before reading the text of his oracles, let us re-read the two versions of his marriage and his personal story (chs. 1 and 3):

Hosea and Gomer

39

| Hosea's marriage |
| :--- |

## First version (Hos. 1)

2 When the Lord first spoke through Hosea,
the Lord said to Hosea,
'Go take to yourself a wife given to prostitution
and children of prostitution,
for the land is prostituting itself by forsaking the Lord.'
3 So he went and took Gomer the daughter of Diblaim,
and she conceived and bore him a son.
4 And the Lord said to him,
'Call his name Jezreel; for yet a little while, and I will punish the house of Jehu for the blood of Jezreel, and I will put an end to the kingdom of the house of Israel.
5 And on that day, I will break the bow of Israel in the valley of Jezreel.'
6 And she conceived again and bore a daughter, and the Lord said to Hosea,
'Call her name Lo-Ruhama, that is, Not Pitied, for I will no more have pity on the house of Israel, to forgive them at all.
But I will love the house of Judah, and I will deliver them by the Lord their God;
I will not deliver them by bow, nor by sword, nor by war, nor by horses, nor by horsemen.'
8 When she had weaned Not Pitied, she conceived and bore a son.
And the Lord said, 'Call his name Lo-Ammi, that is, Not My People, for you are not my people and I am not your God.'

## Second Version (Hos. 3)

1 And the Lord said to me, 'Go again, love a woman who is loved by another and is an adulteress; even as the Lord loves the people of Israel, though they turn to other gods and love cakes of raisins.'
2 So I bought her for fifteen shekels of silver and a measure and a half of barley.
3 And I said to her, 'You must dwell as mine for many days; you shall prostitute yourself, or belong to another man; so I will also be to you.'
4 For the children of Israel shall dwell many days without king or prince, without sacrifice or pillar, without ephod or teraphim.
5 Afterwards the children of Israel shall return and seek the Lord their God, and David their king; and they shall come in fear to the Lord and to his goodness in the latter days.'

These two texts evoke very vivid emotions in us: either we are immediately won over and as it were ravished, or we remain perplexed, disconcerted, intrigued, with a thousand and one questions. So let's try to understand this story more clearly.

## A strange couple: Hosea and Gomer

Let's begin straight away with the main characters, those whom the narrative first presents to us as being called to become a couple, Hosea and Gomer. The former is a prophet and certainly – as we shall see later – connected with the priestly (levitical) sphere, while the latter is a prostitute, either in the most usual sense of the term or in the narrower sense of cultic prostitute who offers herself at a temple.

Here is a marriage which seems to defy all the conventions of the time. On the one hand we know that at least in theory the religion of Israel prohibited any form of prostitution, profane or sacred (Lev.19.29; 21.9; Deut.23.18–19). The Israelite law quite explicitly forbade the marriage of a priest to a prostitute – so think of the reactions of the priests around Hosea! On the other hand – and this is what seems most scandalous in the passage which we have just read – it is hard to see how God could have given such an order to his prophet when the law that he promulgated forbade such marriages.

---

## Hosea 1 and 3: Marriage or Remarriage?

In addition to defying convention, the marriage of Hosea with Gomer raises more than one question for the modern reader. Is such a marriage fictitious or real? And if the latter is the case, is it Hosea's marriage with Gomer which leads to his prophetic vocation or vice versa? All these questions already arise in chapter 1. However, a new series of questions arises in chapter 3: Why is the passage in the first person? What woman is referred to? What about the children? and so on.

To see things more clearly, it is worth putting the two texts (Hos.1 and Hos.3) side by side:

### Hosea 1.2–3

The Lord said *to Hosea,*
Go,
*take a* wife
*who is given to prostitution*

*and children of prostitution*
for *the land is prostituting itself by turning from the Lord'*

*So he went and took Gomer the daughter of Diblaim, and she conceived and bore him a son.*

### Hosea 3.1–2

The Lord said *to me,*
'Go *again,*
*love a* woman
*who is love by another and is an adulteress.*

For *such is the love of the Lord for the people of Israel, though they turn to other gods and love cakes of raisins.'*
*So I bought her for fifteen shekels of silver and a measure and a half of barley*

The symmetry speaks for itself. First of all in the similarities: it all begins with a word of the Lord; the order is addressed to the prophet Hosea and in both cases relates to the marriage of a woman; in both cases the woman is in a matrimonial situation forbidden by Israelite legislation; each time a motivation (*for*) is given and in both cases there is an allusion to the infidelity of Israel. Finally, the whole episode ends with the execution of the order received; a marriage is concluded.

The parallelism is so strong that the two passages should be interpreted in terms of each other and not as two independent stories referring to two distinct events. We must speak, rather, of a deepening: in manifest parallelism to chapter 1, chapter 3 gives the ultimate reason or the foundation for this strange marriage commanded by God. And it is here that the differences count. Two major differences stand out immediately. Let's begin with the second, which is the more important. The second 'for' does not relate to the attitude of the Israelites but to God's atttitude. This is the most amazing thing: God loves a people, unfaithful though it is, and that leads to the second difference. Just as God loves an unfaithful people, so Hosea is invited to love Gomer. The love of God commands the love of others: here we are close to 'Love one another as I have loved you . . .' or 'Be merciful as your Father is merciful.' In other words, the theological controls the theologal. Once one has discovered the true face of God, one is called on to live like him: 'Love a woman . . . for such is the love of the Lord.'

## A strange family!

But not only the parents are astonishing here. The three children whom the couple have bear names which will have sounded as strange to the contemporaries of the prophet as they do to us. Names like *Lo-Ruhama*, i.e. Not Loved, or *Lo-Ammi*, i.e. Not My People, could only be bad omens. The name of the first son could have positive connotations ('God sows'), but God primarily gives it a negative connotation ('God disperses').

This is not good news, far less so when the three children reflect the history of the people of Israel, present and to come . . . And what is to be said of the role that these children are called to play of being witnesses against their mother, in the divorce case undertaken by the prophet? What a strange family this is!

But let's return to the prophet and his main particulars, as they emerge from the verse which is the heading to his book.

## The man and his setting (after Hos.1.1)

'The word of the Lord that came to Hosea the son of Beeri, in the days of Uzziah, Jotham, Ahaz and Hezekiah, kings of Judah, and in the days of Jeroboam the son of Joash, king of Israel.' This is the solemn formula by which the editors of the book of Hosea have chosen to introduce his oracles. We will find a similar formula in the books of Joel, Micah and Zephaniah. In this way the editors indicated the point at which they put the prophet's preaching, indicating at the same time how they wanted it to be accepted by the readers: as nothing less than a 'word of the Lord'.

There is not a word about the prophet's place of origin. All we are told is the name of his father (Beeri), and that hardly gives us any information about his place of origin. Here we must rather refer to the content of the book, which shows close connections with the northern kingdom. In fact, while the prophet does not allude either to Jerusalem or to the cities of Judah, he shows a particular interest in the cities and regions of the North

(Bethel, 4.15; 5.8f.; Gibeah and Rama, 5.8; Mizpah and Tabor, 5.1; Jezreel, chs.1–2; Samaria, 7.1). If Hosea belonged to the northern kingdom, that would also explain why he likes to call the whole of this kingdom by the symbolic name Ephraim, a tribe installed in the northern kingdom in the region of Shiloh and Shechem (cf. Josh.16.1–10).

The historical context is well known to us: mention is made of four kings of Judah, from Uzziah (781–740) to Hezekiah (716–687), as compared with a single king of Israel, Jeroboam II (787–747), under whom Amos also exercised his ministry. However, unlike Amos, Hosea is working in known territory, since he himself comes from the North. However, the mention of the fourth king of Judah takes us to a period later than that of Amos. And since in addition Hosea's book does not allude in any way to the fall of Samaria (722–721), his ministry is generally put around 750–730.

## An extremely troubled period

This period is relatively well known to us, thanks in particular to II Kings 15 and the oracles of the prophet Hosea himself. We could say that the period, which coincides with the end of the reign of Jeroboam II, was still a period of luxury and prosperity. But the succession to Jeroboam II proved to be a very troubled time, and one of extreme political instability. Simply in the period between 747 and 732 there were no less than five kings, two of whom reigned for less than a year. Such a political context presupposes a whole series of intrigues, conspiracies and murderous struggles for power. It was also, according to the well-known refrain of the historian of II Kings, a time of decadence and idolatry: 'He did what was evil in the sight of the Lord . . .' (II Kings 15.9, 18, 24, 28). We are also very far from the expansionist policy of Jeroboam II, and the kings of Israel are beginning to seek alliances with their long-standing enemies, Egypt and Assyria. King Menahem raised a tax to guarantee the protection of the rising star of Assyrian politics, Tiglath-Pileser III (745–727), while

King Ahaz went in person to Damascus to conclude a treaty with the same ruler (II Kings 15–16).

The prophet Hosea is no less implacable in his evaluation of contemporary politics. He denounces in a single-minded way the bloody violence of the dynasty of Jehu: 'I will call the house of Jehu to account for the blood of Jezreel . . .' He condemns, with no less vigour, the coups d'état and the regicides which have become common currency: 'They devour their rulers, all their kings have fallen . . .' (7.7). It is clear to him that God can have nothing to do with such intrigues: 'They have made kings without me, without me they have appointed leaders . . .' He also reproaches Israel for turning heedlessly to Egypt and Assyria: 'Ephraim is like a dove, silly and without sense, calling to Egypt, going to Assyria' (7.11). In short, the political situation is as sombre as could be.

However, the social and religious situation is hardly brighter. Hosea feels obliged to denounce the general corruption: 'There is no faithfulness or kindness, and no knowledge of God in the land; there is swearing, lying, killing, stealing, and committing adultery; they break all bounds and murder follows murder' (4.1–2). And not only are the political leaders responsible for this; the preachers have lamentably failed in their task, and have proved a real 'snare' for the house of Israel (chs.4–5).

So it is in this extremely difficult context that the prophet Hosea was called to bear witness to the God whom he discovered at the heart of his personal difficulties. He knew that the people whom he was called to serve was profoundly unfaithful. But he was himself indwelt by an invincible power, since he had discovered a limitless love, that of a God who takes to heart the happiness of a couple as much as of a whole people.

# II. Three texts for understanding Hosea

## 1. 'Put your mother on trial . . .'
### (Hos.2.4–25)

4 *Put your mother on trial, put her on trial,*
  *for she is not my wife,*
  *and I am not her husband.*
  *Let her remove the signs of prostitution from her face,*
  *and the marks of her adultery from between her breasts.*

5 *Otherwise I will strip her naked*
  *and make her as in the day she was born.*
  *I will make her like a wilderness,*
  *and set her like a parched land,*
  *and slay her with thirst.*

6 *Upon her children also I will have no pity,*
  *because they are children of prostitution.*
  *For their mother has played the prostitute;*
  *she that conceived them has acted shamefully.*

7 *For she said, 'I will go after my lovers,*
  *who give me my bread and my water,*
  *my wool and my flax, my oil and my drink.'*

8 *Therefore I will hedge up her way with thorns;*
  *and I will build a wall against her,*
  *so that she cannot find her paths.*

9 *She shall pursue her lovers,*
  *but not overtake them;*
  *and she shall seek them,*
  *but shall not find them.*
  *Then she shall say, 'I will go*
  *and return to my first husband,*
  *for it was better with me then than now.'*

10 *And she did not know*
  *that it was I who gave her*
  *the grain, the wine and the oil,*

and who lavished upon her silver
and gold which they used for Baal.
11 Therefore I will take back
my grain in its time,
and my wine in its season;
and I will take away my wool and my flax,
which were to cover her nakedness.
12 Now I will uncover her lewdness
in the sight of her lovers,
and no one shall rescue her out of my hand.
13 And I will put an end to all her mirth,
her feasts, her new moons, her sabbaths,
and all her appointed feasts.
14 And I will lay waste her vines and her fig trees,
of which she said,
'These are my hire,
which my lovers have given me.'
I will make them a forest,
and the beasts of the field shall devour them.
15 And I will punish her for the feast days of the Baals
when she burned incense to them
and decked herself with her rings and jewellery,
and went after her lovers,
and forgot me, says the Lord.
16 Therefore, behold, I will allure her,
and bring her into the wilderness,
and speak tenderly to her.
17 And there I will give her her vineyards,
and make the Valley of Achor a door of hope.
And there she shall answer as in the days of her
youth,

as at the time when she came out of the land of
Egypt.
18 And in that day, says the Lord,
you will call me 'My husband',
and no longer will you call me 'My master, my
baal'.
19 For I will remove the names of the Baals from her
mouth,
and they shall be mentioned by name no more.
20 And I will make for you a covenant on that day
with the beasts of the field, the birds of the air,
and the creeping things of the ground;
and I will abolish the bow, the sword, and war from
the land;
and I will make you lie down in safety.
21 And I will betroth you to me for ever;
I will betroth you to me in righteousness and in
justice,
in steadfast love, and in mercy.
22 I will betroth you to me in faithfulness;
and you shall know the Lord.
23 And in that day, says the Lord,
I will answer the heavens
and they shall answer the earth;
24 and the earth shall answer the grain, the wine, and
the oil,
and they shall answer Jezreel;
25 and I will sow him for myself in the land.
and I will have pity on Lo-Ruhama,
and I will say to Lo-Ammi, 'You are my people';
and he shall say, 'You are my God'.

---

This long passage, which commentators have tried desperately to arrange in what might seem a more logical order, is quite in place here and reflects the two extremes which can be found throughout the book of Hosea, namely an implacable plea against the infidelities of Israel and the expression of an infinite tenderness and love on the part of God.

## An implacable plea

The tone is set by the first verse: 'Put your mother on trial, put her on trial . . .' (2.4; cf. also 4.1; 12.3). We already found the equivalent in Amos with the eight oracles which opened his book, but this is the first time that we find the technical term 'trial' to describe an intervention by God in relation to his people. There is even a literary genre to mark the different phases of the trial: the summoning of witnesses, the reminder of obligations and duties contracted in the covenant, accusations, verdict and sentence (cf. Deut.23.21–25; Isa.1.2–3, 10–20; Micah 6.1–8; Jer.2.4–13, 29; Ps.50.4–23).

But these are also divorce proceedings, 'for she is

not my wife and I am not her husband' (2.4). One could not find a more severe judgment. Relations between God and his people have been broken off.

The vocabulary is that of prostitution and adultery. There is nothing to be surprised at in that, given the tone chosen by the prophet for speaking of relations between Yahweh and his people. But the religious connotations of this vocabulary could not be clearer; here there is an inexorable condemnation of idolatry and the Canaanite fertility cults.

The first motif of the condemnation is that of prostitution: 'Yes, their mother is a prostitute . . . Therefore I will hedge her way with thorns . . .' (2.7–8).

But there is a second motif, expressed later on: 'And she did not know that it was I who gave her the grain, the wine, and the oil . . . Therefore I will take back my grain in its time, and my wine in its season . . .' (2.10–11). Even more seriously than acts of prostitution, there is this tragic failure to understand. Israel does not know its good fortune. Even worse, Israel does not recognize the source of that good fortune.

**A happiness beyond all hope**

Verses 21 to 25 are among the finest in the prophetic literature, and they have been often quoted down the ages. Who could not be attracted by words like these?

> Therefore, behold, I will allure her,
> and bring her into the wilderness,
> and speak tenderly to her.
> And I will betroth you to me for ever;
> I will betroth you to me in righteousness and in justice,

in steadfast love, and in mercy.
I will betroth you to me in faithfulness;
and you shall know the Lord.
And in that day, says the Lord,
I will answer the heavens
and they shall answer the earth (2.16, 21–23).

But there is yet more, when we see how these statements are developed by the prophet. Up to this point the trial has been merciless, and with the second 'therefore' (in v.11; the first was in v.8) we might be led to believe that the case has been heard and there is no more hope. That is the perspective which seems to emerge from vv.12 to 15, which announce mourning and devastation, as a reprisal against the infidelities of the people.

And then, in v.16, there is another 'therefore'. Both the logic of the structure and the content of the preceding verses suggest that here the judgment attains an extreme severity, since the prophet has just evoked the faults of the people of Israel, which are also extreme: 'and it has forgotten me, says the Lord'.

Now quite the opposite happens. The tone changes completely, and suddenly it is God himself who takes charge of the future of his people. He begins to speak of seduction, a seduction which will lead to conversion and restoration. The covenant will be re-established again and will reach unsuspected heights of tenderness and reciprocity.

The 'therefore' in v.16 never ceases to surprise. One could not find a better illustration of the gratuitousness of salvation. At the depth of the infidelity of the people, God shows himself to be a God of mercy who still seeks to resume the dialogue and restore the union.

---

## 2. 'Your love is like a morning cloud'
### (Hos.6.1–6)

1 'Come, let us return to the Lord;
  for he has torn, that he may heal us;
  he has stricken, and he will bind us up.
2 After two days he will revive us;

on the third day he will raise us up,
that we may live before him.
3 Let us know, let us press on to know the Lord;
  his going forth is sure as the dawn;

*he will come to us as the showers,*
*as the spring rains that water the earth.'*
4 *What shall I do with you, O Ephraim?*
*What shall I do with you, O Judah?*
*Your love is like a morning cloud,*
*like the dew that goes early away.*

5 *Therefore I have hewn them by the prophets,*
*I have slain them by the words of my mouth,*
*and my judgment goes forth as the light.*
6 *For I desire steadfast love and not sacrifice,*
*the knowledge of God, rather than burnt offerings.*

---

After the tormented history of Hosea's marriage, these few verses are among the most famous in the whole of the book which bears his name. In them we find a completely characteristic tone, with the emphasis on the knowledge and the love of God, on the inconstancy of the love of the people for God, and the debate which this provokes in God himself (v.4), but we also find an undeniable affinity with the New Testament, in particular with the mention of a return to life 'on the third day' and the unequivocal affirmation of the primacy of love over sacrifices.

## A liturgy in due form?

The first part of the text (vv.1–3) reflects a clearly liturgical character: the exhortation in the second person, the communal use of the first person plural, allusions to the return to the Lord, to the efforts to know him and to life in his presence. Furthermore, the second part (vv.4–6) could well be God's response to the community, in the very unfolding of the liturgy.

However, we should not forget the immediate context, which is that of a total but conditional break between God and his people: 'I will return again to my place, until they acknowledge their guilt and seek my face, and in their distress they seek me' (5.15). So God has chosen to remove himself and wait for his people to decide to amend their conduct and to seek him in truth.

The intentions of Israel, expressed in the traditional liturgical vocabulary, might appear quite laudable, except that God's response (vv.4–6) seriously puts in question the motivations and above all the sincerity of this attitude: 'Your love is like a morning cloud, like the dew that goes early

away' (v.4). And above all the conclusion (v.6) shows the inadequacy of the gestures of 'conversion' made by Israel: they are only at the level of rites, sacrifices and burnt offerings, and not at the level of the love and knowledge of God, the only criteria which count in God's eyes.

## God who tears apart and who heals . . .

Hosea is not the only one to talk like this. In Deuteronomy 32.39 we find the same image of a God who strikes in order to go on to heal:

See now that I, even I, am he,
and there is no God beside me;
I kill and I make alive;
I wound and I heal;
and there is none that can deliver out of my hand.

We could also refer to a large number of psalms ('God brings down, God raises up', 'God makes poor, God makes rich') which have a very similar language, and numerous prophetic texts which interpret the misfortunes of Israel.

In all these texts we cannot but admire the unfailing faith and hope of a people which knows that God's last word can only be on the side of healing and the restoration of life. However, we have to recognize that in this vision of things ('God tears apart in order to heal') there is a conception of God which causes some difficulties today. Must we really see God everywhere and make him directly responsible for the way in which his people or innocent victims are smitten and torn apart?

This is a serious and formidable question which will be taken up and turned in every direction by another biblical book, that of Job. The question, with the different answers offered by the biblical and theological tradition, has given rise to radical revisions in recent years. I am thinking, for example, of the impact of works like René Girard's *Violence and the Sacred*, which have obliged us to revise our conceptions of a God whom one can appease or satisfy only by accepting suffering.

So here we have utter mystery and utter paradox. There is something admirable about the prophet's affirmation. However, it should not be understood as a ban which prevents believers from raising the questions which haunt them every time suffering knocks at their door. Happily, the book of Job and numerous psalms of individual or communal lament would later show that these questions are fully justified and would make a definitive contribution towards moving forward the debate on the links between God and human suffering.

### 'The third day'

The expression 'the third day' used by the prophet Hosea cannot fail to arouse the interest of Christian readers for whom the expression has become classic with reference to the resurrection of Jesus (cf. I Cor.15.4; Luke 24.7). The analogy is all the more striking since in the text of Hosea the expression is associated with the vocabulary of life and return to life. However, to be truthful, it is not certain that here we can find even a veiled anticipation of the resurrection of Jesus.

On the one hand it has to be noted that the two texts of the New Testament mentioned earlier do not cite the witness of Hosea to support their presentation of events. For this reason, beyond question, the Church Fathers hesitated to use this text as an argument in favour of the resurrection on 'the third day'. We have to wait for Tertullian (at the beginning of the third century) to have a christological reinterpretation of Hosea 6.1–2.

On the other hand, the ironical, not to say polemical, context of the passage probably forces us to recognize negative connotations here. The expression 'after two days . . . the third day' would express Israel's sentiment of being able to give a good account of itself and would be another way of indicating the fleeting and only transitory character of the people's conversion.

The 'therefore' in v.5 confirms the negative drift of the passage and here is the opposite of the 'therefore' in 2.16, which we looked at earlier: 'Therefore I have hewn them by the prophets, I have slain them by the words of my mouth, and my judgment goes forth as the light.' The word of the prophets reveals and judges the true intentions of Israel's cult.

Certainly the text speaks of a return to life. But what return is this? A sincere and definitive return? Given the context, this does not seem to be the case. If we want to connect Hosea 6.2 with the Christian tradition of the 'third day' of the resurrection of Jesus, that can only be in order to bring out the absolute novelty of what takes place in Jesus: whereas the resurrection hope of Hosea's contemporaries is expressed in the context of an ambiguous and fleeting love, the resurrection of Jesus on 'the third day' is the fruit of a love which is never contradicted, even in death and beyond that . . .

### God's 'emotions' (vv.4–5)

Hosea's language still has surprises in store. After his amazing revelations about his love life, here he presents us with a God debating with himself, in some degree torn between his emotions:' What am I to do with you, Ephraim? What am I to do with you, Judah?' It is as if God were expressing his frailty and his impotence in the face of his people's love. If we often fail to understand God's attitude, the reverse is also true: God does not always understand the causes of our rebellions and our forsaking of him.

God's questions are hard to understand. If one is on the side of Ephraim and Judah, there would be reasons for doubting God's intentions: could he be responding to inconstancy with inconstancy? And to add to the difficulty, the prophet gives us a not very reassuring image of the prophetic word: 'Therefore I have hewn them by the prophets, I have slain them by the words of my mouth . . .' That is not at all the image that we like to have of the word of God. A word which smites and massacres?

Either one loves or one does not love; that is what the text says. The word of the prophets hurts, and it can open deep wounds when one forgets to live in fidelity to the covenant.

However, this is only one stage, and the ultimate aim of the prophetic word lies elsewhere. Even in its harshness and its demands, the prophetic word contributes to making light shine forth: 'and my judgment goes forth as the light'. That is the twofold dimension of every word of God, this 'two-edged sword'; it is a word of both judgment and salvation, good news and the demand for conversion.

## Love and knowledge of God

That is how we are to understand the conclusion of the prophetic oracle: 'For I desire mercy, and not sacrifice . . .' This is both a radical judgment on a cult which makes no sense, and extraordinary good news in which we can rediscover the essentials of the gospel according to Hosea: it is love, and not external rites, which give access to the true God. As we have already seen, the God of Jesus will be no different.

---

## 3.  'Return then, O Israel, to the Lord your God . . .'
### (Hos.14.2–9)

2 'Return then, O Israel, to the Lord your God,
   for you have stumbled because of your iniquity.
3 Take with you words and return to the Lord,
   say to him,
   'Take away all iniquity;
   accept that which is good
   and instead of bulls we will offer as a sacrifice
   the words of our lips.
4 Assyria cannot save us,
   we will not ride upon horses;
   and we will say no more, "Our God",
   to the work of our hand.
   In you the orphan finds mercy.'
5 I will heal their faithlessness,
   I will love them freely,

   for my anger has turned from them.
6 I will be as the dew to Israel;
   he shall blossom as the lily,
   he shall strike root as the poplar;
7 his shoots shall spread out;
   his beauty shall be like the olive,
   and his fragrance like Lebanon.
8 They shall return, those who dwelt under his shadow,
   they shall flourish as a garden;
   and they shall blossom as the vine,
   their fragrance shall be like the wine of Lebanon.
9 O Ephraim, what have I to do with idols?
   It is I who answer and look after you.
   I am like an evergreen cypress,
   from me comes your fruit.

---

Here we are now at the conclusion of the book of Hosea. It is a book which has not failed to make its readers feel a whole range of emotions, from the purest tenderness to the utmost indignation, including the impatience or anger felt at the repeated infidelities of a people which gives itself over to idolatry. But the prophet is about to come to a conclusion. As was the case at the beginning of the book, his message bears a promise of renewal on the part of God.

### 'Return then, O Israel . . .'
The verb 'return' is not a new one for Hosea. It is even part of his favourite vocabulary for indicating

the change that the prophet expects of his hearers in their relations with God: 'Return, then, to your God . . .' (12.7; cf. also 3.5; 6.1; 7.10,16). To 'return to the Lord' is primarily to choose to renew a covenant, certain demands of which one recognizes that one has betrayed. This is clearly a penitential prayer which the people have not perhaps yet made entirely their own, but which the prophet presents as an indispensable condition for them to be able to begin to hope again.

However, the expression does not stop at its penitential dimension. If we accept that this final oracle could have been edited after the exile, it is easy to understand that the verb 'return' could allude to the return from exile, as is the case, for example, in Psalm 126 (v.1): 'When the Lord brought back those who returned to Zion . . .' Furthermore, this sense can be discerned a little later on, in v.8: 'They shall return, those who dwelt under his shadow.' So here we have one more example of re-reading and updating oracles of the prophet in new situations. The return from exile in the sixth century would be a confirmation of the hope preached by the prophet Hosea two centuries earlier.

## A confession of faith

Conversion is not enough. Or at least, it has to be said that it is not enough to change behaviour. What the prophet requires of his people is nothing less than a return to a more authentic faith. By his allusion to the 'words of our lips' he invites Israel to define its faith in God better (vv.3–4). At both the beginning and end of what serves as a creed, the prophet Hosea emphasizes the primordial quality of the God whom he knows, and his mercy: 'You take away all iniquity . . . in you the orphan finds mercy . . .' The prophet has taken stock of the numerous infidelities of his people at length and in a lively way. However, as we have known since the

beginning of his prophetic adventure, the life of the prophet Hosea has been turned upside down by the revelation of free and merciful love for his people.

Then comes the presentation of the offering: 'Accept that which is good, and instead of bulls we will offer as a sacrifice the words of our lips.' Throughout the book, the prophet has denounced the idolatrous practices of the people and the lack of sincerity in its worship of Yahweh. Here, Israel declares itself ready to present 'what is good' and gives up putting the emphasis on bulls and sacrifices, to concentrate more on the sincerity of its profession of faith ('the words of our lips').

Even in its negative formulation, the last verse of the creed proposed by Hosea says a lot about the conversion of the people. Hosea has vividly denounced the illusions of covenants with foreign countries, in particular Assyria (5.13; 7.11), and recourse to military resources (the power of the horse). Now Israel is invited to turn for good to Yahweh who alone can give strength and victory. So here at last the people renounce the idolatry which leads it to say, 'Our God' to the work of our hands.

### 'as the dew . . .'

Verses 5 to 9 pile image upon image to speak of the restoration of the people by God: healing, generous love, abandonment of wrath, flourishing and fertility. But none of these images can show better than that of the 'dew' how God reverses the destiny of his people for its greater happiness. We may remember that God himself reproached his people for showing a love as fleeting and transitory as morning dew. Now God takes up the same image and uses it himself, this time to express the novelty and the beauty of the fruits to come: 'I will be as the dew to Israel . . .' Only God's faithful love, eternally new, can change the destiny of a people whose love is so fragile and so fugitive.

# III. The God of Hosea

## God the spouse

This is the first characteristic of Hosea's God. Hosea was also the first to be bold enough to apply the image of spouse to God, though he was to have prestigious disciples like Isaiah, the author of the Song of Songs, Jesus himself, the apostles Paul and John, and the author of the Apocalypse.

For it is God who must be seen under the features of the lover, now ravished, now torn apart or deceived, but always madly in love, which we rediscover in the first pages of the book of Hosea (chs.1–3). God does not love in an abstract and uncompromising way. He loves by passionately committing himself, even with the characteristics of a spouse.

Certainly there is a risk in using such language, and the image of God the spouse, above all in our days, needs to be supplemented and corrected. But the text itself sees to that. For this is not a role of domination, but a relationship stamped with respect and calling for dialogue and reciprocity. In fact the spouse is no longer the 'baal', i.e. the master or the owner, but the 'husband', i.e. the equal partner. Here we rediscover the original ideal (Genesis 1–2), in which the unity and complementarity of the man–woman couple can be fully the image of God.

Hosea was well aware that this ideal, given by his relationship with his spouse, had been completely transformed by the discovery of what loving really means in God's eyes. If it takes us back to the beauty of the first beginnings, it also has the merits of anticipating what on the lips of Jesus was to become one of the finest images of the presence of God in the world. Jesus in fact describes himself as the spouse who is already present (Mark 2.19): there is a need to rejoice and give up old religious practices. But he is also the bridegroom who is awaited and who will come to consummate the definitive union with his bride, in an infinite communion and dialogue: 'Let us rejoice . . . for the marriage of the Lamb has come. The Spirit and the Bride say "Come"' (Rev.19.7; 22.17).

## A God who is deeply wounded

Hosea's God has nothing to do with an impassible and immovable God, above the hurly-burly of life, whom nothing can affect. On the contrary, Hosea leads us to discover a God full of life and emotions, who has no fear of compromising himself in an alliance and showing his expectations. Hosea's God compromises himself by taking the initiative in tenderness and sincere love: speaking to the heart, plighting his troth in tenderness, loving with tenderness, and leading with human cords – all these are expressions which reveal God's amorous passion for his people.

However, this is also a God who does not hide either his demands or his disappointments. If he does not hesitate to put his people on trial (chs.2 and 4), it is because he feels betrayed: 'But like Adam they transgressed the covenant; there they dealt faithlessly with me' (6.7). This is one of the dominant features of Hosea's God: we feel that he has been deeply wounded and torn apart in his feelings for Ephraim–Israel. Hosea is not afraid of using words to express God's feelings: 'Ephraim has given bitter provocation . . .' (12.15). Don't we have to speak here of the 'suffering' of God?

This wound or suffering of God can equally be felt from the fact that God is often driven to extremes by the ingratitude and infidelities of his people, to the point of debating with himself whether he should put into effect his plans for salvation. His heart 'recoils' (11.8), when he is faced with serious dilemmas:

'What shall I do with you, O Ephraim?' (6.4);

# Speaking of God on the Basis of Human Love and Sexuality

## What the prophet Hosea discovered

Hosea was the first biblical writer to do theology on the basis of his own experience of human love and sexuality. After him one could refer to the fine pages of Genesis 1–2, of Isaiah, of the Song of Songs, then of Jeremiah and Ezekiel, and later, of St Paul. But in one way or another all are heirs of the theological boldness of this great eighth-century prophet.

Later, and again thanks to him, the experience of conjugal love will take on a symbolic dimension. But what makes Hosea original is that this symbolic dimension is an integral part of his own personal experience.

Furthermore, the first three chapters are a concrete and vibrant evocation of Hosea's tormented but prophetic loves. First we learn of the order issued to him to take in marriage Gomer, 'a woman given to prostitution' (1.2). Hosea and Gomer choose to have children, and their three children seem destined for a tragic future (1.3–9).

Then Hosea is tempted to abandon it all. He now thinks only of divorce (2.4–15); nothing works any longer between him and his wife, between him and his children, between the children and their mother. Love is dead between him and Gomer, and there seems to be no more hope of return.

Now at precisely this point the incredible news is given: not only will the divorce not take place, but they will love each other as they did in their youth (2.16–25). Now the talk is of seduction, of mutual appeal, of a loving response and an eternal betrothal. The unloved children again become a living promise of hope (2.25).

So what has happened? In fact there has been a complete reversal of the situation. From the very touching and very true history of Hosea and Gomer, we have moved on to the no less touching and no less true history of God and his people. Indeed the divorce between Hosea and Gomer will never take place. For they have both understood, in the light of God's love for his people, that now they must love in a different way. Chapter 3 does not tell the story of a second marriage of Hosea, but rather the story of the same marriage lived in a different way. The story is still about the couple Hosea and Gomer, but this time the vocation of the prophet goes far beyond the first call that he had heard: 'The Lord said to me, go again and love a woman loved by another . . .' (3.1). And the reason, the theological reason, is given immediately: 'For such is the love of the Lord . . .' Yes, God loves humanity to this degree, even though he knows it to be unfaithful. There is no limit to the love which God has for humankind.

And since God loves like this, Hosea and Gomer will have understood that they must live in the same way. We are already close to 'Be merciful as your Father is merciful' (Luke 6.36) and the new commandment of Jesus, 'Love one another as I have loved you . . .' (John 13.34).

'I would redeem them, but they speak lies against me' (7.13);

'How can I give you up, O Ephraim!
How can I hand you over, O Israel!
How can I make you like Admah!
How can I treat you like Zeboim!

My heart recoils within me,
my compassion grows warm and tender' (11.8);

'Shall I ransom them from the power of Sheol?
Shall I redeem them from death?' (13.14);

'O Ephraim, what have I to do with idols?' (14.9).

Here are serious questions which we would be wrong to take lightly, at the risk of being regarded, like Ephraim–Israel, as 'a dove, silly and without sense' (7.11) . . . God wants to save his people, but cannot do so unless the people shows a sincere desire for conversion.

## A God with a human face

As we read Hosea, we see that his God is intimately connected with human history. Certainly he remains the Wholly Other, the Holy One, and does not give way to anger: 'I will not execute my fierce anger, I will not again destroy Ephraim; for I am God and not man, the Holy One in your midst, and I will not come to destroy' (1.9). But he can also be more human, madly in love with his spouse (2.18), and resolved to lead his people with 'cords of compassion' (11.4).

So Hosea took the risk of speaking of God on the basis of human realities; the love of a couple, with all its risks, its difficulties and its riches (chs.1–3); the love of a father for his son (11.1–4); and also the love of a mother for the fruit of her womb (11.8). All that is deeply human, authentically human, can be found in God.

## A 'seductive' God

Hosea also took the risk of speaking of God in amorous language, and he was bold enough to speak of seduction and betrothal in God. Here is a God who courts humanity. That might seem strange, but isn't this what we find throughout the Bible, and isn't this what John wants to say when he writes that 'God first loved us . . .' The history of Hosea's loves reveals to us a God who will use any means to gain or regain the love of his spouse.

## A God of love

All the features that have been enumerated so far to describe the God of Hosea can be summed up in one word, 'Love'. Comparisons have often rightly been made between the book of Hosea and the Johannine writings because of the importance that they give to love in defining the mystery of God and our relations with him. Hosea must be given the credit for having been the first to offer an account of his experience of God on the basis of his own experience of loving. This is not an idealized or affected language of love. It is an experience which he had in his own history, indeed in his own flesh. The God of Hosea is very much incarnate: how could one be incarnate without experiencing human love? John was to be the theologian *par excellence* of the God of Love. There is nothing surprising about this, since he is also the theologian of the incarnation, of a God who is 'made flesh' (John 1.14). Hosea and John combine marvellously in a single testimony to say that God is infinitely close to all that is human and that the only access to him is through love: 'Beloved, let us love one another, since love is of God and whoever loves is born of God and comes to the knowledge of God . . .' (I John 4.7).

# 5

# Isaiah, The Messenger of 'The Holy One of Israel'

We are now going to embark on the study of the prophet who has been called 'the prince of prophets' and whom some consider to be *the* poet of the Hebrew Bible. His book is colossal, sixty-six chapters, and its composition will have been spread out over almost half a millennium! Here we have a real challenge of condensation: to present in one brief chapter a work which is so impressive and so rich, from both a literary and a theological point of view. Here, more than ever, choices will have to be made; there will have to be summaries and suggestions. However, don't forget that this present volume is an invitation to read the prophets which suggests keys for opening up the book rather than offering a complete and detailed reading.

As with Amos and Hosea, we shall begin with the historical context in which the eighth-century prophet exercised his ministry. We shall also discuss the history of the book which we now have. For the political and religious history which underlies Isaiah 40–66, you will need to refer to the presentation of the prophets of the return, in chapter 8 below.

Isaiah

# I.  A master prophet at the court of Jerusalem: Isaiah, son of Amoz

## The prophet and his time

First let's read again the heading of the book given by the editors:

> The vision of Isaiah the son of Amoz, which he saw concerning Judah and Jerusalem in the days of Uzziah, Jotham, Ahaz and Hezekiah, kings of Judah (1.1).

We are first of all struck by the descriptive title 'vision which he saw'. This presents the prophet as a visionary. Certainly he remains the man of the Word, but the editors wanted to emphasize the importance of the way he looked at persons and events. The visual, not to say aesthetic, aspect of the message takes on a singular importance in Isaiah.

A second remarkable feature is the mention of Judah and Jerusalem. Isaiah has a special link with Judah and its capital. He moves around it easily (see, for example, 7.3), and, more important still, he has his entrées into the royal court.

Finally, the reference to kings Jotham, Ahaz and Hezekiah puts the ministry of Isaiah between 735 and 700. Three major events marked this period and therefore the prophet's message.

### 1. Jerusalem at the hour of choice: the Syro–Ephraimite war (735)

In 735, the northern kingdom – usually called Israel, but also Ephraim by the prophets of the eighth century – had had enough of submitting to Assyrian domination and above all of the heavy taxes which had to be paid to the Assyrian king. It then turned to one of its sworn enemies, Syria (with Damascus as its capital), and sought to make an alliance with Jerusalem and its king to rise against Assyria.

Ahaz, king of Jerusalem, was seized by panic and did not know what to do: 'Then his heart and the heart of his people shook as the trees of the forest shake before the wind' (7.2). Isaiah, still highly regarded at the royal court, did not share this feeling of panic and was opposed to these foreign alliances, which hid a deeper problem, that of a lack of confidence in God. Addressing King Ahaz, he exorcised his fears and called on him and all the people to put their faith in God: 'Take heed, be quiet, do not fear . . . you will not believe, surely you shall not be established' (7.4,9)

### 2. A kingdom becomes extinct: the fall of Samaria (722–721)

The prophet was not directly implicated in this second event, which involved only the northern kingdom, but it is clear that the fall of Samaria will have had repercussions on the southern kingdom. The only clear allusion to the imminent fall of Samaria (here, as in Hosea, designated by the name of Ephraim), is in ch.28:

> Woe to the proud crown of the drunkards of Ephraim,
> and to the fading flower of its glorious beauty,
> which is on the head of the rich valley of those overcome with wine!
> Behold, the Lord has one who is mighty and strong;
> like a storm of hail, a destroying tempest,
> like a storm of mighty, overflowing waters,
> he will cast down to the earth with violence.
> The proud crown of the drunkards of Ephraim will be trodden under foot;
> and the fading flower of its glorious beauty,
> which is on the head of the rich valley,
> will be like a first-ripe fig before the summer;
> when a man sees it, he eats it up
> as soon as it is in his hand (28.1–4).

For a fuller picture we can refer to the account given by the Deuteronomistic historian in II Kings 17. The victories of Shalmaneser V and Sargon II led to the first deportations of Israelites to Assyria and a recolonization of Samaria which was to have profound consequences for relations between Jews and Samaritans.

If in some respects Judah could rejoice at the misfortunes of the northern kingdom, the hour was soon to come when it had in turn to submit to the pressures and murderous attacks of the Assyrian giant. The prophet Isaiah does not fail to put Judah on its guard against the fury of the Assyrian invader (10.5–19, 24–27).

From this point on, Judah would have to come to terms with an unprecedented political and religious situation. The new inhabitants of the northern kingdom had in fact kept their own religious traditions: 'So they feared the Lord but also served their own gods, after the manner of the nations from among whom they had been carried away' (II Kings 17.33). Judah would have to guard against the danger of syncretism.

Furthermore, with the fall of Samaria, we have to note that it is no longer possible to go on speaking of Israel in a political sense – since the kingdom and its capital had been conquered and the local population had been deported – now Israel exists only in a theological sense.

*3. The enemy is at the gates: the Assyrian invasion (701)*

This time, the prophet was directly concerned, indeed personally involved, in the resistance which began to become organized in the reign of Hezekiah. Hezekiah was a king who was pleasing to God, and for this reason merits a highly favourable judgment from the Deuteronomistic historian:

> And he did what was right in the eyes of the Lord, according to all that David his father had done. He removed the high places, and broke the pillars, and cut down the Asherah. And he broke in pieces the bronze serpent that Moses had

made, for until those days the people of Israel had burned incense to it; it was called Nehushtan. He trusted in the Lord the God of Israel; so that there was none like him among all the kings of Judah after him, nor among those who were before him. For he held fast to the Lord; he did not depart from following him, but kept the commandments which the Lord commanded Moses. And the Lord was with him; wherever he went forth, he prospered. He rebelled against the king of Assyria, and would not serve him. He smote the Philistines as far as Gaza and its territory, from watchtower to fortified city (II Kings 18.3–7).

Hezekiah, who readily appealed to the prophet Isaiah, was no dreamer. His faith in God did not lead him to neglect human means. He decided to fortify Jerusalem and the whole of his kingdom, and in particular had a famous tunnel of almost half a mile built to allow Jerusalem always to have access to springs of water, even under siege. Moreover this exploit earned him a special note from the Deuteronomistic historian: 'The rest of the deeds of Hezekiah, and all his might, and how he made the pool and the conduit and brought water into the city, are they not written in the Chronicles of the Kings of Judah?' (II Kings 20.20).

## Five hundred years of prophecy?
## The great Isaianic tradition

You will no doubt have been told or have heard at some point that certain famous passages of Isaiah ('Comfort, comfort my people . . .', 'You are precious in my eyes . . .', 'Behold my servant whom I uphold, my chosen, in whom my soul delights . . .'; 'The spirit of God is upon me . . . he has sent me to proclaim good news to the poor') are passages from Deutero- (= Second) Isaiah. This is a term used for the section which begins with 40.1. Some scholars even distinguish a third section and speak of a Trito- (= Third) Isaiah (Isa.56–66). Given the very great literary, theological and historical affinities between chs.40–55 and chs.56–66, I shall limit myself here to looking at the relations between the two major sections of the book, i.e. chs.1–39 and chs.40–66. Do we have two prophets here, with two different books?

This question is an old one, and the answer given to it by modern exegesis has now commanded assent for more than a century. The vast majority of interpreters in fact distinguish two major sections in the book of Isaiah on the basis of historical, literary and theological facts: the first, made up of chs.1–39, is for the most part to be attributed to the prophet Isaiah from the eighth century; the second, which includes chapters 40–66, will be much later, the work of a school of disciples which sought to translate and update the message of the master in the new context of the return from exile (538 BCE and the very first years of the return).

Granted, these two great collections do not form completely coherent wholes. The first has been augmented and enriched by later elements (e.g. in chs.24–27 and 34–35) which could also very well come from the exilic or post-exilic period. In other words, the activity of bringing to light prophecies of Isaiah, son of Amoz, was pursued for centuries. Some scholars even believe that this takes us down to the Hellenistic period (after 333 BCE), almost five hundred years after the eighth-century prophet. Be this as it may, the theory of an Isaiah school and the division of the book into two major sections (1–39 and 40–66) is based on solid arguments.

### Literary arguments

Independently of any theory, anyone who sets out to read Isaiah 40–66 will soon note the differences in literary presentation as compared with 1–39. First of all, there are no longer verses in prose; there is only poetry. Then, unlike chs.1–39, we do not find any division into individual oracles or any chronological indication, and consequently there is no concrete reference to the eighth-century prophet. Finally, there are numerous significant differences in vocabulary:

- Jerusalem and Judah are mentioned together only once in 40–66, while this pairing recurs constantly in the oracles of 1–39;

- The vocabulary of the *election* of Jacob–Israel is extremely rare in 1–39 (only in 14.1), while we find it nine times in 40–66;

- The root 'evangelize' is unknown in 1–39 and occurs seven times in 40–66;

- The divine attribute 'God of hosts' is a key concept in 1–39 (where it is used fifty-six times), whereas in 40–66 it plays a minor role (only six instances);

- The vocabulary relating to human pride occurs only in 1–39 (around fifteen times).

One could extend the list almost indefinitely. Other differences in vocabulary will appear when we speak of theology later on.

### The references to history

Here again, the differences stand out. Whereas 1–39 is full of allusions to the eighth century (Ahaz, Hezekiah, Isaiah, Sennacherib, etc) for which we find many parallels in II Kings, these are totally absent from 40–66. By contrast, here we have explicit references to the Persian period (538–533) with the mention of Cyrus, king of Persia (45.1), whose victory over Babylon had signified the end of the Babylonian empire and the return of the deportees to Jerusalem. In chs.40–66 we no longer hear Isaiah, son of Amoz, the influential prophet at the royal court, calling for resistance to the Assyrian invasion, but quite a new prophet, exhorting a people held in captivity to depart from Babylon (48.20), return to Zion (51.11) with songs of joy, and rebuild the prosperity of Jerusalem (44.26,28). The historical context could hardly be clearer; here we are in the period of the return from exile, sparked off by the decree of Cyrus in 538, and thus two centuries away from the Judaean prophet of the eighth century.

Certainly there was a time when the idea people had of the prophet, namely a man who under inspiration could predict the future, made it possible to attribute the vast collection of Isaiah 1–66 to a single individual. But it seems much simpler to recognize the historical complexion of the texts and to see them as the result of collective work – just as inspired, if not more so – spread out over several centuries. Specifically that would mean that believers in the sixth century were inspired by oracles of the prophet Isaiah from the eighth century and brought them up to date to fit their time and place.

## Different theological accents

Finally, the literary and historical differences between Isaiah 1–39 and 40–66 point to an even more basic difference, that of theology. It is not that the theology of 40–66 is in contradiction to that of 1–39. However, the accents are different. Very different, as you will see from the table alongside.

## Beyond the differences, a single book

Once the most striking differences have been recognized, the present state of the book still has to be explained. After a long period in which there was an emphasis on the differences, and attempts were made by skilful surgery to indicate them in the text itself, recent research on the book of Isaiah is again stressing the coherence of the book as a whole and the reasons which have led to the fusion in a single book of the two (or, for some scholars, three) great collections. For after all, what is important for us is the book as we now have it. Certainly the history of its formation is most enlightening for us. But we receive it from tradition (the canon of scriptures) as an already constructed whole, and we must interpret it as such.

Now if we keep simply to the broad outlines of more recent interpretations, it is easy to see that the first section (1–39) is essentially the pronouncement of a judgment which ends up announcing the misfortunes which will soon fall on Judah. The second section (40–66) is the expression of a promise of salvation. The reason why it has been grafted on the first section is to show that the word of judgment has effectively been realized, but in no case can it represent God's last word. The dynamic

| From Isaiah 1–39 to Isaiah 40–66: different theological accents | | |
|---|---|---|
| | Isaiah 1–39 | Isaiah 40–66 |
| 1. God of hosts (*YHWH sebaot*) | 56x | 6x |
| 2. First and Last (applied to God) | 0 | 3x |
| 3. Create (always with reference to God) | 1x (in 4.5) | 20x |
| 4. Suffering servant | 0 | 19x |
| 5. Good news | 0 | 5x |
| 6. God who comforts | 3x | 16x |
| 7. Spirit of God | 1x (11.2) | around 20x |
| 8. God the father | 0 | 6x |
| 9. God the spouse | 0 | 50.1; 54.1–13; 62.4–5 |

which operates from one section to another could not be more eloquent: the God who judged his people at the time of the eighth-century prophet and in the events which led to the exile is unfailingly the God who can comfort, heal, renew and gather together his people.

# II. Three texts for understanding Isaiah (1–39)

We really need more than three texts to do justice to the amazing diversity of the book of Isaiah. However, the three passages which follow and which, exceptionally, come after one another in the prophetic book, can be considered as the most famous texts of the prophet of Jerusalem. Here are only three short chapters for such a great collection, but in themselves they reveal the great theological and literary mastery of their author. In them we find successively a song which is transformed into a parable (5.1–7), a theophany which ends up in a call and a mission (6.1–12), and an oracle which borrows from announcements of a marvellous birth and which from now on was to feed centuries of messianic expectation (7.10–17).

## 1. Between love and injustice: the song of the beloved and his vine (Isa.5.1–7)

1 *Let me sing for my beloved*
*a love song concerning his vineyard:*
*My beloved had a vineyard on a very fertile hill.*
2 *He digged it and cleared it of stones,*
*and planted it with choice vines;*
*he built a watchtower in the midst of it,*
*and hewed out a wine vat in it;*
*and he looked for it to yield grapes*
*but it yielded wild grapes.*
3 *And now, O inhabitants of Jerusalem and men of Judah,*
*judge, I pray you, between me and my vineyard.*
4 *What more was there to do for my vineyard,*
*that I have not done in it?*
*When I looked for it to yield grapes,*
*why did it yield wild grapes?*

5 *And now I will tell you*
*what I will do to my vineyard.*
*I will remove its hedge,*
*and it shall be devoured;*
*I will break down its wall,*
*and it shall be trampled down.*
6 *I will make it a waste;*
*it shall not be pruned or hoed,*
*and briers and thorns shall grow up;*
*I will also command the clouds*
*that they rain no rain upon it.*
7 *For the vineyard of the Lord of hosts is the house of Israel,*
*and the men of Judah are his pleasant planting;*
*and he looked for justice, but behold, bloodshed;*
*for righteousness, but behold, a cry.*

## An inoffensive poem?

Isaiah is a great poet, and here he gives us a small masterpiece, remarkable for the beauty of its imagery and the conciseness of its style.

What is striking on a first reading is the way in which the poet uses ordinary language: vineyard, hill, wine vat, tower, grapes, plant, build, dig, clear stones, and so on. All these things and activities are familiar to the inhabitants of Jerusalem and Judah. But at the same time they are so to speak raised to another level by virtue of the fact that the prophet makes a song about them. The verb 'sing' (Hebrew *shir*) and the two cognate nouns, *shir* and *shirah*, are not all that usual in prophetic literature, in which in fact there are only twelve uses of the two nouns out of ninety for the whole of the Old Testament, and only six uses of the verb out of a total of eighty-seven. So from the start there is nothing trivial about the prophet's poem, since it follows a genre which is quite a solemn one.

By first of all presenting his poem as a song, the prophet could not fail to heighten the expectations of his audience. In the Bible, songs are always associated with happy events: the song of exemplary deliverance (Ex.15); Deborah's song of victory (Judg.5); the new song of the captives returning from Babylon (Isa.40); the joyful song of the pilgrims climbing to the Jerusalem temple (all the Psalms of Ascent, 121–134), and finally *the* song, the Song of Songs, celebrating the beauty of love.

The mention right at the start of the twofold object of the song (the beloved and his vineyard) also contributed towards reinforcing the audience's expectation of good news. The beloved and the vineyard are figures which are regularly, if not almost always, associated with happiness.

Let's begin with the beloved. Here, too, everything is done to create confidence. The word beloved (Hebrew *yadid*) is quite rare. We find it only eight times in the Old Testament, two of them here. There is only one occurrence in prophetic literature outside the text of Isaiah. This is Jer. 11.15: 'What right has my beloved in my house, when she has done vile deeds?' There it is used in the feminine, but in a very similar context to that of Isa.5 (judgment), and by correlation it implies that God is like a lover towards his loved one (the people).

There remains the vineyard. Before being given a symbolic connotation, as here, it is first and foremost in the realistic sense a piece of productive property, which contributes to the greater joy of the proprietor. That is how it would appear at first sight, even when it is the object of fraudulent action and plots, as was the case with King Ahab and Naboth of Jezreel: 'Give me your vineyard, that I may have it as a vegetable garden, because it is near my house; and I will give you a better vineyard for it; or, if it seems good to you, I will give you its value in money.' But Naboth said to Ahab, 'The Lord forbid that I should give you the inheritance of my fathers' (I Kings 21.–2–3). Naboth's reaction indicates how important and precious the vineyard

was to every Israelite, as part of his patrimony.

Furthermore, the prophet Amos, who was well up in agriculture and planting, quite naturally refers to the vineyard to describe the happiness to come in the kingdom of David: 'I will restore the fortunes of my people Israel, and they shall rebuild the ruined cities and inhabit them; they shall plant vineyards and drink their wine, and they shall make gardens and eat their fruit' (Amos 9.14). The vineyards are made to be planted, to be cultivated, and to bear fruits which in turn will become the wine which 'gladdens the heart of man, making faces shine brighter than oil' (Ps.104.15).

Everything is perfectly in place here, and the actions of the beloved towards his vineyard are what one would expect from any good vintner. The audience seems to have heard good reasons to be comforted by the song of this prophet and for cherishing the best hopes.

## A disappointed love

However, the disappointment begins to show through at the end of v.2: 'and he looked for it to yield grapes, but it yielded wild grapes'.

With v.3 we have more than a complaint; we have a real summary judgment which is pronounced by the beloved as he calls on the 'inhabitants of Jerusalem and the people of Judah' to take his side. We leave the ground of the fine inoffensive story about a fictitious situation to go on to the more demanding and compromising matter of the judgment to be made 'between me and my vine'.

The judgment relates to two questions which contrast the behaviour of the beloved and the productivity of his vineyard. The behaviour of the beloved has been to give everything for his vineyard: 'What more was there to do for my vineyard, that I have not done in it?' (v.4).

Without warning, in v.5, we learn that the beloved is turning against his vineyard: he is withdrawing all protection from it, letting it go fallow, and refusing it any kind of fertility. Love no longer seems to command the melodic line of the song. What is the explanation for such a change?

## Everything is finally explained!

Then, in v.7, the veil over the identity of the two protagonists in the song, the beloved and the vineyard, is lifted. First we learn that the vineyard is the property of the 'Lord of hosts' and thus that he is the beloved who expresses himself by this song. Secondly, we are left in no doubt about the identity of the vineyard: 'it is the house of Israel'. So the story as told passes over into a second register, that of the parable.

Thus Isaiah is to be credited with having used, for the first time, the vineyard, that concrete and indeed everyday reality, so dear to the inhabitants of the ancient Near East, to denote the people of God and God's particular concern for his people in a symbolic way. The idea, without the word, had already been presented in scripture:

- 'You will bring them in, and *plant* them on your own mountain, the place, O Lord, which you have made for your abode' (Ex.15.7);

- 'And I will appoint a place for my people Israel, and will *plant* them, that they may dwell in their own place, and be disturbed no more' (II Sam.7.10);

---

### Is the 'New Testament' a Brainwave of the Prophets?

The prophets and the New Testament go so well together that it is to the former that we owe two of the most frequent expressions for designating the writings of the latter, namely 'Gospel' and 'New Testament' (which can also be translated 'new covenant'). Two Old Testament writers, two superlative prophets, must be given the credit for having forged these two expressions, which are used to denote either the central part of the totality of the specifically Christian biblical writings.

It is in Isaiah that we find the family of expressions which includes 'evangel' (gospel), 'evangelist' and 'evangelize': 'How beautiful upon the mountains are the feet of him who brings good tidings, who publishes peace, who brings good tidings of good, who publishes salvation, who says to Zion, "Your God reigns"' (52.7). The word is so suitable for describing the whole of Jesus's proclamation that Luke is eager to borrow it from Isaiah to mark the opening of Jesus's ministry in Nazareth: 'And there was given to him the book of the prophet Isaiah. He opened the book and found the place where it was written: "The Spirit of the Lord is upon me, because he has anointed me to preach good news to the poor"' (Luke 4.17–18).

Furthermore, the tradition has borrowed from the prophet Jeremiah the expression 'New Testament' (literally 'new covenant') to denote the totality of the Christian writings accepted by the church in the canon of the scriptures. The tradition is an old one and goes back to the New Testament itself, since the text of Jeremiah 31 is quoted at length (in one of the longest quotations in the New Testament) in the letter to the Hebrews, specifically in order to emphasize the novelty of the event of Jesus Christ:

*For if that first covenant had been faultless, there would have been no occasion for a second. For he finds fault with them when he says:*
*'The days will come, says the Lord,*
*when I will establish a new covenant with the house of Israel*
*and with the house of Judah;*
*not like the covenant that I made with their fathers . . .'*
*In speaking of a new covenant he treats the first as obsolete. And what is becoming obsolete and growing old is ready to vanish away (Heb.8.7–9,13).*

Here, of course, the author is playing on the contrast between newness and oldness, but nothing prevents the old still being useful to him, since he bases his argument on the 'old' text of Jeremiah . . . How one can draw from the 'Old Testament', as from the Gospels, things old and new!

---

- 'I will set my eyes upon them (= those deported from Judah) for good, and I will bring them back to this land. I will build them up, and not tear them down; I will *plant* them, and not uproot them' (Jer.24.6).

So here are three texts which relate to the major periods of the history of Israel: the time of the Exodus and the settlement in Canaan, then the time of the monarchy, and finally, with Jeremiah, the time of the return from exile. God's action makes Israel a choice plant, and, deepening the image of the vine, the prophet Isaiah gives us a real summary outline of the history of salvation, split between the innumerable manifestations of God's love for his people and the numerous acts of ingratitude on the part of the latter.

### The force of a parable

The song becomes a parable. We learn that quite explicitly when we arrive at v.7. But we could already have guessed it on hearing the narrative introduction to the song: 'My beloved *had* a vineyard . . .' Doesn't that make us think of the beginning of numerous parables in the New Testament, like, 'A father *had* two sons . . .' (Luke 15.11); 'A rich man *had* a steward . . .' (Luke 16.1).

The force of a parable is to make people ask questions. This is what Jesus was to do so often: 'What do you think? Which is the most important? Who was the neighbour to the other?' We have the same procedure here: 'What more was there to do? Why did it produce bad fruit?' The answer is never given, to allow the audience to work things out for themselves and draw their own conclusions.

Here, as in other parables of the Old Testament (II Sam.12.1–7; I Kings 20.35–52), the hearers are forced to compromise themselves and pass judgment on the produce of the vine and the care given to it by the beloved. Once they have resolved the enigma, they will be obliged to live with the consequences of their own judgment.

## 2. The vision of the thrice holy God
### (Isa.6.1–13)

1 *In the year that king Uzziah died*
*I saw the Lord sitting upon a throne,*
*high and lifted up;*
*and his train filled the temple.*
2 *Above him stood the seraphim;*
*each had six wings:*
*with two he covered his face,*
*and with two he covered his feet,*
*and with two he flew.*
3 *And one called to another and said:*
*'Holy, holy, holy is the Lord of hosts;*
*the whole earth is full of his glory.'*
4 *And the foundations of the thresholds shook at*
*the voice of him who called,*
*and the house was filled with smoke.*
5 *And I said: 'Woe is me! For I am lost;*
*for I am a man of unclean lips,*
*and I dwell in the midst of a people of unclean lips;*
*for my eyes have seen the King, the Lord of hosts!'*

6 Then flew one of the seraphim to me,
   having in his hand a burning coal
   which he had taken with tongs from the altar.
7 And he touched my mouth, and said:
   'Behold, this has touched your lips;
   your guilt is taken away, and your sin forgiven.'
8 And I heard the voice of the Lord saying,
   'Whom shall I send, and who will go for us?'
   Then I said, 'Here am I! Send me.'
9 And he said, 'Go, and say to this people:
   "Hear well, but do not understand;
   see well, but do not perceive."'
10 Make the heart of this people fat,
   and their eyes heavy,
   and shut their eyes;
   lest they see with their eyes,

and hear with their ears,
   and understand with their hearts,
   and turn and be healed.'
11 Then I said, 'How long, O Lord?'
   And he said:
   'Until cities lie waste without inhabitant,
   and houses without men,
   and the land is utterly desolate,
12 The Lord will remove men far away,
   and the forsaken places will be many in the
   midst of the land.
13 And though a tenth remain in it,
   it will be burned again,
   like a terebinth or an oak,
   whose stump remains standing when it is felled.
   The holy seed is its stump.

---

The triple acclamation 'Holy, holy, holy' (v.3) is one of the best-known pieces in the book of Isaiah. It has crossed the frontiers of Jewish liturgy to find itself, by way of Rev.4, at the heart of the Christian eucharistic liturgy. Verse 10, which speaks of the hardening of the people, is equally familiar to Christian readers, who remember the way in which it was used by Jesus (Matt.13.14–15) to justify speaking in parables, and by the apostle Paul to account for the division of the Jews of Rome when confronted with his teaching (Acts 28.26–27). However, these two verses (Isa.6.3, 10) must be understood with the whole of the passage.

### The account of a call

Here we find all the elements of the account of a call (see e.g. Ex.3; I Sam.3; Judg.6): an encounter with God (theophany), an address, mission, objection, confirmation, sign.

### God and his mystery

Before any mission, the calling of the prophet arises out of the encounter with Someone, out of the discovery of an aspect of the mystery of God. In Isaiah, this dimension stands out quite clearly. In fact the story of his call opens with a great theophany, the context of which is both liturgical and royal.

The context is liturgical, with the mention of the temple and its gates, seraphim, embers and smoke. The distinction between pure and impure, and the mention of the glory and the acclamation of the sanctity of God, are also liturgical. Furthermore, we are put in a royal context simply by the fact that the account is dated by 'the year in which king Uzziah died' and also by the vision of the throne on which the Lord is seated: this recalls the royal psalms (93; 96; 98; 99). Finally, through this liturgy, the prophet himself has no difficulty in recognizing in this God who manifests himself the 'king, the Lord' (v.5).

For the moment the address is not directed towards the prophet, nor does it yet contain any order for mission. At this point in the story everything rests on the proclamation of the holiness of God by the seraphim.

### A sinner among sinners

This proclamation of the holiness of God naturally leads the prophet to recognize his limits and his condition as a sinner. 'Woe is me! For I am lost; for I am a man of unclean lips, and I dwell in the midst of a people of unclean lips; for my eyes have seen the

King, the Lord of hosts!' (v.5). This is not an objection to the mission, since there has as yet been no order to this effect. However, we should note how the prophet expresses his solidarity with the people. He is of the same race as his people, 'a man of unclean lips' living 'in the midst of a people of unclean lips'. Like so many of the other great believers of the Old Testament, Isaiah feels unworthy of the vision which has been forced on him, and in accordance with the idea he has of the holiness of God, he seems to have an impassable abyss between himself and God.

Verses 6–7 make it possible for the prophet to get out of what seems to be an impasse. Before he has even asked anything, he receives forgiveness for his faults and his sin. The experience of salvation and forgiveness comes before mission. God takes the initiative, and at the same time here Isaiah is liberated from the prohibitions relating to God. He can approach the most high and holy God with every confidence, and not only have his life saved, but also become God's messenger.

### Sent, but for what mission?

It is then that 'the voice of the Lord' resounds for the first time. However, we are amazed to hear two questions: 'Whom shall I send? Who will go for us?' No order is given, but rather there is a question, leaving the way entirely free for the prophet's response.

This response is very brief: 'Here am I, send me.' The 'Here am I' is a classic response indicating the availability of the servants of God (Abraham, Gen.22.1; Jacob, Gen.31.11; Moses, Ex.3.4; Samuel, I Sam.3.4). On the other hand, 'Send me' is quite unprecedented in the stories of callings. It indicates the total availability of the prophet for the divine action. The sending can only come from God, but it is perfectly linked with the expression of human freedom and initiative.

The mission, too, is expressed in very classic terms, with the verb 'go' (Abraham, Gen.12.1; Moses, Ex.3.10; Barak, Judg.4.6; Gideon, Judg.6.14). However, what comes next is astonishing: 'Hear well, but do not understand; see well, but do not perceive.' The prophet's mission is described here, as it will be later for Jeremiah, Ezekiel and Jesus, as a pure paradox. On the one hand, the prophet must speak ('speak to this people'), and on the other he invites the people to listen and look. This is the prophet's role, except that it is not for him to decide the result of his mission. Verses 9–10 do not describe an effect which is sought, but rather note an actual situation: the prophet speaks in vain, the people does not understand and does not recognize its God. We have to understand that here we do not have a fatalism which is closed to any possibility of conversion and healing. Verse 11 in fact asks 'How long?', which shows that the prophet perceives the temporary character of the incomprehension. Only the prophetic word serves as a catalyst, as a revelation; it is the 'two-edged sword' which unmasks the intentions of its hearers.

### Is the story in the right place?

In many respects, the story of the calling of Isaiah remains a classic of its kind. However, we may be amazed to find it in ch.6, rather than at the beginning of the book, as is the case, for example, with the calls of Jeremiah, Hosea and Ezekiel. A brief examination of the context will show us better the reason for inserting this story in ch.6.

The first five chapters already bring out the contrast between the holiness of God (5.16) and the sin of the people (1.2, 4; 5.24). They also emphasize the inability of Judah to recognize its God and to understand his ways (1.3; 5.24). In this sense the story of the call confirms what we already know about the hardening of the people.

On the other hand, the story serves as a pivot for the following section, often called 'the book of Immanuel', by introducing the royal typology. Here we shall find the monarchy threatened by the invasion of foreign kings, and the sign given by God to the 'house of David' will ensure the survival of a dynasty threatened with extinction ('the year in which Uzziah the king died').

# 3. The sign of God-with-us: the Immanuel
## (Isa.7.10–17)

10 Again the Lord spoke to Ahaz,
11 'Ask a sign of the Lord your God; let it be as deep as Sheol or as high as heaven.'
12 But Ahaz said, 'I will not ask, and I will not put the Lord to the test.'
13 And he said, 'Hear then, O house of David! Is it too little for you to weary men, that you weary my God also?
14 Therefore the Lord himself will give you a sign. Behold, a young woman shall conceive and bear a son, and shall call his name Immanuel.

15 He shall eat curds and honey when he knows how to refuse the evil and choose the good.
16 For even before the child knows how to refuse the evil and choose the good, the land before whose two kings you are in dread will be deserted.
17 The Lord will bring upon you and upon your people and upon your father's house such days as have not come since the day that Ephraim departed from Judah – the king of Assyria.

With Isa.7.14 and the surrounding verses we are in the presence of one of the most famous and most discussed texts in the Bible. Why this is so can easily be understood, from the Jewish side because of its strong messianic tenor, and from the Christian side, because of the way in which Matthew applies it to Jesus. Virtually no word of the original Hebrew text of 7.14 and its earliest version, in Greek, has not been the object of fierce debate, and we cannot say that the enigma has been entirely resolved. To convince yourself of this it is enough to consult a list of recent literature on the subject; here you can see the cautions the writers express about the hypothetical character of the 'solution' which they propose.

That having been said, the interpretation of the oracle is, on the whole, relatively easy. First of all let's look at the difficulties or ambiguities in the text. The verse which is discussed so much reads as follows: 'Behold, the young woman shall conceive and bear a son, and shall call his name Immanuel' (7.14).

## The Immanuel

The key figure in the oracle – and the section which follows, up to ch.11 – is evidently the Immanuel. So

who is this famous figure? Is he a son of the prophet or a son of the king? Or do we have to envisage a figure in the distant future? Given also that the two verbs in the phrase are participles and that the verb 'to be' is understood, are the conception and the giving birth a fact which has already been realized or is its realization to be expected later? If the latter is the case, how much later? And what are we to think of the diet which is prescribed for him ('Curds and honey he shall eat', v.5). Is this a delicacy, or the food of the needy?

## The *almah*

The identity of the one who is to give birth to Immanuel is no less problematical. First of all, what is the meaning of this term *almah*, which in the Hebrew is preceded by the definite article? In Hebrew it denotes any young woman of child-bearing age, without specifying whether or not she is a virgin. Now we know that on this point the Greek version, the Septuagint, chose a more precise term than the Hebrew, *parthenos*, which explicitly denotes virginity. Certainly this was to be the version on which the Christian tradition, from Matthew onwards, was to base itself. However, in itself the original Hebrew text does not denote a virgin.

64

And then, who could this 'young woman' be? The prophetess, Isaiah's wife, whom we know from elsewhere to have had at least two children? We cannot rule that out. Or perhaps it was the wife of Ahaz. In that case the function of the definite article would be to emphasize the dignity of the person envisaged. Either explanation could also account for the expletive or demonstrative sense of the definite pronoun: the prophet would be thinking of a person present at the moment when he gave his oracle. But the word could also have a symbolic value, and be a collective designation of the totality of the people, of the messianic community, which is going to give birth to the Immanuel.

Finally, what are we to think of the Christian re-reading inspired by Matthew 1.22–23 – and the tradition which has followed it – according to which the oracle will have found its fulfilment in Mary, mother of Jesus? Could the eighth-century prophet have foreseen the circumstances surrounding the birth of Jesus the Christ, and could he have known in advance the principle features of the person who was to be his mother?

## What is a sign?

The very nature of the event raises questions. Since the prophet speaks of a sign, we could ask about the nature and significance of such a sign. What does the word 'sign' (Hebrew *'ot*) mean? Something singular, extraordinary, as the immediate context suggests: 'Ask a sign of the Lord your God; let it be as deep as Sheol or as high as heaven' (7.11)? Do we have to understand by this an event which will soon be fulfilled?

## An oracle for what?

Finally, we must certainly also ask about the sense of the oracle. Was this auspicious or inauspicious? The New Testament interpretation of the oracle certainly leaves no doubt: this is good news. But is that also evident for the oracle in its original context?

So the great diversity of interpretations is understandable, simply because of the ambiguity of the terms used by the prophet. That having been said, the general sense of the oracle can be established with sufficient certainty, if we take certain pointers into account. First, let's look at the literary genre of the oracle.

## First, good news!

The formula 'Behold, X is with child and will bear a son', far from being unprecedented in the time of Isaiah, connects the Immanuel oracle with the literary genre of the announcement of a marvellous birth (Gen.16.11; 18.10; Judg.13.5). 'Marvellous' need not necessarily mean spectacular or outside the laws of nature. Rather, it must be understood as indicating something unexpected and gratuitous. In the two other cases we have a barren woman who now becomes fertile, and that is precisely the import of the good news of the announcement of the birth.

In the case of Isaiah 7.14, then, we must understand the announcement as something unexpected, surprising, which bears witness to the particular benevolence of God towards his people.

## The sign

Is the sign given conditional on faith or aimed more at provoking it? We should note in passing the exceptional importance of the sign: 'as deep as Sheol or as high as heaven'. Another characteristic of the sign is that it is first offered and then given by God, despite the excuse made by the king, who does not want to put the Lord to the test. Finally, the third and last characteristic is that each time the prophet uses the word 'sign' elsewhere than in ch.7 (here we are still keeping within chs.1–39) something near and imminent in time, if not directly contemporary, is always in view:

> Behold, I and the children whom the Lord has given me are signs and portents in Israel from the Lord of hosts, who dwells on Mount Zion (8.18).

> The Lord said, 'As my servant Isaiah has walked naked and barefoot for three years as a sign and a

portent against Egypt and Ethiopia, so shall the king of Assyria lead away the Egyptian captives and the Ethiopian exiles, both the young and the old, naked and barefoot, with buttocks uncovered, to the shame of Egypt. Then they shall be dismayed and confounded because of Ethiopia their hope and of Egypt their boast' (20.3–4).

'And this shall be the sign for you: this year eat what grows of itself, and in the second year what springs of the same; then in the third year sow and reap, and plant vineyards, and eat their fruit' (37.30).

'This is the sign to you from the Lord, that the Lord will do this thing that he has promised: Behold, I will make the dial of Ahaz turn back ten steps. So the sun turned back on the dial the ten steps by which it had declined' (38.7–8).

It is hard to see why the sign announced in ch.7 should be different. Furthermore, the chronological indications that we find in the immediate context (7.16; 8.4) presuppose extremely brief intervals and are orientated on a fulfilment of the prophecy which would be contemporary with Isaiah and his audience.

### The Immanuel

The name given to the child is not only theophoric (i.e. it includes the divine name 'El) but first and above all theological. Historically, we know of no one in the Bible who bore this name as his proper name. The theological significance, though, is quite clear: God-with-us.

But on the historical plane – since the prophecy is rooted in history – who could have been the figure envisaged by the prophet? There are only two possible solutions here: either the son of the prophet and the prophetess or a royal child. Although the former solution would not be unthinkable, it seems preferable to opt for the latter and consequently to see here the son of Ahaz, Hezekiah. It is true that Hezekiah never bore the name Immanuel and was not subsequently identified as being Immanuel. But he is the one who

most corresponds to the prerogatives attributed to Immanuel. The saying is in fact about a royal descendant, since the sign is offered to Ahaz and given to the 'house of David'. Moreover, the chapters to follow will fully develop the royal character of the child who is announced.

Recently the association with Hezekiah has been given important support by research which has demonstrated important literary parallels between Isa.7 (the Immanuel oracle) and Isa.36–39 (the organization of resistance by Hezekiah). This argument (see the box opposite) is convincing and enables us to resolve a number of difficulties in the text of Isa.7. The numerous literary parallels invite us to draw historical parallels: what takes place with Hezekiah is to be understood on the basis of what the prophet had said about Immanuel, and vice versa. Such an interpretation necessarily indicates the answer to be given about the identity of the *almah*; in such a context this has to be the wife of King Ahaz. This interpretation is quite consistent on the one hand with the solemn and royal character of the oracle and on the other with the meaning of the Hebrew word *almah*, which is wider than that of the Greek term *parthenos*, denoting any young woman of childbearing age.

In conclusion, here are some remarks by a specialist on the book of Isaiah:

In our view, the question of the identity of the Immanuel and the *almah* have taken a disproportionate place in the debate provoked by the interpretation of Isa.7.14. The birth of the Immanuel was an event contemporaneous to Ahaz and Isaiah, as v.16 indicates; this element of response is essential to the intelligibility of the sign. It is less important to know whose son the child is: the sign does not reside primarily in the identity of the child but in his very presence, which recalls the radical demand of faith and the tragic consequences of the king's attitude of unbelief . . . The sign given to Ahaz is ambivalent: it expresses both the confirmation of the divine promise and its negative counterpart where there is a lack of trust in Yahweh (J. Vermeylen).

| What if Immanuel was Hezekiah? Two events which can be understood in the light of each other | |
|---|---|
| **Isaiah 7** | **Isaiah 36–39** |
| In the days of Ahaz the son of Jotham, son of Uzziah, king of Judah, Rezin the king of Syria and Pekah the son of Remaliah *came up to Jerusalem* to wage war against it, but they could not conquer it (7.1). | In the fourteenth year of King Hezekiah, Sennacherib king of Assyria *came up against all the fortified cities of Judah* and took them. And the king of Assyria sent the Rabshakeh from Lachish to King Hezekiah at *Jerusalem*, with a great army (36.1–2). |
| And the Lord said to Isaiah, 'Go forth and meet Ahaz, you and Shear-jashub your son, *at the end of the conduit of the upper pool on the highway to the fuller's field . . .*' (7.3). | And he stood *by the conduit of the upper pool on the highway to the fuller's field.* |
| When the house of David was told, 'Syria is in league with Ephraim', his heart and the heart of his people shook as the trees of the forest shake before the wind (7.2). | When King Hezekiah heard it, he rent his clothes, and covered himself with sackcloth, and went into the house of the Lord (37.1). |
| And say to him, 'Take heed, be quiet, *do not fear*, and do not let your heart be faint because of those two smouldering stumps of firebrands . . . thus says the Lord God: "It shall not stand and it shall not come to pass"' (7.4, 7). | When the servants of King Hezekiah came to Isaiah, Isaiah said to them, 'Say to your master, "Thus says the Lord: *Do not fear*, because of the words that you have heard, with which the servants of the king of Assyria have reviled me. Behold, I will put a spirit in him, so that he shall hear a rumour, and return to his own land; and I will make him fall by the sword in his own land"' (37.6–7). |
| Therefore the Lord himself will give you a *sign*. Behold, a young woman shall conceive and bear a son, and shall call his name Immanuel (7.14). | 'And this shall be the *sign* for you: this year eat what grows of itself, and in the second year what springs of the same; then in the third year sow and reap, and plant vineyards, and eat their fruit' (37.30–32). |
| For before the child even knows how to refuse the evil and choose the good, the land before whose two kings you are in dread will be deserted. The Lord will bring upon you and upon your people and upon your father's house such days as have not come since the day that Ephraim departed from Judah – the king of Assyria (7.16–17). | Then Isaiah said to Hezekiah, 'Hear the word of the Lord of hosts: Behold, the days are coming, when all that is in your house, and that which your fathers have stored up till this day, shall be carried to Babylon; nothing shall be left, says the Lord. And some of your own sons, who are born to you, shall be taken away' (39.5–7). |

# III. The God of Isaiah

Isaiah is not only one of the greatest poets of the Bible. He is also one of its greatest theologians, and in him one can discover numerous aspects of the face of God: creator, omnipotent, saviour, consoler, defender, holy one, faithful, solid, indomitable, etc. If we take the book as a whole (Isa.1–66), the collection of divine attributes is almost inexhaustible. However, here we shall be looking only at the first section of the book of Isaiah, chs.1–39, the essentials of which go back to the eighth-century prophet. So we shall be trying to bring out the main features of the face of God which are represented in this section.

## A God of majesty . . .

If the God of Isaiah had to be presented with the help of an architectural image, the one that would immediately come to be mind would be a Gothic cathedral (Notre Dame in Paris, Chartres, Strasbourg, Cologne, Salisbury and so many others). The book of Isaiah is rather like a cathedral, and the God whom it reveals is also the one who is revealed by the monuments of architecture and faith that cathedrals are: lofty towers and belfries, grave sculptures and bas-reliefs, solid buttresses, fine tracery and impressive ogives. All is homage to a God of majesty.

Entering the book of Isaiah is indeed like going into a cathedral. The lines are imposing, powerful, bold, all in the image of the God whom the prophet has encountered, a God who dwells in the heights:

The Lord is exalted, for he dwells on high;
he will fill Zion with justice and righteousness
(33.5).

However, this is not a grandeur to overwhelm believers; on the contrary, they are invited to celebrate joyfully the incomparable grandeur of their God:

Shout, and sing for joy, O inhabitant of Zion,
for great in your midst is the Holy One of Israel
(12.6).

Contrary to what we were able to see in Hosea, and what we shall rediscover to a large extent in Jeremiah, in Isaiah we find no allusions to the suffering of God or to emotions approaching that. In Isaiah, God presents himself with an absolute assurance which shows us nothing of the inner debates attributed to him by the other two prophets. Here is also a God of whom one can say that he keeps his distance, a God whom no one could approach with too much familiarity.

## . . . who challenges the greatness of the powerful

However, there is a reason why the prophet emphasizes the greatness of God to such a degree. Every day he is confronted with the pretensions to greatness of the political authorities and the commercial powers of Jerusalem and neighbouring nations. So there is something provocative and challenging in his language about God which aims to lead the great figures of this world to relate themselves in truth to God, who alone is great.

So it is for theological reasons (God alone is great, God humbles the powerful) that the prophet constantly denounces the pretensions of human pride (mentioned, in one form or another, at least fifteen times in 1–39):

The haughty looks of man shall be brought low,
and the pride of men shall be humbled;

and the Lord alone will be exalted in that day.
For the Lord of hosts has a day
against all that is proud and lofty,
against all that is lifted up and high . . .
And the haughtiness of man shall be humbled,
and the pride of men shall be brought low;
and the Lord alone will be exalted in that day
(2.11–12,17).

## The Lord of hosts

The title 'Lord of hosts' extends Isaiah's vision of the majesty of God. However, the importance that this title assumes in his work invites us to make a special study of it. Isaiah is in fact the biblical writer who uses it by far the most frequently (fifty-six times, rather more than a quarter of all the instances in the Old Testament) to speak of God.

The expression 'God of hosts' (in Hebrew, *YHWH sebaoth*) literally means 'God of armies'. It can sometimes refer to the image of a warlike God who leads Israel to victory (that is often the case in the two books of Samuel: cf. I Sam.4.4; 15.2; 17.45; II Sam. 5.10; 6.20). However, it must not be forgotten that the armies involved here are the heavenly armies, i.e. the stars (cf. Gen.2.1; Deut.4.19; Ps.33.6; 103.21). By invoking God under the title 'God of hosts', Isaiah thus emphasizes equally the power of the creator God, master of the stars and cosmic forces. Furthermore this is the way in which the translators of the Septuagint understood it in rendering the expression by the Greek *pantocrator*.

## The 'Holy One of Israel'

'Holy God': although this quality of God is less frequently attested than omnipotence (the root *qadosh* appears twenty-one times), it equally represents a key concept of Isaiah's theology. By contrast, we may note that it appears only twice in Amos, twice in Hosea and once in Micah. For Isaiah, not only does Yahweh appear as the thrice holy God (6.3: this suggests the idea of fullness),

but he defines himself as the 'holy one of Israel' (eleven times in all: cf. for example 1.4; 10.20; 12.6; 17.7 . . .), and as a result he demands to be treated as such by his people:

'But the Lord of hosts, him you shall regard as holy; let him be your fear, and let him be your dread' (8.13).

If holiness also implies the idea of perfection, first of all it relates to the transcendent character of God, God's otherness. God is the Wholly Other, the one whose mystery is never exhausted.

## A demanding God, but one who knows how to forgive his people

The first six chapters of Isaiah reflect a lively awareness, on the part of the prophet, of the sin of his people and his own condition as a sinner. Through the words of Isaiah we feel the very great disappointment of the 'Holy One of Israel', who sees himself abandoned and betrayed by a sinful nation:

Ah, sinful nation,
a people laden with iniquity,
offspring of evildoers,
sons who deal corruptly!
They have forsaken the Lord,
they have despised the Holy One of Israel,
they are utterly estranged (1.4).

In Isaiah we find a good thirty allusions to sin which, for him, consists essentially in a revolt against God, a scorn, an ignorance and an abandonment of his Torah (1.2, 4, 28; 5.24). But it is also violence against one's neighbour (1.15; 26.21) and contempt for the right:

Wash yourselves, make yourselves clean;
remove the evil of your doings from before my eyes;
cease to do evil, learn to do good;
seek justice, correct oppression;
defend the fatherless, plead for the widow (1.16–17).

Over and above the gravity of the sin, Isaiah announces with no less conviction the amazing reality of the forgiveness offered. If he himself is purified (6.7), it is so that he may become a sign and a witness of the mercy of God towards the whole people:

> Come now, let us reason together, says the Lord;
> though your sins are like scarlet,
> they shall be white as snow;
> though they are red like crimson,
> they shall become like wool (1.18).

> Therefore by this the guilt of Jacob will be expiated,
> and this will be the full fruit of the removal of his sin (27.9).

> And no inhabitant will say, 'I am sick';
> the people who dwell there will be forgiven their iniquity (33.24).

## A 'solid' God on whom one can rely

Of all the prophets, Isaiah is the one who most stresses the importance of faith. In him we find most often the two main roots which evoke the idea of faith, perceived not as adherence to a doctrinal content but as an attitude of trust in God: 'aman and its derivatives (twenty-two times in Isa.1–39 as compared with the twenty-one occurrences in Jeremiah, six in Zechariah, four in Hosea and only two in Ezekiel), and batah (= rely on) and its derivatives (twenty times in Isa.1–39 as opposed to only four times in Isa.40–66 and nine times in the whole of the 'minor' prophets).

The meaning of the first root ('aman) is summed up in the word-play which is at the centre of the prophet's exhortation to King Ahaz:

> If you will not believe, surely you shall not be established (which we might translate, in order to retain the word-play: 'If you do not hold firm (in faith) you will not hold anything' (Isa.7.9).

In Hebrew, the meaning of the root 'aman in its simplest form denotes being firm, solid. Further-more, it is in this sense that the disciples of the prophet make it a divine name, in designating God the 'Amen' (65.16), i.e. the one who is solid, the one on whom one can rely. Used in a derived form, called hiph'il in Hebrew, the root has come to denote the basic attitude of believers: to believe is to declare that God is solid, trustworthy, faithful, and that is to engage in a relationship which one wants to be solid and trustworthy.

The second root (batah) used by the prophet to speak of faith conveys the idea of assurance, of security: faith is trust in Someone. It is based on a relationship of trust and not on intellectual adherence to a collection of truths. Chapters 36–37 (in which we find almost half the usages of this root, nine out of twenty) illustrates the motif well. Confronted with the threat of Sennacherib against Jerusalem, Hezekiah remains confident and calls on the people not to give way under the pressure of fear:

> 'We rely on the Lord our God' (36.7).

## . . . and in whom one hopes

Already from the perspective of this second root, faith presents itself under the aspect of hope: 'to rely on the Lord' is to open oneself to the future which comes from him. Now we meet two other roots in the prophet Isaiah which are also directly attached to the idea of hope, and both of them emphasize this orientation on the future: qawah (= hope) and hikkah (= expect). qawah occurs seven times more in Isaiah 1–39 and as many times in Isaiah 40–66. In 1–39 the verb is even applied to Yahweh, who hoped to see people responding to his love (5.2, 4, 7), but it expresses above all the whole community's expectation of salvation – in the form of a 'creed':

> It will be said on that day, 'Lo, this is our God; we have waited for him, that he might save us. This is the Lord, and we have waited for him' (25.9).

> In the path of your judgments, O Lord, we wait for you;

to respect your name is the desire of our soul (26.8).

O Lord, be gracious to us; we wait for you.
Be our arm every morning, our salvation in the time of trouble (33.2).

The second verb (*hikkah*) is rarer (fourteen instances in the whole of the Old Testament; however, we find it three times in Isaiah 1–39, while not at all in Isa.40–66, Jeremiah and Ezekiel):

I will *wait* for the Lord, who is hiding his face from the house of Jacob, and I will hope in him (8.17).

However, the Lord is *waiting* to be gracious to you;
therefore he is exalting himself to show mercy to you.
For the Lord is a God of mercy,
blessed are all those who *wait* for him (30.18).

Finally, at a symbolic level, Isaiah asserts himself as a prophet of hope by announcing the coming of light in the middle of the night. If he is asked, 'Watchman, what of the night?' (21.11–12), the prophet replies:

Then the Lord will create over the whole site of Mount Zion and over her assemblies a cloud by day, and smoke and the shining of a flaming fire by night (4.5).

But there will be no gloom for her that was in anguish . . .
The people who walked in darkness have seen a great light,
those who dwelt in a land of deep darkness, on them has light shined (9.1, 2).

Moreover the light of the moon will be as the light of the sun,
and the light of the sun will be sevenfold, as the light of seven days,
in the day when the Lord binds up the hurt of his people,
and heals the wounds inflicted by his blow (30.26).

## Saviour of all the peoples

A prophet of Judah passionately attached to the cause of Jerusalem–Zion, Isaiah no less remains a prophet preoccupied with the destiny of nations. Beyond question, it is in him that we find the most universalist accents and the finest perspectives on the future. The God in whom he believes is not only the God of Jerusalem and Judah. On the contrary, he reveals himself as the God who seeks to bring together all the nations and to procure for all an endless happiness, without any hindrances:

It shall come to pass in the latter days
that the mountain of the house of the Lord
shall be established as the highest of the mountains,
and shall be raised above all the hills;
and all the nations shall flow to it, and many peoples shall come, and say:
'Come, let us go up to the mountain of the Lord,
to the house of the God of Jacob;
that he may teach us his ways
and that we may walk in his paths' (2.2–3).

They lift up their voices, they sing for joy;
over the majesty of the Lord they shout from the west.
Therefore in the east give glory to the Lord;
in the coastlands of the sea, to the name of the Lord, the God of Israel.
From the ends of the earth we hear songs of praise,
of glory to the righteous one (24.14–16).

On this mountain the Lord of hosts will make for all peoples a feast of fat things, a feast of wine on the lees, of fat things full of marrow, of wine on the lees well refined. And he will destroy on this mountain the covering that is cast over all peoples, the veil that is spread over all nations. He will swallow up death for ever, and the Lord God will wipe away tears from all faces, and the reproach of his people he will take away from all the earth; for the Lord has spoken (25.6–8).

If here the divine initiative is strongly under-lined, the prophet appeals just as much to human responsibility. The advent of salvation for all peoples will not come about without a profound conversion of relations between them:

And they shall beat their swords into plough-shares,
and their spears into pruning hooks;
nation shall not lift up sword against nation,
neither shall they learn war any more (2.4).

It is then, and only then, that God will be able to restore the original harmony of creation and ensure the definitive victory over evil:

The wolf shall dwell with the lamb,
and the leopard shall lie down with the kid,
and the calf and the lion and the fatling together,
and a little child shall lead them.
The cow and the bear shall feed;
their young shall lie down together;
and the lion shall eat straw with the ox.
The sucking child shall play over the hole of the asp,
and the weaned child shall put his hand on the adder's den.
They shall not hurt or destroy
in all my holy mountain;
for the earth shall be full of the knowledge of the Lord
as the waters cover the sea. (11.6–9)

Isaiah's vision of the destruction of Babylon (Isa. 13.20)

# 6

# Jeremiah: The Passion of the Word

In contrast to Amos and Hosea, it could not be said of Jeremiah that he is unknown. Perhaps it should even be said that he is too well known. His 'confessions' made him famous and soon gave him a reputation for extremely sensitive prophecy, rather miserable, and tormented over his mission. Furthermore, the whole book of Lamentations was attributed to him, as if he alone had to carry the tragedy and the complaint of a whole people.

Did this Jeremiah truly utter only lamentations and 'Jeremiads'? Wasn't he the first to speak of a 'new covenant'? Isn't he the champion of a profound religious renewal which led Israel towards a more deeply inward religion? And isn't it with him that we find the most systematic and radical teaching on the subject of justice? In fact there is more and better in Jeremiah than lamentations and Jeremiads. His message is stamped with courage and humanity. Let's try to rediscover Jeremiah, this deeply human and attractive prophet, whose oracles comprise struggle and courage, torments and happiness, rejection and solidarity, disappointment and hopes, doubts and passion.

## I. Between the dream and exile

### Jeremiah in his time (1.1–3)

The words of Jeremiah,
son of Hilkiah,
one of the priests who were in Anathoth
in the land of Benjamin,
to whom the word of the Lord came in the days of Josiah the son of Amon, king of Judah, in the thirteenth year of his reign.
It came also in the days of Jehoiakim the son of Josiah, king of Judah, and until the end of the eleventh year of Zedekiah, the son of Josiah, king of Judah, until the captivity of Jerusalem in the fifth month.

Jeremiah was a member of a priestly family, and he came from Anathoth, a small village in the suburbs, north of Jerusalem. His prophetic ministry is one of the longest of all the writing prophets. In fact it extends over the reigns of three kings of Judah: Josiah, who reigned from 620 to 609; Jehoiakim, from 609 to 598; and finally Zedekiah, from 597 to 587.

### A promising renewal

Everything had begun well for Jeremiah. He could not have wished for a better situation in which to employ his genius as a prophet. In fact he had had the good fortune to be called to prophesy in the time

# The 'Confessions' of Jeremiah

Traditionally, the term 'confessions' – which recalls the great classic of St Augustine – has come to be applied to a group of six passages in Jeremiah which have three things in common: they are in the first person; they are directly addressed to God and not to the people or its rulers; they express the deep suffering felt by the prophet in exercising his mission. These passages come between chs.11 and 20 of the book of Jeremiah and are made up of 11.18–23; 12.1–6; 15.10–21; 17.12–18; 18.18–23; 20.7–18. No prophet revealed as much as Jeremiah his own states of mind and the suffering inherent in his mission.

This is without doubt the feature which led to the book of Lamentations being attributed to the prophet of Anathoth and to the creation of the term 'Jeremiad', which is hardly flattering to the prophet, as if to say that he complained all too readily.

Now the 'confessions' of Jeremiah are far from expressing a morbid delight in suffering and complaint. On the contrary, here is the protest of someone who is trying to understand what is happening to him, and above all who is trying to discover God's intentions in all this. Though the 'confessions' of Jeremiah give us the impression of matching the prophet's mood, we must not believe that they have only psychological value, as if they were only the reflection of his states of mind.

They are more. These passages which are called the 'confessions' of Jeremiah are also very much the 'word of God', in the twofold sense of the term: a word coming from God (which can be attributed to God) and a word about God. In other words, they, too, are theology.

For we have to ask who is speaking in these texts. Who is the 'I' in the confessions? Jeremiah? The righteous man? The people? Or perhaps even Yahweh?

There is no doubt that the 'confessions' speak of a dramatic experience, that of the prophet himself: 'Then they said, "Come, let us make plots against Jeremiah, for the law shall not perish from the priest nor counsel from the wise, nor the word from the prophet. Come, let us smite him with the tongue, and let us not heed any of his words"' (18.18). Jeremiah's adversaries plot ceaselessly against him and seek to silence him. Another passage of the confessions clearly refers to the 'manoeuvres' and 'sinister plans' of these same adversaries (11.18–19). In fact Jeremiah was persecuted, denounced, arrested, shut up, imprisoned. His complaints have nothing to do with the development of a persecution complex, but derive from a dramatic experience.

In this sense the confessions of Jeremiah have acquired a universal status, so that they have become the prayer of the righteous who suffer. We can easily recognize in the prayer of Jeremiah the accents of the righteous who are persecuted without reason and the protest of the innocent faced with the misfortunes which fall on them from above, whereas the treacherous and the impious seem to prosper with impunity: 'Why does the way of the wicked prosper? Why do all who are treacherous thrive?' (12.1). 'Be not a terror to me, you are my refuge in the day of evil. Let those be put to shame who persecute me, but let me not be put to shame' (17.17–18).

Other righteous have suffered like Jeremiah and, like him, have raised the cry of their suffering to God. However, Jeremiah's prayer does not stop there. It also expresses the suffering of a whole people, and behind the 'I' of the confessions we easily hear the turmoil and the complaint of the people of Judah and Jerusalem: 'How long will the land mourn, and the grass of every field wither?' (12.4; cf. 14.2–6).

Finally, we should never forget that the words of Jeremiah are the word of God (Jer.1), and that for this reason, through the complaint of Jeremiah we must also hear the complaint of God: 'Tell them, My eyes run down with tears night and day, and do not cease, for the virgin daughter of my people is smitten with a great wound, with a very grievous blow . . .' (14.17). Ultimately, who is speaking? Jeremiah receives the order to speak like this, but he is only saying what the Lord is requiring him to say. So it is God himself who deplores the fate of his people ('my people' as the text says). God is not indifferent to the misfortunes of his people; this is what Jeremiah is ultimately bearing witness to in his confessions.

of king Josiah, that almost perfect king ('He did what was right in the eyes of the Lord, and walked in all the ways of David his father, and he did not turn aside to the right hand or to the left', II Kings, 22.2), whom the Deuteronomic historian puts at the head of all the kings of Judah and Israel: 'Before him there was no king like him, who turned to the Lord with all his soul and with all his might, according to all the laws of Moses; nor did any like him arise after him' (II Kings 23.25).

The same historian did not fail to list, in the two chapters preceding this summary (II Kings 22–23), the reasons for such an evaluation:
– It was in his reign that 'the book of the law', also called 'the book of the covenant', was found. King Josiah himself called for it to be read out, first in private and then in public. He was the first to take this book seriously and to require the people to conform to the demands of this book of the covenant:

> And the king stood by the pillar and made a covenant before the Lord, to walk after the Lord and to keep his commandments and his testimonies and his statutes, with all his heart and all his soul, to perform the words of this covenant that were written in this book; and all the people joined in the covenant (II Kings 23.3).

– Following this discovery, Josiah undertook a vast operation of cultic purification all over the country, abolishing priests, altars, idols, pagan rituals, divinatory techniques, and so on.
– More positively, he made Jerusalem the central cult place and reintroduced a celebration of the passover more in keeping with Mosaic requirements:

> And the king commanded all the people, 'Keep the passover to the Lord your God, as it is written in this book of the covenant.' For no such passover had been kept since the days of the judges who judged Israel or of the kings of Judah; but in the eighteenth year of King Josiah this passover was kept to the Lord in Jerusalem (II Kings 23.21–23).

Curiously enough, the text of II Kings 22–23 makes no mention of the prophet Jeremiah, speaking rather of the prophetess Huldah. So it does not seem as if Jeremiah was the architect of the renewal begun by Josiah; rather, he will have been its beneficiary or its product. But we may suppose that Jeremiah's career began in a decidedly favourable atmosphere and that his oracles on inner religion found a more than favourable ground in what has been called the 'Deuteronomic reform'. In this first phase of his ministry we may say that for Jeremiah all hopes, all dreams were possible.

## Bitter tomorrows

Unfortunately for him, and for the people of Judah, Josiah was to die young, at the age of only thirty-nine, and his son Jehoiakim, rather than following in his footsteps, again took up the horrors and abominations of his predecessors, carrying the people of Judah with him: 'And he did what was evil in the sight of the Lord, according to all that his fathers had done' (II Kings 23.37). For Judah and its king, the hour of reckoning for so many crimes and infidelities was soon to strike:

> In his days Nebuchadnezzar king of Babylon came up, and Jehoiakim became his servant three years; then he turned and rebelled against him. And the Lord sent against him bands of the Chaldaeans, and bands of the Syrians, and bands of the Moabites, and bands of the Ammonites, and sent them against Judah to destroy it, according to the word of the Lord which he spoke by his servants the prophets. Surely this came upon Judah at the command of the Lord, to remove them out of his sight, for the sins of Manasseh, according to all that he had done, and also for the innocent blood that he had shed; for he filled Jerusalem with innocent blood, and the Lord would not pardon (II Kings 24.1–5).

It was during this period above all that Jeremiah was to preach 'violence and repression' (20.8). The prophet was then in opposition: alone against the world, he announced the imminent catastrophe.

Not because he wanted it, but because he was convinced that Judah had made a bad choice, and that it was rushing to its doom. The imminent misfortune was not fatal, but it could be explained historically by the failure of the king of Judah and his people to put into practice the words of the 'book of the covenant' and their flagrant contempt for all justice.

As for Jehoiakim, we can understand how Jeremiah did not think much of him from the one oracle, virulent and sarcastic, that he utters about him:

Woe to him who builds his house by
unrighteousness,
and his upper rooms by injustice;
who makes his neighbour serve him for nothing,
and does not give him his wages;
who says, 'I will build myself a great house
with spacious upper rooms,'
and cuts out windows for it,
panelling it with cedar,
and painting it with vermilion.
Do you think you are a king
because you compete in cedar?
Did not your father eat and drink
and do justice and righteousness?
Then it was well with him.
He judged the cause of the poor and needy;
then it was well.
Is not this to know me?
says the Lord?
But you have eyes and heart
only for your dishonest gain,
for shedding innocent blood,
and for practising oppression and violence.
Therefore thus says the Lord concerning
Jehoiakim the son of Josiah, king of Judah:
'They shall not lament for him, saying,
"Ah my brother!" or "Ah sister!"
They shall not lament for him, saying,
"Ah lord!" or "Ah his majesty!"
With the burial of an ass he shall be buried,
dragged and cast forth beyond the gates of
Jerusalem' (22.13–19).

This was an extremely difficult period for Jeremiah, and his confessions bear witness to this (chs.11–20). It was a difficult period by virtue of the very word which he had to convey: 'For whenever I speak, I cry out, I shout "Violence and destruction!" For the word of the Lord has become for me a reproach and derision all day long' (20.8). He does not proclaim his message with a joyful heart, but simply in order to hand on the word of the Lord to his contemporaries. It is also a difficult period because of the opposition that such a message arouses. All are against him – the king, the priests, the other prophets and even his own family: 'For I hear many whispering. Terror is on every side! "Denounce him! Let us denounce him!" say all my familiar friends, watching for my fall. "Perhaps he will be deceived, then we can overcome him and take our revenge on him"' (20.10). Finally, this is a difficult period for Jeremiah himself, who feels the weight of solitude and sees himself exposed to deep questionings. He does not really understand what is going on. Even the behaviour of his God seems difficult to comprehend and he dares to put his questions to God: 'You are righteous, Lord, when I complain to you; yet I would plead my case before you. Why does the way of the wicked prosper? Why do all who are treacherous thrive?' (12.1). Bravery is needed – but his questions are quite legitimate. Sometimes the prophet is even bold enough to reproach God for having 'abused his youthful naiveté': 'Lord, you have deceived me, and I was deceived; you were stronger than I, and you have prevailed. I have become a laughing-stock all the day; everyone mocks me' (20.7).

But Jeremiah does not let God down. At the darkest and most tragic hours in the history of his people he shows an exceptional courage and stakes his hope on every trial. This will be the third and last stage of his prophetic ministry, from 597 to 587, in the reign of Zedekiah.

## The time for courage

The catastrophe, announced by Jeremiah so many times, is now in process of falling on Judah:

Jeremiah

Nebuchadnezzar has had enough spasmodic rebellions in Jerusalem. Now he is going to take radical action and inflict a terrible punishment on it, putting the village to fire and the sword, and deporting part of its population. Let's re-read the succinct description given by the Deuteronomistic historian, in II Kings:

> At that time the servants of Nebuchadnezzar king of Babylon came up to Jerusalem, and the city was besieged. And Nebuchadnezzar king of Babylon came to the city, while his servants were besieging it; and Jehoiachin the king of Judah gave himself up to the king of Babylon, himself, and his mother, and his servants. The king of Babylon took him prisoner in the eighth year of his reign, and carried off all the treasures of the house of the Lord, and the treasures of the king's house, and cut in pieces all the vessels of gold in the temple of the Lord, which Solomon king of Israel had made, as the Lord had foretold. He carried away all Jerusalem, and all the princes, and all the mighty men of valour, ten thousand captives, and all the craftsmen and the smiths; none remained, except the poorest people of the land. And he carried away Jehoiachin to Babylon; the king's mother, the king's wives, his officials, and the chief men of the land, he took into captivity from Jerusalem to Babylon. And the king of Babylon brought captive to Babylon all the men of valour, seven thousand, and the craftsmen and the smiths, one thousand, all of them strong and fit for war (II Kings 24.10–16).

There seems to be a certain schematism in the figures (10,000, 7,000 and 1,000), but this is a national tragedy, the most terrible to strike Jerusalem in the whole history of the New Testament. Lamentations and some psalms which are related to it (e.g. Pss.74; 75; 89) will bear eloquent witness to the magnitude of the tragedy in the consciousness of Judah and Israel.

The disaster which burst upon Jerusalem was terrible. But perhaps – some contemporaries of the prophets might have thought – it was a transitory misfortune and things would soon return to normal.

Quite the opposite happened, and Jerusalem was to experience even more sombre hours. This first wave of deportations in 597 was succeeded by a second in 587 – perhaps less important in terms of the number and quality of the population deported, but no less terrible for the destiny of the city of Jerusalem (see the account in II Kings 25). Most terrible of all, this time it was necessary to come to terms with the idea of a prolonged exile. The exile was to last for at least two generations, until 538.

## Jeremiah confronted with catastrophe

Faced with this tragedy, what was the role and attitude of the prophet Jeremiah? First of all, let us remember that he himself was not deported to Babylon. But that did not spare him, from the depths of his own exile in Egypt, sharing in the torments of his fellow citizens in exile in Babylon. To be brief, we could express Jeremiah's position in the face of the catastrophe of the exile by the following three points.

First, the catastrophe had not come as a surprise to him, since he had tried so many times to alert the people to the gravity of the crisis.

Secondly, in the face of universal opposition, Jeremiah invites the exiles to regroup immediately and at the very heart of the exile to rebuild their lives and their happiness *now*. In this connection we need to read the very fine letter which he sent to those who had been deported (see the box overleaf). In it, what he says in substance is this: 'What has happened to us is terrible . . . the desolation in Jerusalem and Judah is great . . . But life must go on. It is not the end of the world . . . and God is calling on us to work for happiness, where we are, now . . .'

Thirdly, beyond the immediate present in which everything has to be rebuilt, Jeremiah can invent new ways of expressing faith and hope. If he formerly denounced injustice and proclaimed catastrophe, now he can persuade his followers to hope:

The slaughter of the sons of Zedekiah (II Kings 25.7)

# Jeremiah's Letter to the First Exiles (Jer.29.1–23)

Jeremiah is not a prophet of misfortune. He only warns about the unfortunate consequences of the options chosen by the king of Judah and his people; he does not desire them. Moreover, as soon as misfortune breaks out on them, his first concern is one of solidarity. That is the prime aim of his letter to the exiles, the text of which is given below. Note first the resolutely positive tone of the letter, quite the opposite of fatalism: 'Build . . . plant . . . take wives . . . seek the welfare', and the call to hope:

1 *These are the words of the letter which Jeremiah the prophet sent from Jerusalem to the elders of the exiles, and to the priests, the prophets, and all the people, whom Nebuchadnezzar had taken into exile from Jerusalem to Babylon.* $^2$*This was after King Jeconiah, and the queen mother, the eunuchs, the princes of Judah and Jerusalem, the craftsmen and the smiths had departed from Jerusalem.* $^3$*The letter was sent by the hand of Elasah the son of Shaphan and Gemariah the son of Hilkiah, whom Zedekiah king of Judah sent to Babylon to Nebuchadnezzar king of Babylon. It said:*

## While you are waiting, settle down!

4 *Thus says the Lord of hosts, the God of Israel, to all the exiles whom I have sent into exile from Jerusalem to Babylon:* $^5$*Build houses and live in them; plant gardens and eat their produce;* $^6$*take wives and have sons and daughters; take wives for your sons, and give your daughters in marriage, that they may bear sons and daughters; multiply there, and do not decrease.* $^7$*Seek the welfare of the city where I have sent you into exile, and pray to the Lord on its behalf, for in its welfare you will find your welfare.* $^8$*For thus says the Lord of hosts, the God of Israel: Do not let your prophets and your diviners who are among you deceive you, and do not listen to the dreams which they dream;* $^9$*for it is a lie which they are prophesying to you in my name; I did not send them, says the Lord.*

10 *For thus says the Lord: When seventy years are completed for Babylon, I will visit you, and I will fulfil to you my promise and bring you back to this place.* $^{11}$*For I know the plans I have for you, says the Lord, plans for welfare and not for evil, to give you a future and a hope.* $^{12}$*Then you will call upon me and you will make pilgrimages and pray to me, and I will hear you.* $^{13}$*You will seek me and find me; you will seek me with all your heart.* $^{14}$*And I will be found by you, says the Lord, and I will restore your fortunes and gather you from all the nations and all the places where I have scattered you, says the Lord, and I will bring you back to the place from which I sent you into exile.*
15 *If you say, 'The Lord has raised up prophets for us in Babylon' . . .*

## The Judaeans who are still in the country will be punished in their turn

16 *Thus says the Lord concerning the king who sits on the throne of David, and concerning all the people who dwell in this city, your kinsmen, who did not go out with you into exile.* $^{17}$*Thus says the Lord of hosts, Behold, I am sending on them sword, famine and pestilence, and I will make them like vile figs which are so bad that they cannot be eaten.* $^{18}$*I will pursue them with sword, famine and pestilence, and will make them a horror to all the kingdoms of the earth, to be a curse, a terror, a hissing and a reproach among all the nations where I have driven them,* $^{19}$*because they did not heed my words, says the Lord, which I persistently sent to you by my servants the prophets, but you would not listen, says the Lord.*
20 *Hear the word of the Lord, all you exiles whom I sent away from Jerusalem to Babylon.*

## Beware of false prophets

21 *Thus says the Lord of hosts, the God of Israel, concerning Ahab the son of Kolaiah and Zedekiah the son of Maaseiah, who are prophesying a*

↓

> lie to you in my name: Behold, I will deliver them into the hand of Nebuchadrezzar king of Babylon, and he shall slay them before your eyes. [22]Because of them this curse shall be used by all the exiles from Judah in Babylon: 'The Lord make you like Zedekiah and Ahab, whom the king of Babylon roasted in the fire.' [23]Because they have committed folly in Israel, they have committed adultery with their neighbours' wives, and they have spoken in my name lying words which I did not command them. I am the one who knows, and I am witness, says the Lord.

Therefore, behold, the days are coming, says the Lord, when it shall no longer be said 'As the Lord lives who brought up the people of Israel out of the land of Egypt', but 'As the Lord lives who brought up the people out of the north country and out of all the countries where he had driven them.' For I will bring them back to their own land which I gave to their fathers (16.14–15).

Thus says the Lord of hosts, the God of Israel: 'Once more they shall use these words in the land of Judah and in its cities, when I restore their fortunes:

    "The Lord bless you, O habitation of righteousness,

    O holy hill!"
And Judah and all its cities shall dwell there together, and the farmers and those who wander with their flocks. For I will satisfy the weary soul, and every languishing soul will I replenish' (31.23–25).

Thus says the Lord: In this place of which you say, 'It is a waste without man or beast', in the cities of Judah and the streets of Jerusalem that are desolate, without man or inhabitant or beast, there shall be heard again the voice of mirth and the voice of gladness, the voice of the bridegroom and the voice of the bride, the voice of those who sing, as they bring thank-offerings to the house of the Lord: 'Give thanks to the Lord of hosts, for the Lord is good, for his steadfast love endures for ever!' For I will restore the fortunes of the land as at first, says the Lord (33.10–11).

## II. Three texts for understanding Jeremiah

### 1. God watches over the fulfilment of his Word
#### (Jer. 1.4–19)

4 *Now the word of the Lord came to me saying,*
5 *'Before I formed you in the womb I knew you,*
  *and before you were born I consecrated you;*
  *I appoint you a prophet to the nations.'*
6 *Then I said, 'Ah Lord God! Behold I do not know*
  *how to speak, for I am only a youth.'*
7 *But the Lord said to me,*
  *'Do not say "I am only a youth";*
  *for to all to whom I send you you shall go,*
  *and whatever I command you you shall speak.*

8 *Be not afraid of them,*
  *for I am with you to deliver you, says the Lord.*
9 *Then the Lord put forth his hand and touched my*
  *mouth; and the Lord said to me,*
  *'Behold, I have put my words in your mouth.*
10 *See, I give you authority this day over nations and*
  *over kingdoms.*
  *to pluck up and to break down,*
  *to destroy and to overthrow,*
  *to build and to plant.'*

11 *And the word of the Lord came to me, saying, 'Jeremiah, what do you see?' And I said, 'I see a rod of almond.'* [12]*Then the Lord said to me, 'You have seen well, for I am watching over my word to perform it.'*

13 *The word of the Lord came to me a second time, saying 'What do you see?' And I said, 'I see a boiling pot, facing away from the north.'*

14 *Then the Lord said to me,*
   *Out of the north evil shall break forth upon all the inhabitants of the land.*

15 *For lo, I am calling all the tribes of the kingdoms of the north, says the Lord; and they shall come and every one shall set his throne at the entrance of the gates of Jerusalem, against all its walls round about, and against all the cities of Judah.*

16 *And I will utter my judgements against them, for all their wickedness in forsaking me; for they have burned incense to other gods, and worshipped the works of their own hands. But you, gird up your loins; arise, and say to them everything that I command you.* [17]*Do not be dismayed by them, lest I dismay you before them.* [18]*And I, behold I make you this day a fortified city, an iron pillar, and bronze walls, against the whole land, against the kings of Judah, its princes, its priests, and the people of the land.* [19]*They will fight against you; but they shall not prevail against you, for I am with you says the Lord, to deliver you.'*

---

**A story in three panels (vv.4–10, 11–12, 13–19)**

The first lines of this extract (vv.4–10) are well known and often cited among examples of accounts of calls. Everything seems to be there – address, election, consecration, mission, objection, confirmation of the mission – and we may feel justified in reading this passage as a self-contained whole, without any need to refer to the nine following verses.

However, those who wrote these lines arranged them very well, linking them to what follows in such a way that the whole of ch.1 must be read as one unified story of the call of Jeremiah.

The story unfolds in three stages, punctuated by the refrain 'The word of the Lord came to me' (vv.4, 11, 13). The repetition of this formula ensures the unity of the whole chapter. However, the three stages of the structure are not only juxtaposed; they are arranged in relation to one another, so well that the first and third constantly echo each other, while the second is manifestly inserted in the middle to give the main message of the whole account.

Before interpreting the details, let's first look at the correspondence between the extremes (the first and third panels of the picture, between vv.4–10 and vv.13–19):

| First panel (vv.4–10) | Third panel (vv.13–19) |
|---|---|
| Say to them everything that I command you (1.7) | But you, arise . . . say to them everything that I command you (1.17) |
| Be not afraid of them (1.8) | Do not be dismayed by them (1.17) |
| For I am with you to deliver you, says the Lord (1.8) | I am with you, says the Lord, to deliver you (1.19) |
| See, I give you authority this day over nations and over kingdoms . . . (1.10) | And I, behold I make you this day a fortified city, an iron pillar, and bronze walls, against the whole land, against the kings of Judah, its princes, its priests, and the people of the land (1.18) |

The resemblances are too numerous and too precise to be an accident; the two extremes correspond, and each illuminates the other.

This play of parallels is aimed at bringing out vv.11 and 12, which contain the point of the story, the central message, that relates essentially to the fulfilment of the word of the Lord.

Now that we have this overall view of the chapter, we can take up some of the elements of the account.

## A liberating response

First of all the account speaks of the 'consecration' of the prophet 'from his mother's womb'. Some have read this in a deterministic and essentialist way, as if the prophet was not only predestined but predetermined to a certain vocation, and had only to acquiesce the moment that the call was heard. But we have to note the active role which Jeremiah plays throughout the narrative. On the one hand, he makes an objection (v.6), and on the other, in each of the two visions he is called on to react to what he sees. Finally, we should note that the final objective of the mission, the liberation of the people, also includes the liberation of the envoy himself: 'I am with you to liberate you.' Jeremiah's calling presupposes a free response, but it also engages the prophet on new ways of freedom.

## Jeremiah, the new Moses

The prophetic career of Jeremiah coincided with what has been called the Deuteronomic reform and what seems to be the discovery of the scroll containing Deuteronomy. Now we know the importance that Moses has in this book, and in what esteem he is held, specifically as a prophet. Deut.18.18 in fact reflects an expectation widespread at the time of Jeremiah, that of the prophet like Moses: 'I will raise up for them a prophet like you from among their brethren; and I will put my words in his mouth, and he shall speak to them all that I command him.'

The affinities between the account of Jeremiah's call and this verse from Deuteronomy are easy to

Jeremiah's call

recognize: clearly, the author or authors of Jeremiah saw in Jeremiah a worthy rival to the great prophet Moses. Furthermore, the stories of the calls of these two great figures (Ex.3; Jer.1) have other points of similarity. Both men allude to the difficulty they find in speaking, both are reassured by the Lord, who proposes to be with them, and both receive a mission of liberation. Once again, it is difficult to say who has influenced whom, but it is certain that the disciples of Jeremiah soon associated their master with the great prophetic figure of Moses.

## The prophet's uncomfortable mission

If Koheleth (Ecclesiastes), in his admirable poem on the ambivalence of time, could calmly say that there is 'a time to plant and a time to root up . . . a time to pull down and a time to build' (3.2–3), Jeremiah already experienced in his life as a prophet the coexistence and the conflict of these opposites. One could hardly define the ambivalence of the prophetic mission better than is done in Jer.1.10: 'to pluck up and to break down, to destroy and to overthrow, to build and to plant'. One could hardly call the formula an accident, since it recurs as a refrain throughout the book, to some degree confirming how day by day Jeremiah lived out his mission between these two poles.

| The verbs in v.10 in the book of Jeremiah as a whole | | | | | | |
|---|---|---|---|---|---|---|
| 1. *natash*, pluck up | 2. *natats*, break down | 3. *'abad*, destroy | 4. *haras*, overthrow | 5. *banah*, build | 6. *nata*, plant | |
| X | X | X | X | X | X | 1.10 |
| X | X | X | X | X | X | 31.28 + do evil |
| X | X | X | | X | X | 18.7–9 |
| X | | | X | X | X | 24.6 |
| X | | | X | X | X | 42.10 |
| X | | | X | X | X | 45.4 |
| X | | X | | | | 12.17 |
| | | | | X | X | 29.5, 28 |
| | | | | X | X | 31.4–5 |
| X | | | X | | | 31.40 |
| | | | | X | X | 35.7 |

The priority and predominance of negative terms is somewhat surprising: uproot, overthrow, ruin, demolish. There is nothing particularly encouraging here! Except that it corresponds effectively to a need and a reality. Jeremiah's mission – more than that of his predecessors? – was to go against the grain, and would require a singular courage.

However, this phrase must be read in a dynamic way. Certainly the positive terms are less numerous, but isn't their position at the end an indication of the objective that is aimed at: 'to build and to plant'. Furthermore, it is interesting to see that these two verbs recur in a much more constant way throughout the book, whereas the author shows greater freedom in using the other terms, and sometimes drops more than one of them.

So the prophet's mission is to denounce, to overthrow, to demolish, but in order to plant and build better. Certainly this is a mission of judgment, but it is also a mission of salvation: 'to liberate you'.

## The almond tree which speaks of God

At the centre of the text, as I have pointed out, stands the very fine parable of the almond tree. 'Almond tree' in Hebrew is *shaqed*, and this allows the author to produce a magnificent word-play, since by keeping the same consonants and changing only one vowel, with the word *shoqed* he can speak to us of the mystery of God who watches over the fulfilment of his word.

This text truly provides the key for reading Jeremiah. What the prophet says comes as a hard blow, but since it takes up the very words of God, its fulfilment cannot be in doubt.

## Knowing how to look: the prophet's secrets

I have emphasized the links between the first and third panels of the picture. There are also very evident and close links between the second and the third:

| | |
|---|---|
| And the word of the Lord came to me, saying (1.11) | And the word of the Lord came to me a second time, saying (1.13) |
| 'Jeremiah, what do you see?' | 'Jeremiah, what do you see?' |
| And I said, 'I see a rod of almond' | And I said, 'I see a boiling pot, facing away from the north.' |
| And the Lord said to me (there follows an interpretation of the vision given by God) | And the Lord said to me (there follows an interpretation of the vision given by God) |

Here, too, the procedure brings out the complementarity of the two accounts. The prophet is someone who can observe, and to whom God can say, 'Well seen!' But we should also note the difference in the context of the revelation: this is always a created reality (as in the parables of Jesus), but in the first instance nature or creation says something of the mystery of God, whereas in the second God reveals himself from history. These are the two contexts in which the prophets are called to do theology: the world of creation and the world of human history.

### 'A prophet for the nations'

Jeremiah amply deserves this title, even if others before him (Amos and Isaiah, for example) also pronounced oracles against the nations neighbouring on Israel and Judah. However, more than any other prophet, Jeremiah is speaking at a period of history marked by great international upheavals. Jeremiah will certainly be a 'prophet for the nations', since he will experience the devastation caused by the Babylonian army; he will write to the captives in Babylon and will himself have to flee to Egypt. He will also be a prophet for the nations by virtue of the tone of certain oracles (chs.25; 46–51), which show in a very realistic way how Israel's neighbours (Moab, Edom, Damascus, etc.) do not escape the devastation caused by Nebuchadnezzar and his troops. Perhaps we tend to forget the drama which was played out among these nations, certainly with equal intensity, at a time when, as Jeremiah tells us, 'evil is going forth from nation to nation, and a great tempest is stirring from the farthest parts of the earth' (25.32). Perhaps this is not a consolation, but at least Jeremiah has the merit of putting in perspective a tragedy which Jerusalem and Judah were not the only ones to know.

## 2. No knowledge of God without justice!
### (Jer.9.1–11)

1 O that I had in the desert
   a wayfarers' lodging place,
   that I might leave my people
   and go away from them!
   For they are all adulterers,
   a company of treacherous men.
2 They bend their tongue like a bow;
   falsehood and not truth has grown strong in the land;
   for they proceed from evil to evil,
   and they do not know me, says the Lord.

3 Let everyone beware of his companion,
   and put no trust in any brother,
   for every brother is a supplanter,
   and every companion goes about as a slanderer.
4 Every one deceives his companion,
   and no one speaks the truth;
   they have taught their tongues to speak lies;
   they commit iniquity and are to weary to repent.
5 Heaping oppression upon oppression,
   and deceit upon deceit
   they refuse to know me, says the Lord.

6 Therefore thus says the Lord of hosts:
  'Behold, I will refine them and test them,
  for what else can I do, because of my people?
7 Their tongue is a deadly arrow,
  it speaks deceitfully;
  with his mouth each speaks peaceably to his
  neighbour,
  but in his heart he plans an ambush for him.
8 Shall I not punish them for these things,
  says the Lord;
  and shall I not avenge myself
  on a nation such as this?
9 Take up weeping and wailing for the mountains,
  and lamentation for the pastures of the wilderness,

because they are laid waste so that no one passes
through,
  and the lowing of cattle is not heard;
  both the birds of the air and the beasts have fled and
are gone.
10 I will make Jerusalem a heap of ruins, a lair of
jackals,
  and I will make the cities of Judah a desolation,
  without inhabitant.
11 Who is the man so wise that he can understand this?
  To whom has the mouth of the Lord spoken, that he
may declare it?
  Why is the land ruined and laid waste like a
wilderness,
  so that no one passes through?

---

## Who is speaking: God or Jeremiah?

Here is another instance – along with the 'confessions' and several other passages of the book of Jeremiah – where it is difficult to discover precisely who is speaking. Numerous indications certainly point to Yahweh: this is indicated by the threefold 'says the Lord' (vv.2, 5, 8), reinforced by the expression 'thus says the Lord of hosts' (v.6) and by the reference to 'the word which the mouth of the Lord spoke to him'. Furthermore, all ambiguity is removed in v.2, when we hear 'and they do not know me', which manifestly refers to God.

So it is to God himself that we must attribute the 'weeping and wailing' and the 'lamentation' (v.9) which resound in this chapter, and doubtless also in the immediate context.

However, it is very difficult not to see how this lamentation is also that of Jeremiah himself, noting with his own eyes the desolation in the streets of Jerusalem (v.9). Furthermore, the two questions of v.11, the attribution of which remains indeterminate, well translate those of Jeremiah and his contemporaries: 'Why is the land ruined and laid waste like a wilderness, so that no one passes through?' Finally, even v.1 could be understood in terms of

the prophet himself, tempted to break off his solidarity with an adulterous people: 'O that I had in the desert a wayfarers' lodging place, that I might leave my people and go away from them! For they are all adulterers, a company of treacherous men.'

## Injustice is at its height

The verdict given by God is implacable: throughout Jerusalem one finds only injustice and deceit. This is a general situation, and not a matter of a few isolated misdemeanours: 'they are all adulterers, a company of treacherous men' (v.1); 'for every brother is a supplanter, and every companion goes about as a slanderer' (v.3); 'every one deceives his companion' (v.4). What is striking over and above the generalization is the intensity or the degree of injustice that we find among the people, and the author castigates this in an incisive summary: 'Heaping oppression upon oppression, and deceit upon deceit' (v.5).

This is certainly the most astonishing feature of the prophet. Jeremiah has often been described as a spiritual prophet, herald of the new covenant and

Lamentation over the fall of Jerusalem (Lam. 1.1)

| The Vocabulary of Justice and Injustice in Jeremiah | |
|---|---|
| 1. Judge | 5.28 |
| 2. Judgment – right | 5.1, 28; 7.5; 17.11; 21.12; 22.3, 13, 15; 23.5; 33.15 |
| 3. Justice | 22.3, 13, 15; 23.5; 33.15 |
| 4. Just – innocent | 23.5; 33.15 |
| 5. Lie – falsehood | 5.2; 6.13; 7.9; 8.10; 9.2, 4; 23.14 |
| 6. Judge a cause | 5.28; 21.12; 22.16 |
| 7. Someone's cause | 5.20; 21.12; 22.16 |
| 8. Commit adultery | 5.7; 7.9; 9.2; 23.10, 14; 29.23 |
| 9. Do evil | 2.33; 9.2; 23.10, 11, 14 |
| 10. Gain, profit | 6.13; 8.10; 22.17 |
| 11. Oppress | 6.6; 7.6; 21.12; 22.17 |
| 12. Free | 34.9, 10, 11, 14, 16 |
| 13. Faithfulness, loyalty | 5.1, 3; 9.2, 4 |
| 14. Innocent blood | 2.34; 7.6; 22.3, 17 |
| 15. Deceit, fraud | 5, 27; 9.5, 7 |
| 16. Liberation | 34.8, 15, 17 |
| 17. Serve – enslave | 22.13; 34.9, 14 |
| 18. Subject | 34.11, 16 |
| 19. Despoil | 21.12; 22.3 |
| 20. Do violence | 6.7; 22.3 |

author of moving 'confessions'. Certainly he is all that, but he is also an incomparable champion of social justice, a faithful heir and disciple of Amos, Hosea and Isaiah. Of all these prophets, he is the one who offers the most complete and systematic analysis of social injustice, and Jer.9.1–11 is one of the passages which best illustrates this aspect of his message. In fact in addition to the generalization and the intensity already indicated, one is surprised at the abundance of terms related to justice (or its opposite, injustice) in the passage which we are studying: adulterers, traitors, falsehood and untruth, evil, iniquity, slanderer, lies, oppression, deceit, wickedness, deadly arrow, ambushes, and so on. There is a wealth of terms (which can be checked out for the rest of the book from the box opposite, 'The Vocabulary of Justice and Injustice in Jeremiah'), but also a precise analysis. For Jeremiah does not stick to generalities and does not content himself with denouncing injustice in high places. He sets out to challenge and interrogate everyone, down to the sphere of daily, fraternal and social relations.

## Injustices towards brothers and companions

If in fact we look at the whole of the vocabulary of justice and injustice in Jeremiah, we shall see clearly that no category is spared (the king, the rich, the priests, all the people). Now here, in ch.9, Jeremiah's attack is directed more at the whole of the people, and what he denounces is the corruption of relations between brothers and companions. Here we no longer have the foreign adversary, but the close friend, the relative. For here, too, justice makes its demands: in words spoken to others, in consideration for others, in keeping the peace between brothers, and so on. Now Jeremiah has to note that relations between brothers and companions have deteriorated terribly: 'Let everyone beware of his companion, and put no trust in any brother, for every brother is a supplanter, and every companion goes about as a slanderer. Every one deceives his companion' (vv.3–4).

## A question of theology

Thus the judgment passed by the prophet on his contemporaries is very severe in the matter of justice. But in fact the question is more than a simple one of justice. Jeremiah raises the debate to a strictly theological level; in other words, he invokes the knowledge of the true God as the supreme foundation for the demands of justice. That is what emerges from the antithesis formulated in v.2: 'for they proceed from evil to evil, and they do not know me, says the Lord'. To commit injustice 'from evil to evil' is quite simply to fail to know God. Furthermore, the same judgment is passed again in v.5: 'Heaping oppression upon oppression, and deceit upon deceit, they refuse to know me, says the Lord.'

It is only in justice, practised at every level, that the experience of knowledge of the true God is possible. The originality of Jeremiah is precisely the way in which he has explicitly and inseparably linked the themes of the knowledge of God and justice (or, in the negative, of the failure to know God and injustice). The box which follows relates to the former theme ('knowledge of God'), but it is easy to see in the verses quoted or in their immediate contexts how the two themes are inseparable.

## Knowledge of God = respect for justice

These are the principle passages, in Jeremiah, in which one can find, either positively or negatively, a connection between knowledge of God and justice:

> For my people are foolish,
> *they know me not;*
> they are stupid children,
> they have no understanding.
> They are skilled in doing evil,
> but how to do good they know not (4.22).

> Then I said, 'These are only the poor,
> they have no sense;
> for *they do not know* the way of the Lord,
> the law of their God.
> I will go to the great,
> and will speak to them;

for *they know* the way of the Lord,
the law of their God.
But they all alike have broken the yoke,
they have burst the bonds (5.4–5).
(cf. v.2: 'Is there anyone who does justice and seeks
truth?')

They bend their tongue like a bow;
falsehood and not truth has grown strong in the
land;
for they proceed from evil to evil,
and *they do not know me*, says the Lord.
Let every one beware of his companion,
and put no trust in any brother;
for every brother is a supplanter,
and every companion goes about as a slanderer.
Every one deceives his companion,
and no one speaks the truth;
they have taught their tongue to speak lies . . .
*they refuse to know me*, says the Lord (9).

Let him who glories glory in this, that he understands and *knows me*, that I am the Lord who
practise steadfast love, justice and righteousness
in the earth; for in these things I delight, says the
Lord (9.23).

Did not your father (Josiah, father of Jehoiakim) eat
and drink
and do justice and righteousness?
Then it was well with him.
He judged the cause of the poor and needy;
then it was well.
Is not this to *know me*? says the Lord (22.15–16)
(for a contrast, see 22.13, 17).

And no longer shall each man teach his neighbour
saying, '*Know the Lord*,' for they all shall *know me*,
from the least to the greatest, says the Lord; for I will
forgive their iniquity, and I will remember their sin
no more' (31.34).

---

# 3.  The new covenant
## (Jer. 31.31–34)

*[31] Behold, the days are coming, says the Lord, when I will make a new covenant with the house of Israel and the house of Judah, [32] not like the covenant which I made with their fathers when I took them by the hand to bring them out of the land of Egypt, my covenant which they broke though I was their husband, says the Lord. [33] But this is the covenant which I will make with the house of Israel after those days, says the Lord: I will put my law within them, and I will write it upon their hearts; and I will be their God, and they shall be my people. [34] And no longer shall each man teach his neighbour saying, 'Know the Lord,' for they all shall know me, from the least to the greatest, says the Lord; for I will forgive their iniquity, and I will remember their sin no more.*

---

This text is beyond doubt the best-known text from the book of Jeremiah for a Christian public, since the New Testament not only contains it as the longest quotation of a text from the Old Testament (Hebrews 8.8–12, see p.60 above), but even owes its name to it (testament = covenant). This very celebrity represents a danger, to the degree that we Christians risk claiming Jeremiah's prophecy for ourselves, independently of the context in which it arose and the meaning that it could have for the prophet and his contemporaries. It is this content and this significance that we are now going to try to discover, paying attention to the different details of the text, and not just the expression 'new covenant', fine though it is.

### God makes all things new: the context of the new covenant (Jer. 30–33)

Jeremiah's oracle on the new covenant, far from being an isolated oracle and coming as a surprise, is inserted into a group of oracles devoted to the restoration of Israel (ch.30–33). These oracles are full of terms indicating the changes that God will soon bring to the destiny of his people: restore (30.2, 18; 31.23; 32.42), deliver (30.10–11), convalescence and healing (30.17; 33.6), rebuilding (30.18; 31.2,38); rejuvenating (31.1), return to life and flourishing (31.12–13), a future full of hope (31.17), the creation of something new (31.22). The new covenant means first and foremost the happiness which is regained for Judah and Jerusalem: '. . . In the cities of Judah and the streets of Jerusalem that are desolate, without man or inhabitant or beast, there shall be heard again (note the threefold announcement, beginning with 'again' in 31.4–5) the voice of mirth and the voice of gladness . . .' (33.10–11).

## How new?

Jeremiah emphasizes that the covenant will be new and 'not like the covenant which I made with their fathers when I took them by the hand to bring them out of the land of Egypt' (v.32). It is not only more recent in time, as if it were the revised, corrected and enlarged edition of an earlier covenant. The covenant of which Jeremiah speaks is unprecedented, radically new and of a quality superior to the old. Four features express how the covenant announced by Jeremiah is new:

1. The new covenant with the community of Israel will be written 'in their being' rather than in their flesh. The first covenant, made with Abraham, then renewed in the time of Moses, required circumcision for all male children. The new covenant will have nothing to do with ties of blood. There will no longer be any need for tables of stone on which to inscribe the words of the covenant. From now on the new words of God will be communicated in the depths of the conscience of the community, and the covenant which stems from that will be inward and universal.

2. 'I shall be their God and they shall be my people . . .' Unlike the covenant concluded on Sinai, the formulation of which was modelled on the vassal treaties of the ancient Near East, which emphasized the difference between the sovereign and his vassal, the new covenant will be marked by the stamp of mutuality. The two partners, God and the community, will exist for one another and by one another.

3. 'They will all know me, small and great . . .' The first covenant had been sanctioned by the 'ten words', the symbol of the revelation made on Sinai, and the people could hear the word of God only through Moses as intermediary. The whole religion of Israel gravitated around this initial revelation and presupposed the mediation of a prophet of the stamp of Moses, then priests who were charged with instruction. Here each and everyone will be able to have access to the knowledge of God without going through the mediation of prophets, priests or temple.

4. A covenant of forgiveness. The last, and by no means the least, new feature is that even the sin of Israel will not be able to lead to the revoking of the covenant. The new covenant will be eternal and no longer conditional on the obedience of the community. Whereas the first covenant had been bound up with an impressive number of prohibitions, anathemas and curses, the new covenant is sanctioned under the sign of the forgiveness offered: 'I will forgive their iniquity, and I will remember their sin no more.'

## From Jeremiah to Jesus, even greater newness?

In the face of so much newness, the question now arises for us Christian readers how the covenant in Jesus could claim in turn to any newness. The expression 'new covenant' appears only once on the lips of Jesus, at the Last Supper. According to the joint testimony of Paul and Luke, in pronouncing the blessing on the cup, Jesus said, 'This cup is the new covenant in my blood . . .' (I Cor.11.25; Luke 22.20). The expression is manifestly taken from Jeremiah, but neither Paul nor Luke feel any need to comment on the way in which this covenant is new.

Rather, it is the author of the letter to the

Hebrews who will set out to do this, basing himself explicitly on Jer.31 (Heb.8–10). Speaking of Christ as 'a minister in the sanctuary and the true tent which is set up not by man but by the Lord' (Heb.8.1), he writes: 'But as it is, Christ has obtained a ministry which is much more excellent than the old as the covenant he mediates is better, since it is enacted on better promises' (Heb.8.6). Then he adds, immediately after his quotation of Jer.31.34: 'In speaking of a new covenant he treats the first as obsolete. And what is becoming obsolete and growing old is ready to vanish away' (Heb.8.13).

There is a paradox here which is a good illustration of the relationship of continuity and newness between the first covenant and the new covenant. In fact the author of the letter to the Hebrews seeks to demonstrate the newness of the covenant that has been established in Jesus. But to do this he actually bases himself on the text of a prophet who belongs to the first covenant! Furthermore, the argument in the letter to the Hebrews fits remarkably well with the Jeremiah text, which it matches in essentials, in that it sees the newness of the covenant in Jesus as consisting in the forgiveness of sins (Heb.10.15–18) and emancipation from the ritual and mediations of the first covenant (cult and earthly temple, tables of the covenant, sprinkling of blood, etc.: Heb.9). For the author of the letter to the Hebrews, then, Jesus is the one who brings to fulfilment the great newness announced by Jeremiah. It is impossible to understand Jesus without Jeremiah or Jeremiah without Jesus. The two covenants, the first covenant and the new covenant, refer to each other and complement each other.

# III. The God of Jeremiah

## A God of the word

I already remarked at the beginning of this book how Jeremiah was one of the biblical writers who have provided us with the most complete theologies of the word. In many respects he already heralds the heights of the prologue to the Gospel of John (John 1.1–18).

The God of Jeremiah is in fact a God who reveals himself by the word. The Word is omnipresent in his book: a personal, intimate word, but also a word made to provoke dialogue and addressed to the community. It is in Jeremiah that we find most frequently the root denoting word (*dabar*, both noun and verb, more than 300 instances), and the expression 'word of the Lord' occurs no less than fifty-two times (two less than in Ezekiel). In Jeremiah's book, which is the longest in the Bible, God never stops speaking. Nor must we forget that what is presented here as a collection of 'words of Jeremiah' is no less than the very words of God, put on the lips of the prophet (1.7, 9).

The account of Jeremiah's call shows how central the experience of the word was to the prophet's life: 'And the word of the Lord came to me, saying, "Jeremiah, what do you see?" And I said, "I see a rod of almond." Then the Lord said to me, "You have seen well, for I am watching over my word to perform it."'

Jeremiah is also the prophet who puts most emphasis on the mediation of the prophets, all through a history in which God has revealed himself to his people:

From the day that your fathers came out of the land of Egypt to this day, I have persistently sent all my servants the prophets to them, day after day; yet they did not listen to me, or incline their ear, but stiffened their neck. They did worse than their fathers. So you shall speak all these words to them, but they will not listen to you. You shall call to them, but they will not answer you. And you shall say to them, 'This is the nation that did not obey the voice of the Lord your God, and did not accept discipline; truth has perished, it is cut off from their lips' (7.25–28).

So the history of the prophets goes back to the exodus from Egypt, with Moses, and has continued 'persistently . . . day after day'. Through the prophets, the 'voice of the Lord' has truly been presented to the people of Israel. We might think that we were already hearing the review which the author of the letter to the Hebrews would make of the history of revelation: 'In many and various ways God spoke of old to our fathers by the prophets; but in these last days he has spoken to us by a Son . . .' (Heb.1.1–2).

## A God of justice

Jeremiah is the prophet of the word of God in a singular way. That does not prevent him from presenting one of the most vibrant pleas in the Bible for human dignity. The word of God that he is called to pronounce becomes a liberating word for humankind.

Jeremiah is in fact one of the prophets who presses furthest the demands of social justice. We have seen the importance of the discussion of justice in his work. Now this discussion derives directly from what he says about God. The God of Jeremiah is a God of justice, in other words a God who is justice, and if Jeremiah puts so much emphasis on the demands of justice, it is because he believes in a God who is basically just: 'You are righteous, O Lord' (12.1). So his reasoning is: 'Be righteous, because God is righteous.'

According to Jeremiah, one cannot know God truly without knowing justice. Paraphrasing John in the New Testament, one could make Jeremiah say: 'He who does not practise justice has not discovered God, for God is justice' (cf. I John 4.8). This is a conviction shared by all the prophets of Israel, but none pushed it to such extreme consequences as Jeremiah:

Let him who glories glory in this.
that he understands and knows me,
that I am the Lord who practise steadfast love,

justice, and righteousness in the earth;
for in these things I delight, says the Lord
(Jer.9.23).

He judged the cause of the poor and needy;
then it was well.
Is not this to know me?
says the Lord (22.16).

So it is not surprising that Jeremiah is the only biblical author to invoke God under the name 'he is our justice' (23.5–6; cf. also 33.16).

## 'God-for-you'

Of all the prophets, it is beyond question in Jeremiah that we find the most direct references to the covenant. Thus Jeremiah shares the convictions of the Deuteronomistic school and with it thus presents to us a God involved in a covenant. Jeremiah's God is the God of a people, the God who exists for a people, a God who calls himself 'God-for-you' (7.23; 11.4; 24.7) or 'their God'. Certainly he is God of a covenant, but he is also God of a promise whose existence is bound up with the destiny and the happiness of a people: 'Obey my voice, and I will be your God, and you shall be my people; and walk in all the way that I command you, that it may be well with you' (7.23). Here again Jeremiah is already announcing the perspectives of the Gospel of John on the mystery of a God made flesh: 'And the word was made flesh and dwelt among us . . .' (John 1.14). Jeremiah's God is a God incarnate, who does not fear to play a part and involve himself in the history of a people.

## A God who suffers

Precisely because he is a God intimately bound up with the history of a people, Jeremiah's God is a God who suffers. In these hours of national tragedy, God cannot remain insensitive to the suffering of his people. This is what comes out of the 'confessions' of Jeremiah, in which we have seen that the use of the first person necessarily says something about the mystery of God. Thus sayings like:

My grief is beyond healing,
my heart is sick within me.
Hark, the cry of the daughter of my people
from the length and breadth of the land (8.18–19);

My eyes run down with tears night and day,
and do not cease,
for the virgin daughter of my people is smitten
with a great wound,
with a very grievous blow (14.17)

show us that God is affected by the suffering of his people.

## A God who 'plucks up and overthrows' . . .

The mission received by the prophet Jeremiah (1.10) also tells us something about God's attitude towards his people. God plucks up and overthrows. God shakes his people and treats them ruthlessly. The verb 'pluck up' is used no less than eight times in the book of Jeremiah, mainly to refer to the trial of the exile:

Thus says the Lord concerning all my evil neighbours who touch the heritage which I have given my people Israel to inherit: 'Behold, I will pluck them up from their land, and I will pluck up the house of Judah from among them' (12.4).

If at any time I declare concerning a nation or a kingdom, that I will pluck up and break down and destroy it (18.7).

The very real and very concrete experience of being plucked up, experienced by those deported from Israel, is here interpreted theologically as part of God's plan.

## . . . but in order to 'build and plant' better

This plan of God cannot be achieved with misfortune or testing. We have to see that the ultimate aim of the prophet's mission, and thus God's action, is to 'build and plant'. God wants to make new, to restore his people, to bring them to unity and life, to rebuild them:

And after I have plucked them up, I will again have compassion on them, and I will bring them again each to his heritage and each to his land. And it shall come to pass, if they will diligently learn the ways of my people, to swear by name, 'As the Lord lives,' even as they taught my people to swear by Baal, then they shall be built up in the midst of my people. But if any nation will not listen, then I will utterly pluck it up and destroy it, says the Lord (12.15–17).

I will set my eyes upon them for good, and I will bring them back to this land. I will build them up, and not tear them down; I will plant them, and not uproot them (24.6).

If you will remain in this land, then I will build you up and not pull you down; I will plant you, and not pluck you up; for I repent of the evil which I did to you. Do not fear the king of Babylon, of whom you are afraid; do not fear him, says the Lord, for I am with you, to save you and to deliver you from his hand (42.10–11).

At the height of the testing, condemned to exile or flight, Jeremiah, like all the biblical prophets, continues to maintain an unconditional hope.

# 7

# Ezekiel: The Visionary of Glory

After Isaiah and Jeremiah, now we enter the presence of another giant of biblical prophecy, Ezekiel. He is himself the heir of his two predecessors, above all of Jeremiah, from whom he takes over and with whom he shares a great atmosphere of newness, in several respects proclaiming the inward, free and responsible religion preached by Jesus. Furthermore he also recalls the beginnings of biblical prophecy and its great ancestors, Elijah and Elisha.

Ezekiel is undeniably heir to the classical prophets. But he is also and above all an innovator, an initiator. In fact he is the one who gives the tone and inspiration to what is to become the vast current of apocalypses. He was to have a decisive influence on the books of Daniel and the Apocalypse of John, the two great classics of biblical apocalyptic. The authors of these two later works found in Ezekiel a style and a power of imagery which was singularly suited to their purposes.

Indeed, Ezekiel has the honour of having created the images of the four living creatures (with whom later the four evangelists were to be associated), the book which is swallowed, the divine throne, the son of man resplendent in glory, and the new city where God dwells for ever.

To judge from the impressive architecture and the complexity of the book which bears his name, Ezekiel was by no means a commonplace personality. Others would even say that he is strange, and that some of his visions verge on hallucination and schizophrenia. The charge is not a new one, since already in ancient Jewish tradition Ezekiel had a reputation for the obscurity of his remarks, and his book was not accepted into the canon of scripture without difficulty.

So let us try to see better the sometimes transparent, sometimes enigmatic or contrasting features of the person and the message he has given us.

---

## I.  The paradoxes of a prophet

Given the facts in the book, which contains no less than fourteen precise dates for individual oracles, the ministry of Ezekiel can beyond doubt be dated more precisely than that of any other prophet. First let us look at the two extreme dates, given in 1.1–3 and 29.17:

- In the thirtieth year, in the fourth month, on the fifth day of the month, as I was among the exiles by the river Chebar, the heavens were opened and I saw visions of God. On the fifth day of the month (it was the fifth year of the exile of King Jehoiachin), the word of the Lord came to Ezekiel . . . (1.1–3).

- In the twenty-seventh year, in the first month, on the first day of the month, the word of the Lord came to me . . . (29.17).

In both cases the years are dated by the deportation of king Jehoiachin, which on the basis of the Babylonian Chronicle can be put in March 597. The introduction of 1.1–3 is clearly overloaded, and we have to use v.3 as the precise basis for establishing the beginning of Ezekiel's prophetic ministry, 'on the fifth day of the month (it was the fifth year of the exile of King Jehoiachin)'. That brings us to 593, and in the light of the indications given in 29.17, the majority of Ezekiel's oracles were pronounced between summer 593 and spring 571. While the first date puts us almost midway between the two waves of deportation (597 and 587) which affected the inhabitants of Jerusalem, the second goes well beyond the ruin of Jerusalem (which took place in 587) and relates to the experience of deportation to Babylon by a complete generation. For this reason, two major stages can be distinguished in the prophetic ministry of Ezekiel, both before (593–587) and after (587–571) the fall of Jerusalem.

### First stage: before the fall of Jerusalem (593–587)

Although this first stage of the prophetic ministry of Ezekiel lasted only six years, no less than half his book (chs.1–24) is devoted to the oracles of this period. These are essentially oracles of judgment which denounce the sin of Israel (see chs.6; 16 and 23) and announce in unequivocal terms the imminent and definitive fall of Jerusalem (see first ch.7, which is commented on below, and the symbolic actions of the prophet in chs.4; 5 and 12). There is no appeal against the divine judgment, and it leaves no possibility of intercession on the part of the prophet: 'Thus shall my anger spend itself, and I will vent my fury upon them and satisfy myself; and they shall know that I, the Lord, have spoken in my jealousy, when I spend my fury upon them' (5.13).

The judgment is implacable, but the situation is not as desperate as was thought. If there is a glimmer of hope, it is due to the very presence of Ezekiel among the exiles. For this is what makes Ezekiel so original: he is speaking from the very heart of the exile, as one who has been deported: 'among the exiles by the river Chebar' (1.1). Unlike Jeremiah, he himself experienced deportation to Babylon, being taken far away from Jerusalem and its temple. However, God continues to speak to him and to speak to his people. The challenge to Ezekiel during this period was to help the exiles and to struggle against despair. He already did this by giving them the assurance that the Glory of the Lord, far from being bound to physical places, however venerable, is a dynamic presence, which comes to meet and guide God's people in foreign lands, at the very heart of exile and suffering.

### Second stage: after the fall of Jerusalem (587–571)

The transition to the second stage of Ezekiel's prophetic ministry is presented in a gripping way by the announcement of the imminent death of the prophet's wife: 'Son of man, behold, I am about to take the delight of your eyes away from you at a stroke; yet you shall not mourn or weep . . .' (24.16–17). Events were soon to confirm this announcement, since Ezekiel's wife died the same evening. The next day Ezekiel did as the Lord had prescribed and abstained from any funeral rites (24.18). Summoned to explain himself to his neighbours, he announced the imminent fall of Jerusalem, which would come so brutally to spoil the joy of its inhabitants: 'Thus says the Lord God: Behold, I will profane my sanctuary, the pride of your power, the delight of your eyes, and the desire of your soul; and your sons and your daughters whom you left behind shall fall by the sword. And you shall do as I have done; you shall not cover your lips, nor eat the bread of mourners. Your turbans shall be on your heads and your shoes on your feet; you shall not mourn or weep, but you shall pine away in your iniquities and groan to one another' (24.21–23).

Can these bones live? (Ezek. 37.3)

The shock will be terrible, but the fall of Jerusalem will also mark the beginning of a new prophetic activity on the part of Ezekiel: 'On that day a fugitive will come to you to report to you the news. On that day your mouth will be opened to the fugitive, and you shall speak and be no longer dumb. So you will be a sign to them; and they will know that I am the Lord' (24.26–27). The prophet's mission will now be to revive hope in his people, by presenting the future that God means to construct for it: God will be the shepherd of his people (ch.34), to whom he will give 'a new heart and . . . a new spirit' (36.26), and whose dry bones he will raise (ch.37). He will then establish his new dwelling, more perfect than the old (the destroyed temple), and will create a new land, with no lurking dangers and only blessings (chs.43–48).

## From judgment to salvation: the general arrangement of the book

As I have already remarked, the architecture of the book and the individual visions is complex. Nevertheless, the general structure of the book stands out quite clearly, and corresponds to a scheme well known in the prophets. After the three introductory chapters (reporting the vision of the Glory, from which stems the account of the prophet's calling and mission) we find a series of oracles of judgment, directed first against Israel and Judah (chs.4–24) and then against the neighbouring nations (chs.25–32). Then, to conclude the book, come the oracles of salvation with the promise of the restoration of Jerusalem and the people (chs.33–48).

## A man and his paradoxes

With Ezekiel, we get the impression that everything is taken to an extreme, and at the same time that everything is on the move. His text makes us aware of such a complex personality and theology that he seems paradoxical. Opposites meet in him in a tension which becomes magnificently creative. Thus we find in him the priest and the prophet, the fantastic visionary and the man of action, the peerless communicator (with his parables and allegories) and the controversialist, the man resolutely turned towards the future and the prophet always concerned about the present.

## Priest *and* prophet

First of all Ezekiel is presented as belonging to a priestly family; he is 'son of the priest Buzi' (1.3). So it is not surprising that we find a liberal use of liturgical language. Ezekiel shows a remarkable knowledge of the physical geography of the temple, the rituals which take place there, and the calendar of celebrations (see especially chs.40–48). That he belongs to a priestly family is also clear from his concern, clearly expressed, to separate the sacred from the profane (45.1–6; 48.9–14), and the expression of his horror at legal impurities (4.14; 44.17). Finally, his preoccupations with morality and questions of retribution (ch.8) fit in well with the function of the priests who are responsible for the instruction of the faithful.

We have already seen, mainly with Amos, but also with Hosea, Isaiah and Jeremiah, how the prophets reacted vigorously against a certain form of worship and against careless and depraved ministers. Now we have someone who prophesies from the very heart of the priestly milieu. While Ezekiel is a priest, he is nevertheless able to keep all the freedom of the prophet. He knows and respects the temple, but he dares to announce to his exiled brothers and sisters that the Glory of God is not tied to Jerusalem and its temple.

Ezekiel has all the characteristics of the prophet: the irresistible character of his vocation and mission, the power of his visions and symbolic actions, his moral radicalism and calls for conversion, and finally the great freedom which comes to him from hearing the Word and the Spirit. And like his predecessors, his last word is not one of condemnation, but of encouragement and hope.

## Visionary *and* man of action

The fantastic character and what one might almost call the geometrical precision of his visions make Ezekiel very much the speculator, the visionary capable of abstractions and great constructions: we have only to think here of the intricate descriptions of the Glory (chs 1; 10; 43), the great vision of the dry bones (ch.37) and the detailed description of the measuring of the temple (chs.40–48). If here our attention is drawn to see the impetuous use of an inexhaustible imagination, at the same time we are seduced by the regularity, the symmetry and the precision of forms, in which everything seems to have been calculated precisely and proportioned down to the slightest detail.

At the same time we are struck by the visual and concrete aspect of these visions, and by the precision of the details, which betray the man of action, always in contact with everyday life. Ezekiel could present symbolic actions which the people around him were to be able to interpret, like, for example, depicting a city under siege, lying on his left side, preparing a loaf of unclean bread, shaving with a sword (chs.4; 5), or even preparing a bundle of clothes with which to go into exile (ch.12).

---

## The Prophet, This Son of Man

One cannot read the book of Ezekiel without noting the title 'son of man' given to the prophet, always by Yahweh. This expression, which we meet ninety-three times in Ezekiel, would seem to have been coined by him, unless Ps.8.4 indicates otherwise. But whether the formula is an old one or a new one, the frequency and systematic character of its use in Ezekiel invites us to seek its meaning and intent in the prophet himself.

All interpreters agree on one point: the formula emphasizes the *humanity* of the prophet, the fact that he shares in the human condition. There is something very splendid about this: by virtue of his very humanity, on the basis of his human experiences, Ezekiel is called on to prophesy. At the same time we can see here a universalistic openness: his prophecy has human resonances which go beyond the frontiers of Jerusalem and Judah and can combine with all those who participate in the same humanity.

By contrast, by far the majority of commentators have been fond of emphasizing that the expression represents the distance between the Lord of Glory and the prophet, because of the context in which the formula appears – above all in the first instances – and then in the story of his initial call (chs 1–3). The distance is real in the eyes of the prophet, but in the book of Ezekiel the title 'son of man' which he is given never has the negative connotation of smallness or weakness which might be associated with the human condition, as opposed to the greatness or power of the divine glory. On the contrary, the expression, always used in a context of revelation and mission, reveals a particular nobility, so that the title 'son of man' is truly one of the finest titles that can be given to Ezekiel.

This is so for two reasons. First of all because for Ezekiel this title always signifies his dignity before God and the importance of his collaboration in the prophetic work: it is as 'son of man' that he is invited to stand upright (2.1), not to fear (1.6), to prophesy (11.4), and that he is sent (1.3) and called on to perform various missions (attested by the numerous imperatives connected with the use of the expression 'son of man').

On the other hand, even if for Ezekiel the mystery of God remains impenetrable, it has links with human realities. In fact the four living creatures which accompany the glory of God have a human appearance (1.5), with human hands (1.8) and a human face (1.10). Furthermore, it is only the glory itself which does not have a human appearance (1.26). Ezekiel never denied that there is a difference between the human being and God. But far from emphasizing this distance in his work, the expression 'son of man' invites us rather to see the respect that God has for his prophet and the importance that he attaches to his collaboration.

## A misunderstood communicator

Ezekiel presents parables and allegories one after the other; he succeeds in giving them a particularly dramatic twist and through them manages to present a most profound theology. We have to be deeply impressed and touched by the allegory of the two eagles (chs.17; 19) aimed particularly at Nebuchadnezzar and the Pharaoh; or that of the great cedar, also directed against the Pharaoh (ch.31); by the highly personalized story of the guilty loves of Jerusalem–Judah and Israel (chs.16; 23); by the parable of the blighted marriage, a symbol of Jerusalem, the 'bloody city' (ch.24); and finally by the very fine image of God the shepherd of Israel (34.1–16) which will later be taken up by Jesus (John 10).

However, despite such a demonstration of skill in the art of storytelling and doing theology in images, Ezekiel constantly meets with popular incomprehension. Certainly, he had been warned: 'And you, son of man, be not afraid of them, nor be afraid of their words, though briers and thorns are with you and you sit upon scorpions; be not afraid of their words, nor be dismayed at their looks, for they are a rebellious house. And you shall speak my words to them, whether they hear or refuse to hear; for they are a rebellious house' (2.6–7). So he knew that his work would never be easy; it would certainly not be successful from the start. But he would not have put so much effort into communicating had he not had the hope of finding at least one sympathetic ear for what he was saying and of provoking some change.

Now it seems that people were disconcerted rather than won over by Ezekiel's images and symbolic actions. They never stopped asking questions: 'What are you doing?' (12.9); 'Will you not tell us what these things mean for us, that you are acting thus?' (24.19); 'Will you not show us what you mean by these?' (37.18). Fine though they may be for us now, we have to say that for Ezekiel's contemporaries, his images were enigmatic (17.2, 12). Mockingly, the people around him called him the 'maker of allegories' (20.49).

## Visionary of the future and lover of the present

Ezekiel is established as a 'watchman for the house of Israel' (3.17; 33) whom he must serve as a 'sign' (chs.12; 24). In this capacity he must 'direct his gaze' towards the future (6.2; 21.1; 25.1; 29.2). The whole of the last section of the book of Ezekiel (chs.36–48) is specifically devoted to a description of the future which God is reserving for his people: the gathering together and purification of the house of Israel (ch.36); the gift of new breath and resurrection for the dry bones (ch.37); the supreme manifestation of the glory and holiness of God in the confrontation with Gog (ch.39; 40); the building of a new temple and the creation of a new earth (chs.40–48).

These are grandiose visions, which some, including Ezekiel's contemporaries, could describe as utopian: 'The vision that he sees is for many days hence, and he prophesies of times far off' (12.27). But the prophet is not making gratuitous speculations, unconnected with the life of his contemporaries. True 'watchman' that he is, he shakes the inertia of the house of Israel and calls on it to take seriously the demands of the word of God for today: 'Thus says the Lord God: None of my words will be delayed any longer, but the word which I speak will be performed, says the Lord God' (12.27).

As with the other prophets studied so far, I have chosen just three texts to serve as an introduction to the book of Ezekiel. It need hardly be said that the choice was not easy. The visions of Ezekiel seem so closely interconnected that one hesitates to separate them, and each of them could claim to be typical of the prophet's teaching.

Two texts come from the first main section of the book: the first is an oracle of judgment addressed to Israel, whom the prophet leaves in no illusions about its imminent end; the second details at length the priest-prophet's argument about the responsibility of individuals before God. Finally, the third text comes from the last section and presents itself as an oracle of salvation, announcing the restoration of Israel as a nation.

# II. Three texts for understanding Ezekiel

## 1. The end has come

(Ezek. 7)

1 *The word of the Lord came to me:* [2] *'Listen, O son of man, thus says the Lord God to the land of Israel: An end! The end has come upon the four corners of the land.* [3] *Now the end is upon you, and I will let loose my anger upon you, and will judge you according to your ways; and I will punish you for all your abominations.* [4] *And my eye will not spare you, nor will I have pity; but I will punish you for your ways, while your abominations are in your midst. Then you will know that I am the Lord.*

5 *Thus says the Lord God: An unprecedented disaster! Behold, it comes.* [6] *An end has come, the end has come; it has awakened against you. Behold, it comes.* [7] *Your doom has come to you, O inhabitant of the land; the time has come, the day is near, a day of tumult and not of joyful shouting upon the mountains.* [8] *Now I will soon pour out my wrath upon you, and spend my anger against you, and judge you according to your ways; and I will punish you for all your abominations.* [9] *And my eye will not spare, nor will I have pity; I will punish you according to your ways, while your abominations are in your midst. Then you will know that I am the Lord, who smite.*

10 *Behold, the day! Behold, it comes! Your doom has come, injustice has blossomed, pride has budded.* [11] *Violence has grown up into a rod of wickedness; none of them shall remain, nor their abundance, nor their wealth; neither shall there be pre-eminence among them. The time has come, the day draws near.* [12] *Let not the buyer rejoice, nor the seller mourn, for wrath is upon all their multitude.* [13] *For the seller shall not return to what he has sold, even if he lives. For wrath is upon all their multitude; it shall not turn back. Each will live in his iniquity; none will be able to regain strength.*

14 *They will blow the trumpet and make all ready; but none will go to battle, for my wrath is upon all their* multitude. [15] *The sword is without, pestilence and famine are within; he that is in the field will die by the sword; and him that is in the city famine and pestilence will devour.* [16] *And if any survivors escape, they will be on the mountains, like doves of the valleys, all of them moaning, every one over his iniquity.*

17 *All hands are feeble,*
*and all knees weak as water.*

18 *They gird themselves with sackcloth,*
*and horror covers them;*
*shame is upon all faces, and baldness on all their heads.*

19 *They cast their silver into the street,*
*and their gold is like an unclean thing;*
*their silver and gold are not able to deliver them*
*in the day of the wrath of the Lord; they cannot satisfy their hunger*
*or fill their stomachs with it,*
*for it was the stumbling block of their iniquity.*

20 *Their beautiful ornament they used for vainglory,*
*and they made their abominable images and their detestable things of it;*
*therefore I will make it an unclean thing to them.*

21 *And I will give it into the hands of foreigners for a prey,*
*and to the wicked of the earth for a spoil;*
*and they shall profane it.*

22 *I will turn my face from them, that they may profane my precious place;*
*robbers shall enter and profane it,*
*and make a desolation.*

23 *Because the land is full of bloody crimes and the city is full of violence,*
*I will bring the worst of the nations to take possession of their houses;*

24 *I will put an end to their proud might,*
*and their holy places shall be profaned.*

25 *When anguish comes, they will seek peace,*
*but there shall be none.*
26 *Disaster will come upon disaster, rumour follow*
*rumour;*
*they will seek a vision from the prophet,*
*but the law will perish from the priest, and counsel*
*from the elders.*

27 *The king will mourn, the prince be wrapped in*
*despair,*
*and the hands of the people of the land will be*
*palsied by terror.*
*According to their way I will do to them,*
*and according to their own judgments I will judge*
*them;*
*and they shall know that I am the Lord.*

---

## The end has come!

The prophets who preceded Ezekiel, from Amos to Jeremiah, did not fail to evoke the *possible end* of Israel; certainly at the time when Ezekiel speaks this day has already come for the northern kingdom (in 722). But the southern kingdom, with Jerusalem as capital, had survived for more than one hundred years. As the threat was slow in being realized for the inhabitants of Jerusalem, they ended up no longer believing it and thought themselves sheltered from the misfortunes which had struck the other kingdom.

With this new oracle of Ezekiel's we are no longer talking only of a hypothesis but of something which is already well on the way to realization: a first wave of deportation has already taken place, and the second is on the horizon. Soon, very soon, Jerusalem will be burned and ruined. The delays and excuses for the people of Jerusalem will be at an end.

Note in this text the numerous allusions to the end, as if to emphasize the urgent character of the situation: 'The end has come upon the four corners of the land' (v.2); 'An end has come, the end has come; it has awakened against you. Behold, it comes' (v.6); 'Behold, the day! Behold, it comes! Your doom has come . . . there is no more respite for them . . .' (vv.10–11). Ezekiel rightly speaks of awakening; his contemporaries have not seen the catastrophe coming and the awakening will be all the more brutal for them.

This situation, unprecedented in the national history of Israel ('An unprecedented disaster', v.5), explains the radical character of the judgment passed by the prophet on his contemporaries. Ezekiel has no time to take pity on their fate. His phrases are brief and breathless, as if to confront the inhabitants of Jerusalem better with the harsh reality which is coming and to arouse them better from their torpor.

## The end of the world?

The emphasis of the prophet Ezekiel on the end and the success of his visions among authors of apocalypses have led to his being classed among the prophets of the end of the world. The allusion in the passage studied here to the infernal trio of war (the sword), famine and pestilence (v.15) can easily be invoked to confirm such a classification. In fact the Jewish and Christian apocalypses will not fail to associate this trio of calamities with their own scenario of the end of the world. Furthermore, it would be difficult to find a better summary of the events of the end than that made by Ezekiel at the conclusion of the oracle in ch.7:

'When anguish comes, they will seek peace,
but there shall be none.
Disaster will come upon disaster, rumour follow
rumour' (vv.25f.).

The subsequent apocalypses will detail *ad infinitum* the sequence of disasters and bad news which will mark the events of the end. But with this vision of Ezekiel's the essentials have already been stated.

However, we would be wrong to 'reify' and absolutize this vision, as if in fact the prophet were explicitly talking of a total and universal end of the

102

terrestrial universe. We must not forget that he is speaking for his time. He is also speaking for his country, and what he says has nothing to do with generalized considerations about the future of the planet earth. The end which he announces is the end for the country, for 'the land of Israel'. This is a national history, localized in time and space: 'Now the end is upon you, the end has come; it has awakened against you' (vv.3,6). In other words, for Ezekiel, as also without doubt for many other apocalyptists, it is more correct to talk of the end of a world than of the end of the world in general. This is what also follows from vv.26–27, which undeniably gives a local, strictly Judaean, colour to the events of the end:

> They will seek a vision from the prophet,
> but the law will perish from the priest, and counsel from the elders.
> The king will mourn, the prince be wrapped in despair . . .

For the inhabitants of Jerusalem this is certainly the end of a world, or one might say the end of an era, since, as the prophet remarks, the major institutions of Israel, both spiritual and political, will be completely paralysed.

### A just return of things

Ezekiel is not content to announce the end to the inhabitants of Jerusalem and Judah. He presses his reflection further and asks about the causes which have made it inescapable.

In a first stage, God himself is held responsible for the formidable events which are about to take place: 'Now I will soon pour out my wrath upon you, and spend my anger against you . . . and my eye will not spare, nor will I have pity' (vv.8–9; cf. also vv.3–4). Further on, Ezekiel takes up statements already made by Jeremiah (cf. Jer.42.18; 44.6). But here too Ezekiel's statements are more radical: according to him, the wrath of God is at its peak, and his mercy is as it were suspended.

To this theological reading of events, however, Ezekiel hastens to add a critical reading of the conduct of the inhabitants of Jerusalem and Judah. There is no capricious humour about the wrath of God or his fury. They express God's just reaction to Israel's conduct: 'I will judge you according to your conduct . . .' (v.3; cf. also vv.9, 27). The judgment is severe but fully merited, since Israel has committed 'abominations' (vv.3–4, 8–9). The word, which has cultic connotations, also serves in Ezekiel to describe any form of injustice (cf. ch.22, where the different forms of abomination with which Israel is charged include murder, theft, sexual abuse, exclusion of the foreigner, exploitation of the poor and unfortunate, and so on). Israel is thus in process of reaping the violence which it has itself sown (vv.11, 23).

Is everything lost? The few allusions to penitential practices or religious activities (vv.18, 26–27) give hardly any glimpse of hope of a sincere and lasting conversion on the part of Israel. But all the same, some hope remains, marked by the repetition of the formula 'then you will know (or they will know) that I am the Lord' (vv., 4, 9, 27). The ultimate aim of God's judgment, implacable though it may be, is not to annihilate Israel but to lead it to recognize its God. It is at the price of confrontation with the just judgment of God that Israel will finally be able to know who its God is, and it is from this recognition that God will be able to recreate his people and invent a radically new future for them.

## 2. Living by one's choices
### (Ezek.18)

*1 The word of the Lord came to me again: ²'What do you mean by repeating this proverb concerning the land of Israel, "The fathers have eaten sour grapes, and the children's teeth are set on edge?" ³As I live, says the Lord God, this proverb shall no more be used by you in Israel. ⁴Behold, all souls are mine; the soul of the father as well as the soul of the son is mine: the soul that sins shall die.'*

5 'If a man is righteous and does what is lawful and right – ⁶if he does not eat upon the mountains or lift up his eyes to the idols of the house of Israel, does not defile his neighbour's wife or approach a woman in her time of impurity, ⁷does not oppress any one, but restores to the debtor his pledge, commits no robbery, gives his bread to the hungry and covers the naked with a garment, ⁸does not lend at interest or take any increase, withholds his hand from iniquity, executes true justice between man and man, ⁹walks in my statutes, and is careful to observe my ordinances – he is righteous, he shall surely live, says the Lord God.

10 'But if he begets a son who is a robber, a shedder of blood, who does none of these duties, ¹¹but eats upon the mountains, defiles his neighbour's wife, ¹²oppresses the poor and needy, commits robbery, does not restore the pledge, lifts up his eyes to the idols, commits abomination, lends at interest, ¹³and takes increase; shall he then live? He shall not live. He has done all these abominable things; he shall surely die; his blood shall be upon himself.

14 But if this man begets a son who sees all the sins which his father has done, and does not do likewise, ¹⁵who does not eat upon the mountains or lift up his eyes to the idols of the house of Israel, does not defile his neighbour's wife, ¹⁶does not wrong anyone, exacts no pledge, commits no robbery, but gives his bread to the hungry and covers the naked with a garment, ¹⁷withholds his hand from iniquity, takes no interest or increase, observes my ordinances, and walks in my statutes; he shall not die for his father's iniquity; he shall surely live. ¹⁸As for his father, because he practised extortion, robbed his brother, and did what is not good among his people, behold, he shall die for his iniquity.

19 Yet you say, "Why should not the son suffer for the iniquity of the father?" When the son has done what is lawful and right, and has been careful to observe all my statutes, he shall surely live. ²⁰The soul that sins shall die. The son shall not suffer for the iniquity of the father, nor the father suffer for the iniquity of the son; the righteousness of the righteous shall be upon himself, and the wickedness or the wicked shall be upon himself.

21 But if a wicked man turns away from all his sins which he has committed and keeps all my statues and does what is lawful and right, he shall surely live; he shall not die. ²²None of the transgressions which he has committed shall be remembered against him; for the righteousness which he has done he shall live. ²³Have I any pleasure in the death of the wicked, says the Lord God, and not rather that he should turn from his way and live? ²⁴But when a righteous man turns away from his righteousness and commits iniquity and does the same abominable things that the wicked man does, shall he live? None of the righteous deeds which he has done shall be remembered; for the treachery of which he is guilty and the sin he has committed, he shall die.

25 Yet you say, "The way of the Lord is not just." Hear now, O house of Israel: Is my way not just? Is it not your ways that are not just? ²⁶When a righteous man turns away from his righteousness and commits iniquity, he shall die for it; of the iniquity which he has committed he shall die. ²⁷Again, when a wicked man turns away from the wickedness he has committed and does what is lawful and right, he shall save his life. ²⁸Because he considered and turned away from all the transgressions which he had committed, he shall surely live, he shall not die. ²⁹Yet the house of Israel says, "The way of the Lord is not just." O house of Israel, are my ways not just? Is it not your ways that are not just?'

30 Therefore I will judge you, O house of Israel, every one according to his ways, says the Lord God. Repent and turn from all your transgressions, and the obstacle which makes you sin will no longer exist. ³¹Cast away from you all the transgressions which you have committed against me, and get yourselves a new heart and a new spirit! ³²Why will you die, O house of Israel? For I have no pleasure in the death of any one, says the Lord God; so turn, and live.'

This is one of the most famous texts in Ezekiel, which has earned him the title of champion of individual freedoms and responsibilities among the Old Testament authors. Jeremiah had already set down the first markers (Jer.31.29–30); Ezekiel pursues his reflection and pushes it to radical conclusions. If we are to understand the novelty of Ezekiel's teaching, we must first recall the current theory which he meant to refute.

## A tenacious theory

Ezekiel attacks bluntly, by taking up a popular saying which expresses a theory well rooted in the mentality of Israel: 'What do you mean by repeating this proverb concerning the land of Israel, "The fathers have eaten sour grapes, and the children's teeth are set on edge?"' (v.2). The saying, already quoted by Jeremiah (31.29), translates the impatience and the sense of injustice among the Judaeans in exile, who have the impression of having to pay for the faults of previous generations.

However, the saying has deeper roots and rests on a twofold conviction on the part of Israel. By all accounts there was first of all the conviction of a national solidarity in all things. The collective destiny comes before the individual destiny. There is solidarity in both good and evil. Certainly, in the Bible individuals may be set apart, but their actions can never be dissociated from the collective destiny of Israel. Beyond doubt this has its admirable side, but it also leads to impasses, like connecting the destiny of generations with the faults of the past. The theory is an old one, indeed more than venerable, since it is connected with the revelation on Sinai:

> The Lord passed before him, and proclaimed, 'The Lord, the Lord, a God merciful and gracious, slow to anger, and abounding in steadfast love and faithfulness, keeping steadfast love for thousands, forgiving iniquity and transgression and sin, but who will by no means clear the guilty, visiting the iniquity of the fathers upon the children and the children's children, to the third and the fourth generation' (Ex.34.6–8).

The saying quoted by Ezekiel therefore has solid support in the theological tradition of Israel. Furthermore, this saying reflects another conviction, which one might call the theory of retribution. In the Israelite mentality, good moral conduct should lead to a happy moral outcome, while conversely, bad moral action must necessarily lead to misfortune. Some biblical proverbs will be enough to illustrate this theory of retribution, which can be found throughout the Bible from Genesis to the Apocalypse:

> He who walks in integrity walks securely,
> but he who perverts his ways will be found out (Prov.10.9).

> The fear of the Lord prolongs life,
> but the years of the wicked will be short (Prov.10.27).

> A wicked man earns deceptive wages,
> but one who sows righteousness gets a sure reward (Prov.11.18).

So deeply rooted in the mentality of the biblical authors is the idea of retribution, i.e. of a God who rewards or punishes depending on whether one acts well or badly, that one could continue the quotations indefinitely. In this context, when a misfortune takes place, one looks for a guilty person: there must have been a fault somewhere. That is the whole problem, in particular, in the book of Job, in which the hero has to debate with all his might against the theory of his friends, who try to explain or justify his sufferings by referring to the theory of retribution.

This, then, is the set of problems which leads to Ezekiel's comments. If his argument is so closely woven, not to say casuistic, it is because the theory is so deeply held by his audience (vv.2, 19, 25, 29), and he will have to work hard to lead them to adopt a new vision of things.

## To each according to his acts!

Ezekiel does not beat about the bush. Systematically, and with an impregnable logic, he refutes the theory held by his hearers. He does this in two stages, first by attacking the specific problem of a transgression having consequences from one generation to another (vv.1–20), and then by broadening what he says to speak of the 'evil person' and the 'righteous person' in general (vv.21–32). However, Ezekiel's position is the same in the two panels of his discourse, and for this reason marks the transition between the two (v.20):

> The soul that sins shall die. The son shall not suffer for the iniquity of the father, nor the father suffer for the iniquity of the son; the righteousness of the righteous shall be upon himself, and the wickedness of the wicked shall be upon himself.

The principle is clear: each individual must be responsible for his acts. To arrive at this statement, Ezekiel imagines two opposed scenarios. Take the case of a righteous father who has a 'son who is a robber' (vv.5–10) and that of a father who does injustice but whose son turns from the sins committed by his father (vv.14–18). In neither case does heredity play any role in the final destiny of the two sons: ' the soul that sins will die', and the one who is righteous 'shall certainly live' . . . There is no question of bearing 'the sin of the father' any more than of being saved by the justice of the father.

## A liberating speech . . .

This is a clearly liberating speech which gives responsibility to each individual and endorses each of the choices which that individual makes. The good news in this text is twofold. First, everyone is free and the exercise of his freedom counts for something. The second good news relates to God: if God gives freedom to human beings, this is not to trap them, but to give them access to life: 'For I have no pleasure in the death of any one, says the Lord God; so turn, and live' (v.32). Each person is free to choose, but life and only life interests God.

Salvation, which is presented here in terms of 'life', cannot be lived without the demands of justice. What justice is this? Beyond question one could call it legalistic, if one simply noted that it takes up the prescriptions of the Decalogue (Ex.20), the Book of the Covenant (Ex.20–24) and the Holiness Code (Lev.17–26). But we should also note in the purest prophetic tradition the importance of social duties (respect for the poor and the good of others, help for the starving and the impoverished, etc.). Salvation necessarily involves the doing of justice and attention to the poor. So there is no question of a salvation which is purely spiritual and detached from every-day commitment.

## . . . which is also formidable

Admirable and innovative though it is, Ezekiel's position does not resolve all the problems. First, for those who hold the theory which he tries to refute, we may say that the problem is only half solved. Though the prophet has demonstrated well the liberation of generations from each other in both justice and injustice, he maintains the theory of retribution in all its rigour: injustice can only lead to death and justice to life. That may well be the case, but is the opposite true? Do we have to infer injustice every time that we encounter death? And justice every time we are in the presence of life? Despite its nobility, Ezekiel's position does not settle everything, as is also witnessed by the book of Job, the final redaction of which is certainly later than that of Ezekiel.

There is also a danger of wanting to account for everything: if we keep strictly to the chronological scheme presented by the prophet, it would seem that injustice at the last moment could efface a whole life of justice (vv.24–26). Then the question arises: does God judge each person according to his works, or only according to the last choices that he made in his life? Doesn't such a perspective risk engendering fear and paralysing freedom, the freedom which the prophet specifically wants to rehabilitate? Finally, it must be remembered that Ezekiel's position, while representing a significant advance, marks only one stage of revelation; subsequently there will be numerous biblical texts which affirm the gratuitousness of salvation and the

# The Fall of an Angel?

Among the oracles pronounced by Ezekiel against the nations, the most famous after the oracle of Gog and Magog is the one addressed to the prince of Tyre (ch.28). This is not because the history of interpretation is particularly interested in the historic figure of the prince of Tyre, one of the rare political leaders to have dared to resist Nebuchadnezzar, but because of the numerous references in the oracle to the creation myth and what was to become the legend of the fall of the angels. First let's read the most significant part of the chapter in this connection:

11 *Moreover the word of the Lord came to me:*
12 *'Son of man, raise a lamentation over the king of Tyre, and say to him,*
*Thus says the Lord God:*
*You were the signet of perfection,*
*full of wisdom and perfect in beauty.*
13 *You were in Eden, the garden of God;*
*every precious stone was your covering,*
*carnelian, topaz and jasper,*
*chrysolite, beryl and onyx,*
*sapphire, carbuncle and emerald;*
*and wrought in gold were your settings*
*and your engravings.*
*On the day that you were created*
*they were prepared.*
14 *With an anointed guardian cherub I placed you;*
*you were on the holy mountain of God;*
*in the midst of the stones of fire you walked.*
15 *You were blameless in your ways*
*from the day you were created,*
*till iniquity was found in you.*
16 *In the abundance of your trade*
*you were filled with violence, and you sinned.'*

## The myth of origins

The language of creation and the imagery of paradise play an important part in this passage, as in the whole of ch.28. In fact there are numerous features which recall the story of paradise in Gen.2–3.

- the dream of becoming like God (vv.2, 6, 9);
- the importance attached to intelligence and wisdom
in achieving the realization of this dream (vv.3–5, 12–17);
- the explicit mention of the garden of God, Eden (v.13);
- the allusion to 'the day of your creation' (v.13);
- the mention of the cherubim (vv.14, 16);
- the reference to sin and the fall (vv.15, 16–18);
- the announcement of punishment and expulsion (vv.16–19);
- the link between sin and death (vv. 8, 18–19).

## A satanic being?

The mention of the 'glittering cherubim' has led some Christian writers, from the fourth century up to the resurgence of fundamentalist interpretations in recent years, to read this account as that of the fall of angels and to see in it a description of the one whom other texts will call Lucifer.

This is certainly not the perspective of the prophecy. It is a complaint with a historical reference which could not be clearer, since the oracle is addressed to someone who is at one point called 'the prince of Tyre' (v.2) and elsewhere 'the king of Tyre' (v.12). Moreover he is neither the first nor the last to claim to be equal to God; that is a theme which is already touched on in Isa.14, and we shall see it again in the book of Daniel and, much later, in the Apocalypse of John. The whole of the chapter is equally full of allusions to the commercial practices of the famous Phoenician city of Tyre. Certainly the reference back to the primitive account of paradise gives a touch of mythological colour to Ezekiel's complaint, but the myth is there to interpret a historical situation and not vice versa. So we would be ill-advised to rely on such a text to make any kind of statement about an alleged fall of the angels at the beginning of creation.

numerous surprises which God has reserved for its fulfilment (cf. for example the book of Jonah and in the New Testament Jesus' parables of the kingdom). Salvation is much more than a question of retribution and a calculation of proportions: on the part of human beings it calls for a constant commitment to justice, but in the end it always depends on an infinitely generous and merciful Love.

## 3.  The water which heals and restores life
### (Ezek. 47.1–12)

1 *Then he brought me back to the door of the temple; and behold, water was issuing from below the threshold of the temple toward the east (for the temple faced east); and the water was flowing down from below the south end of the threshold of the temple, south of the altar.* *²Then he brought me out by way of the north gate, and led me round the outside to the outer gate, that faces toward the east; and the water was coming out on the south side.*

3 *Going on eastward with a line in his hand, the man measured a thousand cubits, and then led me through the water; and it was ankle-deep.* *⁴Again he measured a thousand, and led me through the water; and it was knee-deep. Again he measured a thousand, and led me through the water; and it was up to the loins.* *⁵Again he measured a thousand, and it was a river that I could not pass through, for the water had risen; it was deep enough to swim in, a torrent impossible to cross.* *⁶And he said to me, 'Son of man, have you seen this?'*

7 *Then he led me back along the bank of the river. As I went back, I saw upon the bank of the river very many trees on the one side and on the other.* *⁸And he said to me, 'This water flows toward the eastern region and goes down into the Arabah; and when it enters the stagnant waters of the sea, the water will become fresh.* *⁹ And wherever the river goes every living creature which swarms will live, and there will be very many fish; for this water goes there that the waters of the sea may become fresh; so everything will live where the river goes.* *¹⁰Fishermen will stand beside the sea; from En-gedi to En-eglaim it will be a place for the spreading of nets; its fish will be of very many kinds, like the fish of the Great Sea.* *¹¹But its swamps and marshes will not become fresh; they are to be left for salt.* *¹²And on the banks, on both sides of the river, there will grow all kinds of trees for food. Their leaves will not wither or their fruit fail, but they will bear fresh fruit every month, because the water from them flows from the sanctuary. Their fruit will be for food, and their leaves for healing.*

The vision reported here by the prophet describes in a gripping way the great newness which God is on the point of bringing about, to change the whole destiny of his people.

### The desert which flowers again

First let us note the geographical orientation of the spring which God shows to his prophet: it comes out of the temple 'towards the east' (v.1). Now as we know, it is east of Jerusalem, just beyond the Mount of Olives, that the desert of Judaea begins, stretching right to the shores of the Dead Sea.

Furthermore, the association of this region with the desert is emphasized: '. . . this water flows toward the eastern region and goes down into the Arabah' (v.7) – the very region which is recognized as desert (Deut.1.1; I Sam.23.24; and above all Isa.35.6).

Now what happens? The spring coming from the temple flows through the region of the Arabah and fertilizes it, to the point of forming a 'torrent which is impossible to cross' (v.6). The desert will no longer be the desert, and 'very many trees' will grow on both sides of the river. The miracle has taken place (cf. again Isa.35.6). Nothing is impossible for God: he makes the desert flower again.

## The Dead Sea regains life!

The revitalization of the desert is only a first stage. The water coming from the temple also revives the Dead Sea (sometimes called the Sea of the Arabah: Deut.3.17; 4.49; Josh.3.16): 'and when it enters the stagnant waters of the sea, the water will become fresh' (v.8). Could one conceive of a finer image for regeneration and salvation than that of a resurrection of the Dead Sea and its surroundings? From now on, 'its fish will be of very many kinds, like the fish of the Great Sea (= the Mediterranean)' (v.10). The biblical authors often use the two seas (the Mediterranean and the Dead Sea) to indicate the western and eastern frontiers of the Promised Land (Num.34.3, 12; Josh.15.2,5; Ps.72.8; Micah 7.12; Amos 8.12). Ezekiel's vision thus refers us back to an idealized image of the Promised Land: the eastern frontier will be comparable with the 'Great Sea' set on the western frontiers of Israel.

## Paradise regained

The account in Genesis 2 spoke of a river which divided into four branches in paradise. On its banks were to be found the tree of life and the tree of the knowledge of good and evil – which was to lead to the fall of the first couple. Though the prophet does not speak here of a division into four branches, the universalism of his vision is no less great than in the account of Genesis: 'so everything will live where the river goes' (v.9). But even more than the universalism, we should note the permanence of the fruit produced by the trees which grow round the river:

And on the banks, on both sides of the river, there will grow all kinds of trees for food. Their leaves will not wither or their fruit fail, but they will bear fresh fruit every month, because the water of the river flows from the sanctuary. Their fruit will be for food, and their leaves for healing (v.12).

There will no longer be any prohibition about eating the fruit, and the trees will no longer be able to inflict death. Their fruit and their leaves will only be a source of blessing, and God will constantly renew them for the life of his people.

---

# III. The God of Ezekiel

## The ineffable Lord of Glory

The tone is set by the first lines of the book: Ezekiel's vocation derives directly from his perception of the mystery of God ('the heavens opened and I had divine visions..', 1.1). The prime object of his visions is not the unfolding of the national history of Israel, present or imminent, but the mystery of God: 'divine visions'.

The vision of the Glory, reported in the first three chapters, admirably underlines the greatness of the mystery of God. God is the Wholly Other whom one can perceive only in an imprecise and distant way behind the screen of 'a stormy wind', 'a great cloud' and 'fire' (v.4). God is the ineffable, and can be spoken of only with approximations: 'And in the midst of the fire, as it were gleaming bronze . . . And from the midst of it came the *likeness* of four living creatures . . . Over the heads of the living creatures there was the *likeness* of a firmament, shining like crystal . . . And above the firmament . . . there was the *likeness* of a throne; and seated above the *likeness* of a throne was a *likeness* as it were of a human form. And I saw as it were gleaming bronze, *like* the *appearance* of fire enclosed round about . . . and downwards I saw as it were the *appearance* of fire, and there was brightness round about him. *Like* the *appearance* of the bow that is in the cloud on the day of rain, so was the *appearance* of the brightness round about. Such was the *appearance* of the *likeness* of the glory of the Lord . . .' (1.4–5, 22, 26–28).

As we saw, the call of the prophet Isaiah was also marked by a vision of the Glory and the Holiness of God. But the difference is immediately obvious. In Isaiah the account remains sober and bare. By contrast, in Ezekiel it is overloaded and bears witness to a more complex experience. In this respect the experience of the prophet Isaiah would seem more transparent, while the God of Ezekiel remains always veiled in a certain mystery.

The prophet will need to produce many parables and symbolic acts to bring out progressively the features of the God whom he has encountered. While in his accounts and oracles we hear of gleaming, fire and brightness, Ezekiel sees God only through a screen or, to use St Paul's language, 'through a mirror'.

## Master of history

For all that, the God of Ezekiel is not detached from human history. On the contrary, he appears as the source of all that happens in the collective history of Israel, as in each of Ezekiel's prophetic experiences.

That for Ezekiel God is master of the history of Israel appears in many ways. First of all from the fact that the vast majority of oracles are uttered in the first person, and attribute directly to God the actions which are to mark the course of history: 'I, even I, am against you; and I will execute judgment . . .' (5.8); 'Behold I, even I, will bring a sword upon you and I will destroy your high places . . .' (6.3); 'Therefore I will deal in wrath . . .' (18.18); 'I will gather you from the peoples, and assemble you out of the countries where you have been scattered . . .' (11.17), etc. Secondly, the great allegories of chs.16 and 23 bring out well God's hold on the history of Israel and Judah, from their origins and through all the phases of their growth. Finally, the 'recognition formula', 'then they (you) will know that I am the Lord', which is typical of Ezekiel – it appears fifty-four times in his book – clearly shows that it is through his interventions in history that God makes himself known.

Ezekiel's prophetic experiences are also attributed to the grasp of God's hand (1.3; 3.14, 22; 33.22; 37.1; 40.1) or his spirit (3.12, 14; 8.3). It is God who directs his prophet and through him seeks to change the destiny of his people.

## The Living One

Ezekiel differs from his predecessors even in his language about God. In his work we note significant absences from the theological vocabulary: the word *hesed* (loving tenderness) so characteristic of the covenant is unknown in him, while the term often associated with it, *rehem* (mercy), is used only once with reference to God (39.25). Finally, the most regular root for denoting salvation (*yashua*) appears only three times in his work (as opposed to twenty times in Jeremiah and fifty-six times in Isa.40–66).

On the other hand, Ezekiel applies the primordial attribute of life to God more often than all the other Old Testament writers put together. For Ezekiel, God is the Living One *par excellence*; no less than fifteen oracles are introduced by the formula 'by my life' (literally, 'I am alive': 14.16, 18, 20, etc.). God is also the one who gives or restores life (cf. the whole of ch.18 and above all the vision of the dry bones in ch.37). Where other prophets refer to God's love and mercy for his people, Ezekiel chooses to refer to the extraordinary power that God has over life: 'And you shall know that I am the Lord, when I open your graves, and raise you from your graves, O my people. And I will put my spirit within you, and you shall live, and I will place you in your own land; then you shall know that I, the Lord, have spoken, and I have done it, says the Lord' (37.13, 14).

## The Shepherd of Israel

Ezekiel is to be credited with having developed the double image of the shepherd and the flock to speak of the relations between God and his people (ch.34). Others had already begun to use this metaphor (Pss.23; 80.2; I Kings 22.17; Jer.10.21), but Ezekiel presses it furthest, thus preparing the way for Jesus' splendid parable (John 10).

Some special features may be emphasized in connection with ch.34. First of all Ezekiel addresses the shepherds of Israel. In so doing he puts himself in the context of the ancient Near East, where the title shepherd was given to the kings. However, unlike neighbouring peoples, Israel never lost sight of the realistic sense of the term, even when it was used for the king (David was a shepherd, and the Song of Songs which probably denotes King Solomon and also speaks of him as a shepherd). However, in Ezekiel the symbolism of the image is directed towards a regular criticism of the political and spiritual leaders of Israel: 'Woe to the shepherds of Israel who have been feeding themselves' (34.2).

Secondly, note here a dynamic tension between the singularity of the election of Israel and the universalism suggested by the last use of the expression 'my flock' in ch.34. Whereas the first fourteen instances of this expression manifestly refer to Israel, the fifteenth and last opens up universal perspectives encompassing all humanity: 'And you are my sheep, the sheep of my pasture, and I am your God, says the Lord God' (34.31). God is not a shepherd only for Israel, but for the whole of humankind.

## A Presence for ever

One of the greatest tragedies for Israel at the time of the exile was the feeling of having been abandoned by God: 'For they say, "The Lord does not see us, the Lord has forsaken the land"' (8.13). In these hours of extreme trial, when the temple is destroyed, the king taken prisoner and the people deported from the holy city and the holy land, God is the great absentee. A psalm from this period well represents the disturbance caused by the feeling of the absence of God: 'Why should the nations say, "Where is their God?"' (Ps.79.10). Will the God of Israel always be absent?

Now Ezekiel's response on this matter could hardly be clearer. God remains present to his people. The Glory, habitually identified with the temple, is now mobile and will go to a foreign land (chs.1–3; 12) to comfort the exiles. From there it will depart in order once again to dwell in the new temple, the true dimensions of which correspond to the people of God, gathered together in its fullness (chs.47–48). From now on God will dwell at the heart of his people:

> While the man was standing beside me, I heard one speaking to me out of the temple; and he said to me, "Son of man, this is the place of my throne and the place of the soles of my feet, where I will dwell in the midst of the people of Israel for ever"' (43.6–7).

The God of Ezekiel is very much this *YHWH Shammah* (48.35), i.e. the God-who-is-there, and who transcends the institutions. It is no longer the temple built in stone or the city built by the kings which are to be the pride of Israel, but the certainty of a presence.

> And the name of the city henceforth shall be *YHWH shammah* – the Lord-is-there (48.35).

We might believe that we could already be hearing Christ's promise to his disciples, 'I will be with you always, even to the end of time' (Matt.28.20), or that of the Creator who makes 'all things new': 'Behold the dwelling place of God is with men. He shall dwell with them' (Rev.21.3).

# 8

# The Prophets of the Return

The prophets who have been discussed so far exercised their ministry from the beginning of the eighth century up to and including the time of the exile. The last two of them, Ezekiel and Jeremiah, experienced the dark hours of the Babylonian invasion and the deportation. Did they survive the exile and continue to exercise their ministry once the shock of the catastrophe had passed? In the case of Jeremiah, we do not really know whether he uttered oracles after the first wave of deportation in 597. Ezekiel certainly experienced the second wave and his ministry was extended over two decades. However, in both cases the ministries of the prophets themselves hardly went beyond the first quarter of the sixth century.

In this chapter we are now going to look at the 'prophets of the return', i.e. those who exercised their ministry immediately after the return from exile, an event which extended over several decades from 538 on. Their interventions and their writings cover a period of just over half a century (from 535 to around 480), from Deutero–Isaiah to Malachi. Different terms are used to denote the prophets of this period: 'post-exilic prophets', 'prophets of the Persian period' or 'prophets of the restoration'. I shall call them 'prophets of the return' here, in view of the specific problems and challenges they had to face in rebuilding a

community which had been decimated, even devastated, and in looking for new religious points of reference.

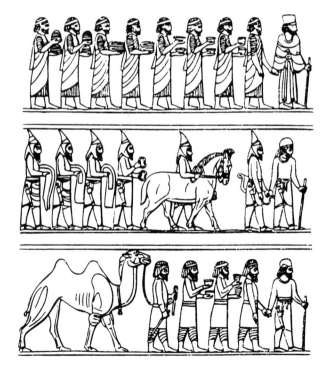

# I. The time of the return: between the dream and the disillusionment

At first sight, the proclamation of the edict of Cyrus in 538 could only be good news for the Jewish exiles who were still detained in Babylon. At last they were going to regain their liberty and saw themselves authorized to return to Jerusalem to rebuild the temple there in its first splendour. The historical situation could not have been more favourable, and would no doubt have pleased a Jeremiah, who complained loudly that he had other things to proclaim than 'ruin and violence'. The hour had struck, it seemed, for resolutely optimistic and enthusiastic prophecies, and that is what came about, at a first stage, with the oracles of Deutero–Isaiah. However, the rejoicing was short-lived. Other prophets were to arise, like Haggai, Zechariah and Malachi, and they would soon 'put the clock back' and remind the community of the demands of a real and profound reconstruction.

## The return celebrated with joy

The Psalmist well expressed the feeling of euphoria which inspired the exiles on the day of their return to Jerusalem: 'When the Lord restored the fortunes of Zion, we were like those who dream. Then our mouth was filled with laughter, and our tongue with shouts of joy . . .' (Ps.126.1–2).

The same enthusiasm is shared, not to say amplified, by the poet, the prophet of the return, who has given us the very fine pages of Isaiah 56–66:

The nations shall see your vindication,
and all the kings your glory;
and you shall be called by a new name
which the mouth of the Lord will give.
You shall be a crown of beauty in the hand of the Lord,
and a royal diadem in the hand of your God.
You shall no more be termed 'Forsaken',
and your land shall no more be termed 'Desolate';
but you shall be called 'My delight is in her',
and your land 'Married';
for the Lord delights in you,
and your land shall be married.
For as a young man marries a virgin,
so shall your sons marry you,
and as the bridegroom rejoices over the bride,
so shall your God rejoice over you.
Upon your walls, O Jerusalem,
I have set watchmen;
all the day and all the night
they shall never be silent . . . (Isa.62.2–6).

From all the evidence, the return was first experienced as one of the great acts of salvation performed by God for his people, comparable to the exodus from Egypt. So it is that Isa.44–45 present a eulogy of Cyrus, the man who decreed the return of the people of Israel: 'I confirm the word of my servant, and perform the counsel of my messengers; I say of Jerusalem, "She shall be inhabited," and of the cities of Judah, "They shall be built, and I will raise up their ruins"' (Isa.44.26).

However, it is to a 'historical book', the book of Ezra, that we must turn to have a more concrete idea of the events which marked the return.

It all began with the edict of Cyrus: 'Thus says Cyrus, king of Persia: "The Lord, the God of heaven, has given me all the kingdoms of the earth, and he has charged me to build him a house at Jerusalem, which is in Judah. Whoever is among you of all his people, may his God be with him, and let him go up to Jerusalem, which is in Judah, and rebuild the house of the Lord, the God of Israel – he is the God who is in Jerusalem; and let each survivor, in whatever place he sojourns, be assisted by the men of his place with silver and gold, with goods and with beasts, besides freewill offerings for the house of God which is in Jerusalem"' (Ezra 1.2–4). The author then gives, in a rapid summary, the reaction of the exiles: 'Then rose up the heads of the fathers' houses of Judah and Benjamin, and the priests and Levites, every one whose spirit God had stirred to go up to rebuild the house of the Lord which is in Jerusalem' (Ezra 1.5). The role of Cyrus is not limited to proclaiming an edict liberating the exiles: he is equally concerned to send back 'the vessels of the house of the Lord which Nebuchadnezzar had carried away from Jerusalem and placed in the house of his god' (1.7), a total of 5,400 objects of gold and silver (1.11).

If we are to believe the figures given by Ezra, the total of those 'who came up out of the captivity of those exiles . . . and who returned to Jerusalem and Judah, each to his own town' (2.1) was 42,360 persons (2.64). On their arrival in Jerusalem, 'Some of the heads of families made freewill offerings for the house of God, to erect it on its site' (1.68).

However, it was not until the 'seventh month' that the people of Israel could finally dream of celebrating with dignity the return from Jerusalem and re-establish the cult, under the direction of Zerubbabel and Joshua (Ezra 3). The rebuilding was done, again according to Ezra, with the utmost emotion and the completest joy:

And when the builders laid the foundations of the temple of the Lord, the priests in their vestments came forward with trumpets, and the Levites, the sons of Asaph, with cymbals, to praise the Lord, according to the directions of David king of Israel; and they sang responsively, praising and giving thanks to the Lord, 'For he is good, for his steadfast love endures for ever toward Israel.' And all the people shouted with a great shout, when they praised the Lord, because the foundation of the house of the Lord was laid. But many of the priests and Levites and heads of fathers' houses, old men who had seen the first house, wept with a loud voice when they saw the foundation of this house being laid, though many shouted aloud for joy; so that the people could not distinguish the sound of the joyful shout from the sound of the people's weeping, for the people shouted with a great shout, and the shout was heard afar (Ezra 3.10–13).

There was rejoicing in Jerusalem, and with good reason, since the people, gathered around the Levites, were again resuming a long tradition of joyful celebrations in the temple precincts.

## The disenchanted return

However, the enterprise of rebuilding was to prove much more arduous than the euphoria of the first moments suggested. In that regard, the prophet Haggai, himself involved in the process of rebuilding, strikes another note than that of the book of Ezra. According to the prophet, his arrival in Jerusalem, far from taking place with enthusiasm, came as more of a shock: the temple was no more than a 'house in ruins' (1.4) and the community remained divided over its reconstruction: 'This people say the time has not yet come to rebuild the house of the Lord' (Hag. 1.2). This was the first great challenge for the prophets of the return: to mobilize people for the rebuilding of the temple. Haggai was the one who was most committed to this cause, with the aid of Zerubbabel, governor of Judah, but he had to press hard to persuade the latter to begin work.

This, the material rebuilding of the temple, was the most obvious problem. Other problems haunted the community, including a disastrous economic situation, the result of a drought which had smitten the land (1.11): 'Consider how you have fared. You have sown much, and harvested little; you eat, but you never have enough; you drink, but you never have your fill; you clothe yourselves, but no one is warm; and he who earns wages earns wages to put them into a bag with holes' (Hag. 1.6). Even in this difficult context, the prophet calls on the people to arise from their torpor, 'Is it a time for you yourselves to dwell in your panelled houses, while this house lies in

The restoration of the temple vessels by Cyrus (Ezra 1.7)

ruins?' (Hag.1.5), and to involve themselves generously in the rebuilding of the temple, which can only be a source of blessing and prosperity (Hag.2.15–19).

Rebuilding the temple was one thing, but it was also necessary to rebuild the community and ease the tensions within different groups. Isaiah 56 clearly refers to such tensions, and according to the prophet salvation can only arrive (Isa.56.1) for the exiles if they open the gates of the rebuilt temple to 'eunuchs' and 'foreigners' (Isa.56.1–8). Only at the cost of a radical conversion will the temple be able to play its true role, which is to be a 'house of prayer for all peoples' (Isa.56.7).

The process of conversion was to be a long one, since almost eighty years later, the scribe Ezra, first so positive in his evaluation of the return, had to deplore in his turn the practices of his people. They had soon allowed themselves to be assimilated to the local populations, either through marriages with foreign women or by the adoption of their idolatrous practices (Ezra 9.1–2). Ezra is quite 'appalled' at this 'faithlessness of the exiles' (Ex.9.3–4) and does not fail to express his shame and his confusion before God: 'O my God, I am ashamed and blush to lift my face to you, my God, for our iniquities have risen higher than our heads, and our guilt has mounted up to the heavens' (Ezra 9.6).

Furthermore, Nehemiah's successive journeys to Jerusalem, around a century after the return, would show that the rebuilding of Jerusalem and its walls had remained a task which had constantly to be repeated. The report which Nehemiah receives from some men 'concerning the Jews that had survived, who had escaped exile, and concerning Jerusalem', was scarcely encouraging: 'The survivors there in the province who escaped exile are in great trouble and shame; the wall of Jerusalem is broken down, and its gates are destroyed by fire' (Neh.1.3). Furthermore, Nehemiah would have occasion to see for himself the extent of the damage on his first journey to the holy city: 'You see the trouble we are in, how Jerusalem lies in ruins with its gates burned. Come, let us rebuild the wall of Jerusalem, that we may no longer suffer disgrace' (Neh.2.17).

In short, the 'return' did not come about magically and instantaneously. It took several generations, and several attempts at restoration, with the intervention of bold and clear-sighted prophets, were needed before the profile of a new community and new theological perspectives could be seen.

# II. Prophets for reconstruction

## The prophets of the return and their writings

So who are these prophets of the return who accompanied and guided the people at the time when everything had to be rebuilt? Among them must certainly be counted Haggai, Zechariah and Malachi, whose writings have been grouped together at the end of the book of the Twelve Prophets. As I said earlier, to these three prophets must be added the disciples of the great prophet Isaiah who have given us chapters 40–55 and 56–66, collections known under the names of Deutero–Isaiah and Trito–Isaiah respectively. There remains the difficult case of Joel, whom commentators date sometimes to the seventh century and sometimes to the fourth. Because of this uncertainty, and also because a dating in the fourth century brings us into a very different context from the first decades which marked the return, we shall not include his book among the group of the prophets of the return. For the same reason, the book of Jonah will be considered separately in the next chapter.

That leaves us with the books of Haggai, Zechariah and Malachi and the last twenty-seven chapters of Isaiah. A brief description of each of these will allow us to put them in their time and indicate their general orientation.

Nehemiah's secret inspection of Jerusalem

## Isaiah 40–66

It is in Isaiah that we find the first – and also the most flamboyant – echoes of the return from exile. His message is addressed to the whole of the first generation of exiles who are returning to Judah. We all know the famous 'Comfort, comfort my people' (40.1) which has been put at the beginning of the collection, and which sums it up admirably. Furthermore, surely we must see the description of the messenger of good news mentioned in 52.7 as a portrait of the author of this work:

> How beautiful upon the mountains
> are the feet of him who brings good tidings,
> who publishes peace, who brings good tidings of good,
> who publishes salvation,
> who says to Zion, 'Your God reigns!'

The author of chs. 40–55 never tires of praising Cyrus (cf.44.28; 45.1), whose famous edict of 538 was to spark off the process of return. There are frequent allusions to Babylon, and these form the framework of an epic which recalls that of the exodus from Egypt. In fact the return from Babylon is presented as a new exodus, even more marvellous than the first:

> Go forth from Babylon, flee from Chaldaea,
> declare this with a shout of joy, proclaim it,
> and send it forth to the end of the earth;
> say, 'The Lord has redeemed his servant Jacob' (48.20).

> Thus says the Lord,
> who makes a way in the sea,
> a path in the mighty waters,
> who brings forth chariot and horse,
> army and warrior . . .
> Remember not the former things,
> nor consider the things of old (43.16–19).

We have to see the last eleven chapters of the book of Isaiah (56–66) as following in the footsteps of the disciple who has given us Deutero–Isaiah.

The author of this collection certainly shares the enthusiasm of his predecessor:

> For Zion's sake I will not keep silent,
> and for Jerusalem's sake I will not rest,
> until her vindication goes forth as brightness,
> and her salvation as a burning torch (62.1).

However, he differs from him in his realistic evaluation of the tensions which are alive within the community, which still hesitates to accept eunuchs and foreigners (56.1–8). The lesson learned in a foreign land has soon been forgotten: the community is turning in on itself and already forgetting that the presence of God is not tied to a place or to a people, even the chosen people.

So the return is not without its problems. The joy and euphoria of the first hours are things of the past, and the community will have to sort out its internal tensions and redefine the expression of its faith. It will be the role of the prophets Haggai, Zechariah and Malachi to support them in this work of reconstruction.

## Haggai

The interventions of the prophet Haggai are easy to date. The five oracles which he pronounced are all set in 'the second year of the king of Darius', in 520, between 'the sixth month, the first day of the month' and 'the twenty-fourth day of the new moon', i.e. over a period of four months. At this time the Persian empire was experiencing a major political crisis, when Darius had to quash a series of internal revolts to support his power. We could see an illusion to this political agitation in the expression 'shake heaven and earth' (2.6–7).

The book of the prophet comprises no more than thirty-eight verses. The prophet is concerned above all to convince the inhabitants of Jerusalem that the time has come to resume the work of rebuilding the temple, which was suddenly interrupted in 537 by the hostility of the Samaritans. The brevity of Haggai's ministry reflects a degree of urgency, since the time when God will re-establish the splendour of Jerusalem and its temple is not far off:

'For thus says the Lord of hosts, Once again, in a little while, I will shake the heavens and the earth and the sea and the dry land; and I will shake all nations, so that the treasures of all nations shall come in, and I will fill this house with splendour, says the Lord of hosts' (2.6–9). According to the chronicler who has given us the final version of the book, the impact of the prophetic word of Haggai was little short of formidable: 'Then Zerubbabel the son of Shealtiel, and Joshua the son of Jehozadak, the high priest, and all the remnant of the people, obeyed the voice of the Lord their God, and the words of Haggai the prophet . . . and they came and worked on the house of the Lord of hosts, their God' (1.12, 14).

## Zechariah

The prophet Zechariah is a contemporary of Haggai, since his first oracle dates from the 'eighth month, the second year of the reign of Darius', November 520. However, only the first eight chapters of his book in fact date from this period, which extends at least to 518 (7.1: 'The fourth year of the reign of Darius . . . the fourth day of the ninth month'). These first eight chapters present visions, aimed essentially at consoling Jerusalem, as is clear from the ending of the first and third of them:

> And the Lord answered gracious and comforting words to the angel who talked with me (1.13).

> For I will be to her a wall of fire round about, says the Lord, and I will be the glory within her (2.9).

Furthermore, the fourth and fifth visions (chs.3 and 4) have a clearly messianic tone and eulogize the high priest Joshua and the governor Zerubbabel, the two architects of the rebuilding of the temple. Then the book ends by recalling the causes of the exile (ch.7) and presenting a series of oracles of salvation (ch.8).

The second part of the book of Zechariah is quite different. We no longer find any precise reference to the rebuilding of the temple, the oracles are more developed and the personality of the prophet fades away completely behind the message. This section is usually referred to as Deutero–Zechariah – in parallel to Deutero–Isaiah – and the date of the book is put in the Greek period, towards 330, around two centuries after the return, in a historical context which is quite different from Zechariah 1–8.

## Malachi

The book of Malachi comes right at the end of the scroll of the Twelve Prophets; its prophetic activity takes place around the 480s. The book is not very long (only three chapters in Hebrew, four in English), but its message remains incisive and striking. The life of the temple has resumed its normal course for some time now, since the prophet can launch out into vigorous criticisms of the offerings brought by the faithful (1, 6–14) and the practice of the priesthood (2.1–9). His criticism of social life is just as fierce (2.10–16). Finally, the preaching contained in ch.3 takes a messianic and eschatological turn, and in Judaism this was to give rise to the expectation of the return of Elijah (3.23–24).

There, in broad outline, are the main witnesses to the return from the exile. Now let us look rather more closely at the main challenges which the prophets of the return were called to meet. Two in particular called for their attention and their creativity.

### To rebuild or not to rebuild the temple?

The rebuilding of the temple was clearly the first task to be undertaken by the exiles who returned to Jerusalem. After all, it was the reason for Cyrus's edict, and the population of Judah could enjoy his financial support. But nothing worked out smoothly. On the one hand, a royal decree was not enough to assure the success of an operation of this kind. It needed the support of the population, and the population was soon caught up in its own economic difficulties (Hag.1.2–6). On the other hand, the question arose in more radical terms, above all in prophetic circles: was it only desirable to rebuild the temple which the prophets of the past had so often criticized, and the practices in which the prophets Jeremiah and Ezekiel had rightly denounced as having directly led to the catastrophe of 587 (Jer.7.1, 15; Ezek.8–9)? Could one forget these deviations so quickly, and be open to lapsing into them again? Certainly Ezekiel had announced the restoration of the temple (Ezek.40–48), but his intention had not been to propose a project of realistic architecture; rather, he had in view an ideal temple, first and foremost based on the complete and entire rebuilding of the people of God.

The option of the prophet Haggai is very clear: the temple must be rebuilt. This is in fact almost the sole substance of what he says to the governors and the whole of the people. He himself is very aware of the difficulties of the project, since he knows the objections of the population (1.2) and the lamentable state of the place (2.3). Hence his general appeal for *courage*: 'Yet now take *courage*, O Zerubbabel, says the Lord; take *courage*, O Joshua, son of Jehozadak, the high priest; take *courage*, all you people of the land, says the Lord; work' (2.4). The prophet Zechariah will also show a great attachment to the temple and will utter encouraging words in favour of rebuilding: 'Thus says the Lord of hosts, "Behold, the man whose name is the Branch: for he shall build the temple of the Lord . . ."' (Zech.6.12).

But as one might expect, the rebuilding of the temple is not an end in itself for these two prophets. Haggai is engaged in polemic with the priests (1.10–14), in the course of which he shows the limits of a holiness based on the cult. For him, as for the prophets before the exile, the true test takes place in life: it is obedience which sanctifies, and not the rite. Now the task of rebuilding the temple is required by God himself, and the fulfilment of this task will prove more a source of blessing than all the ritual practices of the priests around the altar. As for Zechariah, he too engages in a discussion with the 'priests attached to the temple' (ch.7), whom he charges with having distorted the meaning of the fast: 'When you fasted and mourned in the fifth month and in the seventh, for those seventy years, was it for me that you fasted? And when you eat and when you drink, do you not eat for yourselves and drink for yourselves?' (Zech 7.5–6). Zechariah suggests substituting for this egocentric fast 'days of gladness, of rejoicing, of joyous festivities' (Zech 7.19) and above all a life inspired by love of 'truth and peace' (Zech. 7.19). Here we find once more the great demands of social justice characteristic of the classical prophets (see also 7.9–10).

## Is the time of the prophets past?

The prophets Haggai, Zechariah and Malachi had to confront another challenge which was just as important: that of confirming or denying the validity of the prophetic word. In fact they emerged in a period when the credibility of the classic prophets had seriously been put in question and when the question was arising of the status that had to be given to the prophetic word, yesterday and today. Two questions were asked. Does the word of the prophets of yesterday lead to an impasse? And today, in this situation of extreme crisis, is there room for new prophets?

To judge from the witness of Zechariah, the crisis was a real one and its roots went far back into the past:

Be not like your fathers, to whom the former prophets cried out, 'Thus says the Lord of hosts, Return from your evil ways and from your evil deeds.' But they did not hear or heed me, says the Lord. Your fathers, where are they? And the prophets, do they live for ever? But my words and my statutes, which I commanded the prophets, did they not overtake your fathers? So they repented and said, As the Lord of hosts purposed to deal with us for our ways and deeds, so has he dealt with us (Zech.1.4–7).

So this is the basic problem which Zechariah has to tackle before even presenting his own visions: what credit is to be given to the prophetic word? For

The rebuilding of the temple (Ezra 3.12)

him there is no doubt that God has acted in conformity with the word that he made known through 'my servants the prophets'. Their word always remains topical and must be taken seriously.

This is also the sense in which we are to understand the end of the book of Malachi, which claims for the prophet of the return an authority comparable to that of the two great prophetic figures of Moses and Elijah:

> Remember the law of my servant Moses, the statutes and ordinances that I commanded him at Horeb for all Israel. Behold, I will send you Elijah the prophet before the great and terrible day of the Lord comes. And he will turn the hearts of fathers to their children and the hearts of children to their fathers, lest I come and smite the land with a curse (Mal.4.4–6).

The same concern to legitimate the prophetic ministry can be found in Haggai, who is designated no less than five times by the title 'prophet' and once with the title 'messenger of the Lord' (1.13). In him we find a remarkably heightened use of the 'messenger formula' (1.2, 5 ,7, 8; 2.6, 7, 9, 11) and the expression 'thus says the Lord' (twelve times in two chapters), so typical of classical prophecy.

Though they are few, the prophets of the return are aware of standing in the tradition of the classical prophets and continuing their work. In so doing they formally deny the popular feeling which manifested itself after the catastrophe of 597 and the thought that prophecy was totally in eclipse: 'We do not see our signs; there is no longer any prophet, and there is none among us who knows how long' (Ps.74.9).

### The time of re-readings

Even after the exile, the word of the prophets was still very much alive. We would be wrong to believe that the literary production of prophetic circles was limited to the works of the prophets mentioned in this chapter. Quite the contrary. Far from marking the end of prophecy, the exile saw strong literary activity in prophetic circles. It was during the exile and the return that the prophetic books that we have looked at so far (from Amos to Ezekiel) underwent their final redaction, so that we can find in them oracles uttered in the light of events experienced during the exile.

Surprised by the magnitude of the catastrophe, the exiles felt the need to return to the classical prophecies, and it was through them that new prophets arose in the post-exilic community. There is not a prophetic book which does not contain re-readings in the light of the events which marked the end of Israel and Judah. We can judge this from the following extracts, taken from the books of the eighth- and seventh-century prophets, whose message was presented to revive the hope of the exiles from Judah:

> In that day I will raise up
> the booth of David that is fallen
> and repair its breaches,
> and raise up its ruins,
> and rebuild it as in the days of old . . . (Amos 9.11).

> In that day, says the Lord,
> I will assemble the lame
> and gather those who have been driven away,
> and those whom I have afflicted;
> and the lame I will make the remnant;
> and those who were cast off, a strong nation;
> and the Lord will reign over them in Mount Zion
> from this time forth and for evermore.
> And you, O tower of the flock,
> hill of the daughter of Zion,
> to you it shall come,
> the former dominion shall come,
> the kingdom of the daughter of Jerusalem (Micah 4.6–8).

> At that time I will bring you home,
> at the time when I gather you together;
> yes, I will make you renowned and praised
> among the peoples of the earth,
> when I restore your fortunes before your eyes,
> says the Lord (Zeph.3.20).

Even within the first section of Isaiah (1–39), we find chs. 13 and 14 on the fall of Babylon and the restoration of Israel. From all the evidence here we have additions made long after the eighth century, in a late period when Babylon came to the forefront of international politics and exercised a domination from which Israel sought to liberate itself:

> The Lord will have compassion on Jacob and will again choose Israel, and will set them in their own land, and aliens will join them and will cleave to the house of Jacob.
> And the peoples will take them and bring them to their place, and the house of Israel will possess them in the Lord's land as male and female slaves; they will take captive those who were their captors, and rule over those who oppressed them (Isa.14.1–2).

Of course, it is not always easy to determine precisely which texts have been retouched. But it is certain that the drama of the exile in some way forced the exiles to try to understand what was happening to them. The word of prophets like Amos and Isaiah, so hard for its original audience to understand, suddenly served as a beacon in the night. Hence this intense activity of re-reading their oracles which has provided us with new texts, bringing a singular hope.

---

# III.  Decline or renewal of prophecy?

The prophets of the return have suffered, and still suffer, by comparison with their predecessors from before the exile, who are rightly recognized as the 'classic' prophets in Israel. Because they do not have the stature of a Hosea, an Isaiah or a Jeremiah, prophets like Haggai, Zechariah and Malachi have been neglected or judged very severely by researchers. There are relatively few works on this period, and until recently the major syntheses of the Bible have tended to regard the writings of the prophets of the return as being more or less a by-product of the great prophetic literature. In particular the prophets of the return are accused of paying too much attention to the temple and to worship and of being orientated on a more legalistic and less innovative type of Judaism than that of the classical prophets.

So it is not surprising that these prophets have found a more than limited place in the Christian liturgy and have remained little known to the Christian public. The Roman Sunday lectionary contains no passage from either Haggai or Zechariah 1–8, and it offers only a meagre quotation of six and a half verses (!) from Malachi, distributed between two different Sundays of the triennial cycle. By contrast, Deutero–Isaiah is the prophetic book which is most quoted in the same lectionary; however, we cannot presume that it is perceived as dating to the return from exile. Without doubt the name of the great eighth-century prophet alone has gained it this privileged place in the liturgy.

### Actors and witnesses of a new era

However, despite the fact that the prophets of the exile are little known, we can never emphasize the importance of their contribution too much, coming as it does at a turning point of the religious history of Israel. Several factors need to be taken into account if we are to grasp the importance of the changes which took place on the basis of the preaching and writings of the prophets of the return.

- First, the short books of Haggai, Zechariah and Malachi close the book of the Twelve Prophets. If only for this reason, they deserve particular attention. The definitive and canonical form of the Twelve Prophets, the first books of which are none other than the magnificent works of Hosea and Amos, can only be interpreted if we take the last three books into consideration. In other words, there is a literary and beyond question a theological continuity between Hosea and Malachi. This is an aspect which has been too much neglected in the past, and recent research has rightly tended to bring it out as a principle for reading the biblical texts.

- Secondly, we know that the exile marked a turning point, and that the return marks the beginning of a new era which in Jewish circles is called the period of the 'second temple', extending to the year 70 of our era. This was a period of intense literary activity, with the definitive redaction of the Pentateuch, the prophetic books and the Deuteronomic history; it was a time of very deep questions, with the problems tackled in the books of Job and Jonah; and a time of great religious reforms, with Ezra and Nehemiah. How could we ignore those who supported and guided the people in the first hours and the forerunners of these changes?

- Thirdly, with Zechariah, there is a decisive transition towards apocalyptic, which for the most part was to take over from classical prophecy. Should we see a conflict between theocratic and eschatological hopes? The two tendencies are represented in Haggai, Zechariah, Malachi and Deutero–Isaiah, but the debate is far from being settled by their writings. At the very least, we cannot understand the apocalyptic and messianic effervescence of the last two centuries before our era without an in-depth examination of the writings of the prophets of the return.

## Beyond prophecy

Heirs of the classical prophets, the prophets of the return no less mark the transition – and a major transition – to a new era in what was now to become Judaism. Prophecy is not dead, but now revelation will pursue new ways and the biblical writings will develop in another direction. Without in any way denying the prophetic tradition, scribes, wise men and apocalyptists are to take over. The majority of the post-exilic biblical writings derive from wisdom (Job, Koheleth [Ecclesiastes], Song of Songs, some sections of Proverbs, etc.) and the first two centuries before our era were above all to see the flourishing of apocalyptic (Daniel and the non-biblical apocalypses).

Should we deplore this, with nostalgia, like the author of I Maccabees in the second century before our era: 'Thus there was great distress in Israel, such as had not been since the time that prophets ceased to appear among them' (I Macc.8.27); '. . . And the Jews and their priests decided that Simon should be their leader and high priest for ever, until a trustworthy prophet should arise . . .' (I Macc.14.41)? Or should we rejoice to see that there are other ways of speaking of God and of perceiving the relations between faith and the world, faith and history? It would be an insult to the prophets to imprison God and his revelation in a single model and reject other theological approaches. The theology of the prophets is extremely rich and very relevant to the present day. But it does not dispense us, any more than the believers who experienced the return from exile, from inventing our own re-readings and imagining new ways of expressing the presence of God in history.

# 9
# Jonah, or the Prophet 'Despite Himself'

## An invitation to smile

In tackling the prophet Jonah we need to depart from the well-trodden paths. Both the prophet and the author who imagined his story are unconventional characters. It is not every day that one meets a prophet who has made a return journey in a sea monster and who despite all his reticences and subterfuges leads a whole city to repent. And by no means a small city, since this was the famous Assyrian capital of Nineveh, the sworn enemy of Israel . . . We can already foresee that the story that we are going to read will be full of surprises.

There is no better way of getting off the beaten track than to savour the text itself, immediately. All of it. For the four short chapters which make it up are written to be read at a sitting. They are skilfully arranged and will produce the desired effect on the reader only if they are read one after the other.

So good reading, and above all prepare yourself for some surprises and numerous knowing winks, along with some jokes, from the author. Finally, you are forbidden not to laugh!

# Why Jonah?

The book of Jonah is a fiction: it is the fruit of the imagination, the theological openness and the profound faith of a brilliant author whose name remains unknown. But why of all the prophetic figures choose Jonah?

We might try some explanations. In the first place, we need to recognize that while the story itself is fictitious, the person is not. The Bible already knows the existence of a 'prophet Jonah, son of Amittai': 'He (Jeroboam II) restored the border of Israel from the entrance of Hamath as far as the sea of the Arabah, according to the word of the Lord, the God of Israel, which he spoke by his servant Jonah the son of Amittai, the prophet, who was from Gath-hepher' (II Kings 14.25). This was in the eighth century, in almost the same period as the prophet Amos. Now in its very brevity the note in II Kings could explain the choice of the author of the book of Jonah, written some five centuries after the Jonah of history.

The prophet Jonah of the eighth century is thus presented in relation to King Jeroboam II and his expansionist prowess, which Jonah seems not only to have approved but to have declared as being in conformity with the word of God. We have already seen the diametrically opposed judgment which the prophet Amos made on the conquests and the reign of Jeroboam II. This could help us to explain why the author chose Jonah. On the one hand, by choosing a little-known figure, he had great freedom to embroider his person. On the other hand, in Jonah he had an ideal candidate for incarnating an accommodating and restrictive theology which regarded the salvation of Israel as a right and not as a grace, and again, as an exclusive right which would not be extended to the other nations.

A second attempt at an explanation could be put forward on the basis of the meaning of the name Jonah in Hebrew. Jonah in Hebrew means 'dove'. The dove (*yonah*) was the messenger of good news after the flood (Gen.6–8). Now the wickedness of the inhabitants of Nineveh suggests the wickedness that prevailed over the surface of the earth at the time of the flood (Gen.6). Similarly, the delay of forty days announced by Jonah could be understood as a reference to the forty days which marked the duration of the flood (Gen.7.12). Finally, in both stories the conclusion is the same: God 'repents', salvation wins out over the planned misfortune and God proves to be a God of mercy for all.

Thus simply by virtue of his name, Jonah is the bearer of good news. Here again there is a humorous touch. While Jonah resists with all his might, he is destined – but without knowing it and perhaps without wanting it – to bear the good news of salvation for all.

---

## Jonah 1

*Jonah flees the Word of God*

1 Now the word of the Lord came to Jonah the son of Amittai, saying, ²'Arise, go to Nineveh, that great city, and cry against it; for their wickedness has come up before me.' ³Jonah rose, but to flee to Tarshish from the presence of the Lord. He went down to Joppa and found a ship going to Tarshish, so he paid the fare, and went on board, to go with them to Tarshish, away from the presence of the Lord.

4 But the Lord hurled a great wind upon the sea, and there was a mighty tempest on the sea, so that the ship threatened to break up. ⁵Then the mariners were afraid, and each cried to his god; and they threw the wares that were in the ship into the sea, to lighten it for them. ⁶As for Jonah, he had gone down into the inner part of the ship, laid down, and was fast asleep. So the captain came and said to him, 'What do you mean, you sleeper?

↓

126

Arise, call upon your god! Perhaps the god will give a thought to us, that we do not perish.'

7 And they said to one another, 'Come, let us cast lots, that we may know on whose account this evil has come upon us.' So they cast lots, and the lot fell upon Jonah. ⁸Then they said to him, 'Tell us, on whose account this evil has come upon us? What is your mission? Where do you come from? What is your country? And of what people are you?' ⁹And he said to them, 'I am a Hebrew; and I fear the Lord, the God of heaven, who made the sea and the dry land.' ¹⁰Then the men were exceedingly afraid and said to him, 'What is this that you have done!' For the men knew that he was fleeing from the presence of the Lord, because he had told them.

11 Then they said to him, 'What shall we do to you, that the sea may quiet down for us?' For the sea grew more and more tempestuous. ¹²He said to them, 'Take me up and throw me into the sea; then the sea will quiet down for you; for I know it is because of me that this great tempest has come upon you.' ¹³Nevertheless the men rowed hard to bring the ship back to land, but they could not, for the sea grew more and more tempestuous against them. ¹⁴Therefore they cried to the Lord, 'We beseech you, O Lord, let us not perish for this man's life and lay not upon us innocent blood; for you, Lord have done as it pleased you.' ¹⁵So they took up Jonah and threw him into the sea; and the sea ceased from its raging. ¹⁶Then the men feared the Lord exceedingly, and they offered a sacrifice to the Lord and made vows.

# Jonah 2

*Jonah, in the depths of the abyss, prays to the Lord, who saves him*

1 And the Lord appointed a great fish to swallow up Jonah; and Jonah was in the belly of the fish three days and three nights.

2 Then Jonah prayed to the Lord his God from the belly of the fish, saying,

3 'I called to the Lord, out of my distress, and he answered me;
out of the belly of Sheol I cried,
and you heard my voice.

4 For you cast me into the deep,
into the heart of the sea,
and the flood was round about me;
all your waves and your billows passed over me.

5 Then I said, 'I am cast out from your presence;
how shall I again look upon your holy temple?

6 The waters closed in over me,
the deep was round about me;

weeds were wrapped about my head
at the roots of the mountains.

7 I went down to the land
whose bars closed upon me for ever;
yet you brought up my life from the Pit,
O Lord my God.

8 When my soul fainted within me,
I remembered the Lord;
and my prayer came to you,
into your holy temple.

9 Those who pay regard to vain idols
forsake their true loyalty.

10 But I with the voice of thanksgiving
will sacrifice to you;
what I have vowed I will pay.
Deliverance belongs to the Lord!'

11 And the Lord spoke to the fish, and it vomited out Jonah upon the dry land.

# Jonah 3

*Jonah preaches, the Ninevites are converted, and God forgives*

1 Then the word of the Lord came to Jonah the second time, saying, ²'Arise, go to Nineveh, that great city, and proclaim to it the message that I tell you.' ³So Jonah arose and went to Nineveh, according to the word of the Lord. Now Nineveh had become an exceedingly great city, three days journey in breadth. ⁴Jonah began to go into the city, going a day's journey. And he cried, 'Yet forty days, and Nineveh shall be overthrown!' ⁵And the people of Nineveh believed God; they proclaimed a fast, and put on sackcloth, from the greatest of them to the least of them.

6 Then tidings reached the king of Nineveh, and he arose from his throne, removed his robe, and covered himself with sackcloth, and sat in ashes. ⁷And he made proclamation and published through Nineveh, 'By the decree of the king and his nobles: Let neither man nor beast, herd nor flock taste anything; let them not feed, or drink water, ⁸but let man and beast be covered with sackcloth, and let them cry mightily to God; yes, let everyone turn from his evil way and from the violence which is in his hands. ⁹Who knows, God may yet repent and turn from his fierce anger, so that we do not perish.'

10 When God saw what they did, how they turned from their evil way, God repented of the evil which he had said he would do to them; and he did not do it.

# Jonah 4

*Jonah is angry and the Lord explains*

1 But it displeased Jonah exceedingly, and he was angry. ²And he prayed to the Lord and said, 'I pray you Lord, is not this what I said when I was yet in my country? That is why I made haste to flee to Tarshish; for I knew that you are a gracious God and merciful, slow to anger and that you repent of evil. ³Therefore now, O Lord, take my life from me, I beseech you, for it is better for me to die than to live.' ⁴And the Lord said, 'Do you do well to be angry?' ⁵Then Jonah went out of the city and sat to the east of the city and made a booth for himself there. He sat under it in the shade, till he should see what would become of the city.

6 And the Lord God appointed a plant, and made it come up over Jonah, that it might be a shade over his head, to save him from his discomfort. So Jonah was exceedingly glad because of the plant. ⁷But when dawn came up the next day, God appointed a worm which attacked the plant, so that it withered. ⁸When the sun rose, God appointed a sultry east wind, and the sun beat upon the head of Jonah so that he was faint; and he asked that he might die, and said, 'It is better for me to die than to live.' ⁹But God said to Jonah, 'Do you do well to be angry for that plant?' And he said, 'I do well to be angry, angry enough to die.' ¹⁰And the Lord said, 'You pity the plant, for which you did not labour, nor did you make it grow, which came into being in a night, and perished in a night. ¹¹And should not I pity Nineveh, that great city, in which there are more than a hundred and twenty thousand persons who do not know their right hand from their left, and also much cattle?'

Jonah preaches to the people of Nineveh

## A historical account or fiction?

The most important question for the interpretation of the book of Jonah is that of its literary genre. Do we have to understand this account as a 'true story' and take the trouble to discover for example, the type of ship on which Jonah might have embarked, or the kind of sea monster which could have swallowed him up, or historical evidence for the 'conversion' of Nineveh? Or on the contrary, do we have to see this as a story constructed entirely by the author for theological reasons?

Sadly, too often people have stopped at the story of the 'whale', to the detriment of the message.

It must be said straight away that everything in the text points in the direction of fiction. A literary fiction, rather like Aesop's fables, but a fiction which marvellously conveys the theological conceptions of an age and succeeds in presenting from the perspective of caricature and humour a theological message which has a revolutionary aspect.

To grasp the fictitious and imaginary character of the individuals and events, it is enough to re-read a certain number of verses and note everything in them that is 'improbable', or at least strange, unexpected. They can be read in the same way as newspapers and magazines which offer their readers exercises in observation and ask them to spot 'the mistake', i.e. the feature that is out of place. In the case of the book of Jonah, the author is so much a master of telling the humorous story that one could do this with almost every line. Judge for yourself!

| Spot the 'mistake'! | |
|---|---|
| **Text** | **The 'improbabilities' in the account'** |
| Jonah rose, but to flee to Tarshish from the presence of the Lord. He went down to Joppa and found a ship going to Tarshish, so he paid the fare, and went on board, to go with them to Tarshish, away from the presence of the Lord (1.3). | Jonah has just received a mission for the north-east: he immediately leaves for the west and looks for a ship which will take him more to the west and south. 'Flee from the presence of the Lord' is not at all what one would expect from one of his prophets. And in fact can one find anywhere on earth which would escape the 'presence of the Lord'? |
| Then the mariners were afraid, and each cried to his god; and they threw the wares that were in the ship into the sea, to lighten it for them. As for Jonah, he had gone down into the inner part of the ship, laid down, and was fast asleep (1.5). | The sailors, who are pagans, immediately have a reaction of religious fervour, while the prophet, this 'man of God', can find nothing better to do than to sleep. On the one hand there is fervour, and on the other torpor. In telling a story, it is good to exaggerate: all 'the wares that were in the ship' are said to have been thrown into the sea . . . But in that case, how does one explain that the sailors then found the necessary items to cast lots and offer sacrifices . . . and also food for the rest of the voyage? |
| And they said to one another, 'Come, let us cast lots, that we may know on whose account this evil has come upon us.' So they cast lots, and the lot fell upon Jonah (1.7) | Lots are consulted. But the reader already knows that the dice are loaded and that Jonah will be found responsible. Surely that's obvious? ↓ |

| | |
|---|---|
| Therefore they cried to the Lord, 'We beseech you, O Lord, let us not perish for this man's life and lay not upon us innocent blood; for you, Lord, have done as it pleased you.' So they took up Jonah and threw him into the sea; and the sea ceased from its raging. Then the men feared the Lord exceedingly, and they offered a sacrifice to the Lord and made vows (1.14–16). | Though the sailors were pagans at the beginning of the voyage, now they have become fervent Yahwists. They also show a moral sense that the prophet himself would have done well to adopt, and make a real profession of faith in the sovereign freedom of the Lord.<br><br>The sea also connives: it is enough for Jonah to be thrown overboard for calm to return. That is real magic!<br><br>The whole world is saved . . . except the prophet, whose misadventures are far from being at an end. |
| And the Lord spoke to the fish, and it vomited out Jonah upon the dry land (2.11). | Another impressive magic trick. Jonah was somewhere in the Mediterranean, and the fish vomited him up on dry land, probably in the region of Nineveh . . . It must have had quite some breath! |
| Jonah began to go into the city, going a day's journey. And he cried, 'Yet forty days, and Nineveh shall be overthrown!' And the people of Nineveh believed God; they proclaimed a fast, and put on sackcloth, the greatest of them to the least of them (3.4–5). | The author has just said that crossing Nineveh is a three days' walk, and Jonah does the trip in less than a day. Either he was very quick, or he had transport: this is not enthusiasm, far less perfectionism!<br><br>The sudden (already) and unanimous (from the great to the small) conversion of the people of Nineveh is completely overwhelming, all the more so since Jonah has only spoken five words (in Hebrew). Furthermore, his message is enigmatic in the extreme, and contains no call to conversion. And that is not to take into account the linguistic problem: in what language could Jonah have made himself understood . . .? A mystery! |
| And he (the king of Nineveh) made proclamation and published through Nineveh, 'By the decree of the king and his nobles: Let neither man nor beast, herd nor flock taste anything; let them not feed, or drink water, but let man and beast be covered with sackcloth, and let them cry mightily to God; yes, let everyone turn from his evil way and from the violence which is in his hands' (3.7–8). | It is the king rather than the prophet who begins to reflect on the divine action (cf. also v.9) and immediately decrees what measures are to be taken to obtain God's forgiveness. The author adds more: now even the animals (herd and flock) are ordered to fast, to be covered with sackcloth and call 'mightily' on God. Here is something unprecedented in the history of Israel. |
| 'And should not I pity Nineveh, that great city, in which there are more than a hundred and twenty thousand persons who do not know their right hand from their left, and also much cattle?' (4, 11). | The figure of 120,000 for the population of Nineveh would seem exaggerated, and would be quickly disproved by archaeology if it had to be taken literally. Unless it was about something else, and the figure had a symbolic value . . .? |

## A theology made from caricature

Everything in this account is a caricature. We might say that the world has been turned upside down! On the one hand, the pagans turn spontaneously to God and hasten to amend their behaviour to please him. The prophet is less keen to adjust to God's will and mode of action towards humanity: he flees, he sleeps, he does things quickly and without conviction, he even sulks after his success and asks to die. One has seen better prophets!

On the other hand, the text introduces a God who does not cease to surprise. Certainly he remains the Lord of hosts who can command the elements of nature: the storm, the fish, the plant, the sun, the worm. But in other respects he seems impotent when faced with the resistance and narrow-mindedness of his prophet. It is somewhat amazing to see how God can be obeyed by everyone, including the pagans and the elements of nature, but not by his prophet. Does God lag behind human frailness and narrowness? Be this as it may, God seems to have more work to do on Jonah than on the rest of creation. There is some disproportion here: we get the impression that God cannot leave Jonah alone for a moment and that each time he has to invent new ways of bringing him back to his mission.

Here we clearly have a caricature. It is a caricature of a certain kind of theology, but such an accurate caricature that it becomes theology itself. In other words, the caricature that the author makes of the prophet Jonah, far from coming to a sudden end, itself becomes the vehicle of a basic theological message.

On a first glance, it is easy to see that with the figure of Jonah the author is drawing a caricature of a certain Israel which believed itself to be the exclusive beneficiary of salvation and had difficulties in accepting that God could show mercy to other nations, above all if these were hostile. All the narrowness is here attributed to a single figure, so that the lesson is more impressive. But we should not attribute all this to Jonah: in his account the author has wanted quite simply to be the mirror of a theology which was prevalent in his time. And to put forward a counterpart, he had to enlarge the features of an attitude akin to that of Jonah and show how ridiculous it was.

So we must not 'reify' the account and believe that historically Jonah could have merited all the misadventures the account attributes to him. Quite the contrary, the attitude which the author attributes to him was only too real within Israel at the time when he was writing. That is the whole force of his caricature: with humour and laughter he could lead his readers to become aware how ridiculous such a narrow and childish attitude as that of the prophet was. The prophet is angry instead of rejoicing simply because the pagans have just as much right to the love of God and his mercy as he does.

## Smile! God forgives sinners!

Like the parables of Jesus, the story of Jonah conveys essentially one lesson – what in parables has been called the 'point'. This is theological and not moral, in the sense that it reveals to us something of the true face of God. Only subsequently, as in the parables, will the 'moral' or rather 'theologal' demand come: human action will have to adjust to divine action.

Now in the book of Jonah, as in a good many of the parables of Jesus, God appears first and foremost as a God of mercy who forgives sinners. At the beginning of his account the author leaves no doubt as to the 'wickedness' of the Ninevites (1.3), and later, the king of Nineveh himself explicitly recognizes the violence of which each one has been guilty: 'yes, let everyone turn from his evil way and from the violence which is in his hands' (3.8). This is the problem which the book tries to resolve: the people of Nineveh have sinned. Jonah's brief preaching suggests a 'solution' along the lines of a certain classical theology of retribution: the Ninevites have sinned, so Nineveh will be destroyed!

This is the 'solution' chosen by one kind of theology, but it is not the solution chosen by God.

Contrary to all expectations (truly?, at any rate for Jonah), Nineveh is not destroyed. 'When God saw what they did, how they turned from their evil way, God repented of the evil which he had said he would do to them; and he did not do it' (3.10). The text does not yet speak of mercy, but that is what it is about, as moreover Jonah understands when he interprets what has just happened: 'I pray you Lord, is not this what I said when I was yet in my country? That is why I made haste to flee to Tarshish; for I knew that you are a gracious God and merciful, slow to anger and that you repent of evil' (4.2).

The cause seems understood, but now there is a new twist: though the Ninevites are forgiven, there is still someone who resists and is not very happy: 'But it displeased Jonah exceedingly, and he was angry' (4.1). Jonah is annoyed, more than a little. He insists, 'I do well to be angry, angry enough to die' (4.9). So much so that the real problem – as we may in any case have felt on seeing the misfortunes falling upon him – is Jonah, and not the Ninevites, just as later, in the famous parable of Jesus about the forgiveness given by the father to his 'son who is found' (Luke 15.11–32), it is the older brother, not the younger, who will be the problem. In other words, the question raised by the story, and in particular by the personal attitude of the prophet, is that of the acceptance or rejection of the good news of a God who forgives sinners. God has forgiven: instead of rejoicing, Jonah is angry and asks to die. Would a God who forgives be more difficult to accept than a God who punishes? Like the father in the parable in the case of the older son, God will do anything and go to any lengths to make Jonah understand that he should rejoice and not be sad about the forgiveness given to sinners. Will he or won't he enter into God's joy? That is the question which remains open with Jonah and the older son at the end of the two parables.

---

## A Parable Worthy of the New Testament

*A comparison between Jonah and Luke 15.11–32*

Its length apart, which is exceptional, the book of Jonah compares favourably with Jesus' parables on mercy. The most significant comparison that one can make is between Jonah and Luke 15.11–32, which we call the parable of the prodigal son.

- In both cases the point is the same: God forgives sinners (the Ninevites who turn from their evil way and the prodigal son who returns from afar). Also in both cases, it is not sin which is the problem, but rather the fact that God forgives sinners. Is Jonah angry? So too is the older brother! Both find it difficult to imagine that God could rejoice at the return of sinners and welcome them with open arms.

- The two stories equally show the patience of God, who takes the trouble to engage in dialogue with someone who does not understand the ways of his mercy, whether he meets up with an angry Jonah, settled east of the great city, or takes the first steps on leaving the house to go to meet the son who refuses to join the festival.

- Nor is it by chance that the two stories keep the last word for God; for it is God's point of view that the author of Jonah and Jesus want to convey to their readers and hearers. Finally, it must be emphasized that by virtue of this fact the two stories are 'open parables': God having spoken last, we still await the response of Jonah and that of the older son. Will they finally have understood? Will they finally join the feast and have the experience of a God of infinite mercy?

And what if Jonah, the older brother, were us? Would he go in to the feast? Or wouldn't he? . . .

## Salvation for all!

I have already said that a parable like that of Jonah teaches just one lesson. But this lesson is so rich that one find several facets in it. The basic message is clear: God has forgiven the Ninevites. But immediately we must reflect on the implications which that could have for those to whom the book of Jonah is addressed. Nineveh is not just any city, but the capital of an empire which was Israel's greatest enemy during the period of the monarchy, greater and even more formidable than Babylon, which was responsible for the fall of Jerusalem and the deportation of its inhabitants. In taking account of the forgiveness granted to the Ninevites, the author of the book of Jonah is saying no less than this: Nineveh the great, Nineveh the pagan, Nineveh the enemy is also loved by God and is the object of God's tenderness and mercy. In other words, the God of Israel, formerly revealed to Moses, who today speaks by the prophet, is the same for all. God's mercy is not a quality that he puts to work for Israel alone, but is for all the nations. If Nineveh can be forgiven, all can have access to salvation.

## Because God is God . . .

However, a superficial reading of the story could suggest that it has scarcely got past the theology of retribution and that when all is said and done, if God has forgiven, it is because the Ninevites have been converted. This is at least what comes out of the calculations made by the king of Nineveh: 'Let everyone turn from his evil way and from the violence which is in his hands. Who knows, God may yet repent and turn from his fierce anger, so that we do not perish.' These calculations seem right, since in the next verse the author concludes: 'When God saw what they did, how they turned from their evil way, God repented of the evil which he had said he would do to them; and he did not do it' (3.10)

But it is at precisely this point that the real theological debate begins, which now takes place between Jonah and God. Without knowing it, it is Jonah who provides the best explanation: 'I knew that you are a gracious God and merciful, slow to anger and that you repent of evil' (4.2). There is one reason which can be given for the divine forgiveness: the very being of God, whose nature is 'gracious and merciful, slow to anger and repenting of evil'. This is a reason of a theological order. God's forgiveness should not depend on human conduct; on the contrary, it is essentially the fruit of a gratuitous love, deeply rooted in God.

Finally, that forgiveness can only be explained in terms of God and what God is towards humanity, also emerges from the fact that the author gives God the last word (4.10–11). God alone can justify his conduct. And how does he do it? In a conclusion full of hints, but stamped with an infinite tenderness, God proves an incomparable teacher. On the one hand his long experience of a sinful humanity leads him to make himself the defender of the weakness and the ignorance of these Ninevites (these 'human beings who cannot tell their right hand from their left'). On the other, the comparison which he uses for the benefit of Jonah tell us how attached he is to humankind. If Jonah believes that he is right to lament the disappearance of a plant over which he has not taken a moment's trouble, with how much more reason is God right to be moved and have pity 'on Nineveh, that great city, in which there are more than one hundred and twenty thousand human beings' (in other words 'over creating whom I myself took pains'). Here again, what a lesson in universalism we have here! The God revealed to Moses, and to whom Jonah explicitly alludes, is by the very fact of his work in creation a God of goodness and mercy for all men and women.

# The Bible Re-read with a Smile

One cannot escape the fact that the story of Jonah is a fantasy and the account of his adventures is presented in a humorous way. That is what comes out on a first reading. Now far from undermining this first impression, a deeper reading of Jonah reveals how the author has been able to apply his talent as a theological humorist to other biblical traditions. In fact behind the scenario of the misadventures of Jonah we can see the outline of a skilful theological construction, a fabric of biblical reminiscences; and thanks to this, the author can transmit his message in an even more striking way. Now let's survey some of these biblical reminiscences.

First of all we feel the influence of the Genesis story of Cain. In fact Jonah is the only person, apart from Cain, who according to the Bible fled 'from the presence of the Lord' (1.3, 10; cf. Gen.4.16). The author already presents Jonah to us in an unfavourable light, and the comparison with Cain suggests that Jonah is reacting to his mission rather as Cain reacted to his crime. Not a very flattering comparison!

For the moment, let us say that this comparison could be simply a coincidence. However, the author emphasizes that it is not. In chapter 4 we learn that Jonah is very angry at God's conduct and that God feels obliged to accost him and ask him to explain his anger (4.1, 4, 9). Here is a new parallel between Jonah and Cain: Cain was equally annoyed at the conduct of God, who had accepted his brother's sacrifice (Gen.4.5), and God had also challenged the legitimacy of his anger (Gen.4.6). So Jonah has as many problems with mercy as Cain had with the freedom of this same God.

We have already seen, in the box 'Why Jonah?', the parallels between the story of Jonah and that of the flood. Another Genesis story, related to that of the flood, has also left traces on the book of Jonah: the destruction of Sodom and Gomorrah (Gen.18; 19). There too, as with the flood and Nineveh, the initial situation is one of generalized corruption (Gen.18.20). But it is above all on the subject of the very nature of the catastrophe, realized or projected, that the two episodes meet: Sodom and Gomorrah have gone down in history by reason of the famous 'overthrow' (Gen.19.25, 29) brought about by the Lord. Now in the Hebrew text the book of Jonah uses exactly the same root when it makes Jonah say: 'Yet forty days, and Nineveh shall be overthrown' (3.4). These are the only two overthrows which the Bible attributes to God . . . So in the ordinary course of events, Nineveh would have been doomed to the same fate as Sodom and Gomorrah; this makes its salvation seem all the greater and more gratuitous.

Finally, to refine his caricature of the prophet Jonah, the prophet even imagines certain similarities to the great prophet Elijah. In addition to the other allusions already indicated, the delay of forty days could suggest Elijah's journey to Horeb (I Kings 19.18), and above all death as a deliverance. 'Therefore now, O Lord, take my life from me, I beseech you' suggests the pathetic cry of Elijah: 'And he asked that he might die, saying, "It is enough; now, O Lord, take away my life"' (I Kings 19.4). What the two prophets have in common is to have experienced total success, but to have been unable to bear the long-term consequences of their success. But here again the comparison only brings out the contrast: contrary to Jonah, Elijah is devoted body and soul to his mission, and the encounter with God on Horeb is to bring him peace. We cannot say as much of Jonah: he fulfils his mission only by paying lip-service to it, and who knows whether he ever recovered his serenity . . .?

We might also make comparisons with the accounts of the Exodus and the crossing of the Red Sea, or with the psalms, or again with some passages of Joel and Jeremiah. However, these few possible examples should indicate how much the author is a past master in correcting with a smile. While showing a profound knowledge of the biblical traditions, he equally displays extreme freedom. With finesse and all kinds of nuances, he succeeds in demonstrating into what an impasse a certain theology of salvation can lead, and calls for a more joyful theology, theology with a smile, focussed on God's mercy and the care God shows to all his creatures. Smile, God loves you!

# Conclusion

## The two sides of the prophetic word

We have now come to the end of a long journey which has led us from the 'roaring' prophet Amos to Jonah, the prophet who makes us smile. These two prophets are a remarkable illustration of the two sides of the prophetic message. On the one hand, with the percussive and ruthless language of Amos, the prophetic word proclaims the undeniable urgency of conversion to justice. On the other hand, with Jonah, the pedagogy of the prophetic word also takes on a humorous tone, so that it helps us to get a better grasp of the unpredictable newness and tenderness of God and God's love for humanity. From Amos to Jonah, through Hosea, Isaiah, Jeremiah, Ezekiel, Haggai, Zechariah and Malachi, the prophetic word will always develop along these two aspects of God's love for his people: on the one hand the almost impatient demand for faithfulness, and on the other the assurance of an infinite tenderness, always ready to forgive.

I have tried to keep to this essential character of the prophetic word in the course of this study, while being well aware that nothing can replace careful attention to the whole of the texts. I have tried to give the flavour of reading the biblical prophets, and to suggest ways of doing so. By listening each time to the contemporary history of the prophets, to certain key texts drawn from their books, and their vision of the mystery of God, we have been able to grasp something of the diversity and extreme riches of the prophetic movement in Israel. Not everything has been said, and we would need to look at many more texts if we were to appreciate yet other colours of the mosaic formed by the writings and theology of the prophets. But the most important thing has been to open up the way, to make you want to read the prophets, and to suggest an approach.

## The direction of a journey

As we conclude this study, let's briefly recall the object of the itinerary that we've followed.

For each of the prophets studied, we began with a reference to history. More than one reader may have felt that this first stage was merely a matter of intellectual curiosity, history to improve one's biblical knowledge. However, this was an essential and decisive step towards understanding the meaning and purpose of what the prophets say. It is not that we must historicize everything and take each of the prophetic books as a chronicle. But the prophets are bound up with quite specific events, and their texts attest a sensitivity rare in the history of their time. They have thus revealed to us a God who is interested in human history and who invites believers to be interested in it in their turn. In allowing ourselves to be displaced in order to rediscover the historical context in which the prophets proclaimed the word, we have taken a first step towards helping this same word to come to transform our faith today.

Secondly, we chose three key texts for each prophet. This is where the enterprise was riskiest. Three texts are not many in comparison with the literary production of the prophets whom we have studied and the length of their prophetic ministries. A host of other texts could have been chosen, and these could claim to be just as important or as representative of the message of the prophet in question. Certainly, and it is to the credit of the prophets that they have given us such precious collections.

However, the risk had to be taken. Sometimes I chose very well-known texts like the account of the call of Isaiah or his famous Immanuel oracle, or the story of the call of Jeremiah and his oracle of the new covenant; sometimes I chose texts often overshadowed by more familiar ones, like God's trial of Israel in Amos 2 and Hosea 2, or Jeremiah's plea for justice (Jer.9). But whatever the choice may have been, the importance of returning to the text can never be stressed often enough. Whether famous or not, the prophetic texts always have some surprise in store, and whatever the chosen text may be, we always find in them a bold, stimulating and challenging word. I only hope that the soundings we have made of these texts will make you want to pursue your research further and make other discoveries.

Finally, the last stage led us to consider the God of each of the prophets we studied. Certainly it is always the same God, but each of the prophets had a unique experience of him to which his writings bear witnesses. One could discuss nuances or degrees of difference between one prophet and another, but we shall soon agree on the essential point. The heart of the message of the prophets is theological: their mission reflects and actualizes their perception of the mystery of God. Essentially, this mission consists in revealing one or more aspects of the mystery of God.

We do not read the biblical prophets to learn what will happen in the future, but to discover what God means to be for humankind. That is beyond question where the treasure of the prophetic word lies. Through the preaching and the writings of the prophets, we discover step by step the 'thrice holy' God and the God who is infinitely near, the God who 'roars' and the God who 'plucks up and overthrows', and also the God who wants to 'build and plant'. He is the God of those who are near and those who are far, whose presence fills the whole universe and gives it meaning:

> Am I a God at hand, says the Lord,
> and not a God afar off? . . .
> Do I not fill heaven and earth?
> says the Lord (Jer.23.23–24).

If only for their reply to the one question, 'Who is God?', we could never give up reading the biblical prophets, so enthusiastic for God and the human adventure.

# For Further Reading

## Basic works

Blenkinsopp, J., *A History of Prophecy in Israel*, Darton, Longman and Todd and Westminster Press 1983

Brueggeman, W., *The Prophetic Imagination*, Fortress Press 1983 and SCM Press 1992

Charpentier, E., *How to Read the Old Testament*, SCM Press and Crossroad Publishing Company 1982

Coggins, R., et al. (ed.), *Israel's Prophetic Traditions. Essays in Honour of Peter R. Ackroyd*, Cambridge University Press 1982

Heschel, A.J., *The Prophets*, Harper and Row 1962

Limburg, J., *The Prophets and the Powerless*, John Knox Press 1977

Lindblom, J., *Prophecy in Ancient Israel*, Blackwell 1972

McKane, W., 'Prophecy and the Prophetic Literature', in *Tradition and Interpretation: Essays by Members of the Society of Old Testament Study*, ed. G.W. Anderson, Clarendon Press 1979, 163–88

Paul, S.M., et al., 'Prophets and Prophecy', *Encyclopaedia Judaica* 13, 1971, 1150–81

Vawter, B., 'Introduction to Prophetic Literature', in *The New Jerome Biblical Commentary*, ed. R.E. Brown, J.A. Fitzmyer and R.E. Murphy, Prentice Hall and Geoffrey Chapman 1990, 186–200

Von Rad, G., *The Message of the Prophets*, SCM Press 1968

Wilson, R.R., *Prophecy and Society in Ancient Israel*, Fortress Press 1980

## Amos

Auld, A.G., *Amos*, JSOT Press 1986

Barré, M.L., 'Amos', in *The New Jerome Biblical Commentary*, ed. R.E. Brown, J.A. Fitzmyer and R.E. Murphy, Prentice Hall and Geoffrey Chapman 1990, 209–16

Barton, J., *Amos's Oracles against the Nations: A Study of Amos 1.3–2.5*, SOTS Monographs 6, Cambridge University Press 1980

Brueggemann, W., 'Amos IV 4–13 and Israel's Covenant Worship', *Vetus Testamentum* 15, 1965, 1–15

Coote, R.B., *Amos among the Prophets: Composition and Theology*, Fortress Press 1981

Hayes, J.H., *Amos: The Eighth-Century Prophet. His Times and His Preaching*, Abingdon Press 1988

Mays, J.L., *Amos. A Commentary*, Old Testament Library, SCM Press and Westminster Press 1969

Smith, G.V., *Amos: A Commentary*, Library of Biblical Interpretation, Zondervan 1989

Soggin, J.A., *The Prophet Amos*, SCM Press 1987

Story, C.I.K., 'Amos, Prophet of Praise', *Vetus Testamentum* 30, 1980, 67–80

Wolff, H.–W., *Joel and Amos: A Commentary*, Hermeneia, Fortress Press 1977

## Hosea

Andersen, F.I., and Freedman, D.N., *Hosea*, Anchor Bible, Doubleday 1980

Mays, J.L., *Hosea*, Old Testament Library, SCM Press and Westminster Press 1969

McCarthy, D., and Murphy, R.E., 'Hosea', in *The New Jerome Biblical Commentary*, ed. R.E. Brown, J.A. Fitzmyer and R.E. Murphy, Prentice Hall and Geoffrey Chapman 1990, 217–28

Wolff, H.–W., *Hosea: A Commentary*, Hermeneia, Fortress Press 1977

## Isaiah

Brueggemann, W., 'Unity and Dynamic in the Isaiah Tradition', *Journal for the Study of the Old Testament* 29, 1984, 89–107

Conrad, E.W., 'The Royal Narrative and the Structure of the Book of Isaiah', *Journal for the Study of the Old Testament* 41, 1988, 67–81

Evans, C.A., 'On the Unity and Parallel Structure of Isaiah', *Vetus Testamentum* 38, 1988, 129–47

Hayes, J.H., and Irving, S.A., *Isaiah, the Eighth–Century Prophet: His Times and His Preaching*, Abingdon Press 1987

Jensen, J., 'Isaiah 1–39', in *The New Jerome Biblical Commentary*, ed. R.E. Brown, J.A. Fitzmyer and R.E. Murphy, Prentice Hall and Geoffrey Chapman 1990, 229–48

Seitz, C.R., *Reading and Preaching the Book of Isaiah*, Fortress Press 1988

## On Isaiah 7.10–17

Conrad, E.W., 'The Royal Narratives and the Structure of the Book of Isaiah', *Journal for the Study of the Old Testament* 41, 1988, 67–81

Jensen, J., 'The Age of Immanuel', *Catholic Biblical Quarterly* 41, 1979, 220–39

Lust, J., 'The Immanuel Figure: A Charismatic Judge–Leader. A Suggestion Towards the Understanding of Is. 7, 10–17 (8.29–9.6; 11.1–9)', *Ephemerides Theologicae Lovanienses* 47, 1971, 464–70

Nielsen, K., 'Is.6:1 – 8:18 as Dramatic Writing', *Studia Theologica* 40, 1986, 1–16

Rice, G., 'A Neglected Interpretation of the Immanuel Prophecy', *Zeitschrift für die Alttestamentliche Wissenschaft* 90, 1978, 220–7

Schoors, A., 'The Immanuel of Isaiah 7, 14', *Orientalia Lovaniensia Periodica* 18, 1987, 66–77

Scullion, J.J., 'An Approach to the Understanding of Isaiah 7, 10–17', *Journal of Biblical Literature* 87, 1968, 288–300

## Jeremiah

Carroll, R.P., *Jeremiah: A Commentary*, Old Testament Library, SCM Press and Westminster Press 1986

Clements, R.E., *Jeremiah*, Interpretation, John Knox Press 1988

Holladay, W.L., *Jeremiah 1: A Commentary on the Book of Jeremiah chs.1–25*, Hermeneia, Fortress Press 1986

Holladay, W.L., *Jeremiah 2: A Commentary on the Book of Jeremiah chs.26–52*, Hermeneia, Fortress Press 1989

McKane, W., *A Critical and Exegetical Commentary on Jeremiah, Vol.1, chs.I–XXV*, ICC, T.& T. Clark 1986

Perdue, L.G., and Kovacs, B.W. (eds.), *A Prophet to the Nations. Essays in Jeremiah Studies*, Eisenbrauns nd

Smith, D.L., 'Jeremiah as Prophet of Non-Violent Reisistance', *Journal for the Study of the Old Testament* 43, 1989, 95–107

## Ezekiel

Allen, L.C., *Ezekiel 20–48*, Word Biblical Commentary, Word Books 1990

Blenkinsopp, J., *Ezekiel*, Interpretation, John Knox Press 1990

Boadt, L., 'Ezekiel', in *The New Jerome Biblical Commentary*, ed. R.E. Brown, J.A. Fitzmyer and R.E. Murphy, Prentice Hall and Geoffrey Chapman 1990, 305–28

Brownlee, W.H., *Ezekiel 1–19*, Word Biblical Commentary, Word Books 1986

Eichrodt, Walter, *Ezekiel*, Old Testament Library, SCM Press and Westminster Press 1970

Klein, R.W., *Ezekiel: The Prophet and His Messsage*, University of South Carolina Press 1988

Lust, J. (ed.), *Ezekiel and His Book*, Louvain University Press 1986

Zimmerli, W., *Ezekiel 1: A Commentary on the Book of Ezekiel chs.1–24*, Hermeneia, Fortress Press 1979

Zimmerli, W., *Ezekiel 2: A Commentary on the Book of Ezekiel chs.25–48*, Hermeneia, Fortress Press 1983

## The Prophets of the Return

Ackroyd P.R., *Exile and Restoration*, SCM Press and Westminster Press 1968

Blenkinsopp, J., *A History of Prophecy in Israel*, Darton, Longman and Todd and Westminster Press 1983

Mason, R.A., 'The Prophets of the Restoration', Coggins, R., et al. (ed.), *Israel's Prophetic Traditions. Essays in Honour of Peter R.Ackroyd*, Cambridge University Press 1982

## Isaiah 40–66

Stuhlmueller, C., 'Deutero–Isaiah: Major Transitions in the Prophet's Theology and in Contemporary Scholarship', *Catholic Biblical Quarterly* 42, 1980, 1–29

Stuhlmueller, C., 'Deutero–Isaiah and Trito–Isaiah', in *The New Jerome Biblical Commentary*, ed. R.E. Brown, J.A. Fitzmyer and R.E.

Murphy, Prentice Hall and Geoffrey Chapman 1990, 328–48

Watts, J., *Isaiah 34–66*, Word Biblical Commentary, Word Books 1987

Westermann, C., *Isaiah 40–66. A Commentary*, Old Testament Library, SCM Press and Westminster Press 1969

Whybray, *The Second Isaiah*, JSOT Press 1983

## Haggai, Zechariah and Malachi

Cody, A., 'Haggai, Zechariah, Malachi', in *The New Jerome Biblical Commentary*, ed. R.E. Brown, J.A. Fitzmyer and R.E. Murphy, Prentice Hall and Geoffrey Chapman 1990, 348–61

Coggins, R.J., *Haggai, Zechariah, Malachi*, JSOT Press 1987

Petersen, J.L., *Haggai and Zechariah 1–8: A Commentary*, Old Testament Library, SCM Press and Westminster Press 1984

Pierce, R.W., 'Literary Connectors and a Haggai/Zechariah/Malachi Corpus', *Journal of the Evangelical Theological Society* 27, 1984, 401–11

Smith, R.L., 'Haggai, Zechariah, Malachi', in *Micah–Malachi*, Word Biblical Commentary, Word Books 1984

Wolff, H.W., *Haggai: A Commentary*, Augsburg Publishing House 1988

## Jonah

Burrows, M., 'The Literary Category of the Book of Jonah', in *Translating and Understanding the Old Testament. Essays in Honour of H.G. May*, ed. H.T. Frank and W.L. Reed, Abingdon Press 1970

Edwards, R.A., *The Sign of Jonah in the Theology of the Evangelists and Q*, Studies in Biblical Theology II.18, SCM Press 1971

Harvianen, T., 'Why Were the Sailors Not Afraid of the Lord before Verse Jonah 1.10?', *Studia Orientalia* 64, 1988

Landes, G.M., 'The Kerygma of the Book of Jonah. The Contextual Interpretation of the Jonah Psalm', *Interpretation* 21, 1967, 3–31

Limburg, J., *Jonah: A Commentary*, Old Testament Library, SCM Press and Westminster Press 1993

Lubeck, R.J., 'Prophetic Sabotage: A Look at Jonah 3:2–4', *Trinity Journal* 9, 1988, 37–46

Magonet, J., *Form and Meaning. Studies in Literary Techniques in the Book of Jonah*, Lang 1976

Miles, J.A., 'Laughing at the Bible: Jonah as Parody', *Jewish Quarterly Review* 65, 1974–75, 168–81